The Ski Patroller's Manual

The Ski Patroller's Manual

Fourteenth Edition

National Ski Patrol System, Inc.
133 South Van Gordon Street, Suite 100
Lakewood, Colorado 80228
303-988-1111
FAX: 1-800-222-I SKI
or 303-988-3005

National Ski Patrol System, Inc. is a federally chartered educational association serving the ski and outdoor recreation community by providing exceptional education programs.

Credits

Education Director: Judy Over
Education Assistant: Elizabeth Mason
Editors: Rebecca W. Ayers, Wendy Schrupp, Jessie Halverson
Graphic Design: Ken Grasman
Cover Illustration: Bruce Holdeman

ISBN: 0-929752-07-4

Printed in the United States of America

The National Ski Patrol System, Inc. is a federally chartered
educational association serving the ski and outdoor recreation
community by providing exceptional education programs.

The *NSP Policies and Procedures* as amended constitutes the
approved national policies of the National Ski Patrol System, Inc.
All other publications are educational documents and may or
may not reflect current NSP policies.

Table of Contents

Acknowledgments

Producing a manual of this magnitude would have been impossible without the many useful contributions and suggestions of members of the National Ski Patrol and others interested in ski patrolling.

The NSP Board of Directors wishes to thank the following persons in particular for their contributions to the review of this manual.

Publication Review Committee

Marc Bond, National Legal Counsel
David Olson, National Assistant Legal Counsel
Jeff Olsen, Assistant National Chairman
Mike Baker, Assistant National Chairman
Chuck Martschinke, Executive Committee
Hilbert Finn, Past Assistant National Chairman
Mary Davis, Past Board Representative
Jack Mason, Past National Chairman
John Clair, National Chairman
David Skitt, Alaska Division

National Education Program Directors

Lin Ballard, Avalanche
Cindy Holben, Instructor Development
Eileen Barlage, Leadership Development
Mary Murrett, Outdoor Emergency Care
Sue Gormley, Outdoor Emergency Care Assistant
John Wiley, Ski and Toboggan
Keith Underwood, Ski and Toboggan—Snowboard
Bill Rostad, Ski and Toboggan—Nordic
Ron Clark, Mountaineering

National Volunteer Staff

Gretchen R. Besser, Ph.D., Historian
Tim Politis, Awards Coordinator

Additional Contributors

Peter W. Rietz, Attorney at Law, White and Steele
Janet Bell, Central Division OEC Supervisor
Jim Miller, Eastern Division OEC Supervisor
Jim Fillmore, Intermountain Division OEC Supervisor
Jeff Schmidt, Central Division Nordic Supervisor
Richard Todd, Pacific Northwest Division Nordic Supervisor
Carla D. Marcus, Sugarloaf Safety Services Manager

As is the case with many NSP publications, much of the material in this manual has been excerpted or revised from previous NSP manuals. A debt of gratitude is expressed to the many authors of past editions of this publication.

Introduction

The purpose of *The Ski Patroller's Manual* is to provide prospective patrollers and members with information on the National Ski Patrol's (NSP) membership requirements and education programs.

The basic membership requirements and education programs detailed in this manual have been established by the national board of directors and are designed to help patrollers maintain and improve NSP membership. All of the NSP units—divisions, regions, sections, and patrols—strive to deliver the NSP education programs to the membership as efficiently and effectively as possible.

While all NSP members are required to participate in certain education programs and meet specific skill proficiency and knowledge objectives, each area manager is an independent entity that establishes its own specific requirements for local patrollers. Area management standard operating procedures and regulations for day-to-day patrolling activities should not be confused with NSP directives or requirements for membership. Area management often directs its patrollers to participate in activities that are not covered in any of the NSP education programs or sanctioned by the organization.

The information and principles presented in this manual may not be applicable in all situations that arise in the day-to-day operations of a given ski area or center and are subject to change or modification by applicable ski area management or government agencies. The National Ski Patrol, its board of directors, its employees, and its membership assume no liability whatsoever arising out of, or related to, any loss, damage, or injury that may arise from the application of the information and principles presented in this manual.

NSP Policies and Procedures

The *NSP Policies and Procedures* manual, as amended annually, constitutes the approved national policies of the National Ski Patrol System, Inc. All other publications are educational documents and may or may not reflect current NSP policies.

An updated edition of *NSP Policies and Procedures* is distributed each fall to every patrol director, region and division director, and program director and supervisor in the association. The manual contains the NSP Federal Charter, Bylaws, a summary of board actions since 1983, and the application of board policies in the appropriate chapters.

This manual also is available through the *NSP Winter Catalog.*

Dedicated
to the memory of

Charles Minot Dole
(1899-1976)

and to the hard-working, loyal patrollers
who have contributed significant portions of their lives
to making winter sports safer and more enjoyable.

History

Since it was founded in 1938, the National Ski Patrol (NSP) has evolved from a handful of ski patrollers into the world's largest patrol organization, which supports, participates in, and influences the outdoor recreation community at large. Throughout the history of the NSP, its members have devoted a significant part of their lives to providing the public with emergency care, rescue services, and education programs that promote the safety and enjoyment of mountain recreation. As a result, thousands of injured people have received prompt, skillful emergency care, and numerous lives have been saved.

Charles Minot Dole— National Director, 1938–1949

Before 1932, alpine skiing was relatively unknown in the United States. Until then, the sport primarily had been the pastime of a few rural families and the descendants of Northern European immigrants. Most Americans got their first exposure to skiing through media coverage of the 1932 Olympics at Lake Placid, New York. Inevitably, the sport took off.

In the 1930s, skiing was a hardy activity that required a long drive on poorly maintained roads to an area that had snow-covered hills or mountains. The only mode of uphill transportation was climbing—which required a couple of hours of huffing and puffing—all for a few minutes of a well-earned downhill thrill.

The skier's cry, "Track!" originated at that time, and when skiers climbing uphill heard that shout, they did the best they could to give the right-of-way to the approaching downhillers. Since ski lessons were virtually nonexistent, few skiers had learned to turn well and some could not turn at all, thanks to primitive equipment on unpacked snow. Accidents were common, and most skiers

accepted them as the price to pay for participating in the sport.

Charles Minot "Minnie" Dole, an insurance broker from Greenwich, Connecticut, realized the need for emergency care and rescue services for injured skiers back in 1936. Dole was skiing at Stowe, Vermont, with his wife, Jane, and their friends, Frank and Jean Edson, when he took a fall, heard a bone snap in his ankle, and lay helpless in the snow. Frank Edson stayed with him while Jane Dole and Jean Edson skied down the mountain for help.

The first person they met was a local farmer who said anyone foolish enough to ski deserved whatever fate offered, and he went on his way. The women finally located two people who helped haul Dole off the mountain on a makeshift rescue toboggan improvised from a piece of corrugated tin roofing. X-rays showed a break so severe that Dole was told he might

never walk again, let alone ski. But he was determined to recover, and he did.

That same determination compelled Dole to help improve emergency care for skiers when, two months after Dole's accident, Frank Edson was killed in a ski race. At the suggestion of Roland Palmedo, president of the Amateur Ski Club of New York, Dole was put in charge of a ski safety committee for the club. In March 1938, Dole organized a volunteer ski patrol for the National Downhill Races at Stowe. Roger Langley, president of the National Ski Association (NSA), now the United States Ski Association, was so impressed with the patrol that he asked Dole to organize a similar patrol on a national basis. Then and there, the National Ski Patrol came into being—originally as a subcommittee of the NSA.

A tremendous organizational effort took place under Dole's leadership during the next few years. Soon, the National Ski Patrol had five geographical divisions and a small core of patrollers, including Olympic racers Bob Livermore, Dick Durrance, and Alex Bright, whose names lent prestige to the new organization. In 1941, the first *National Ski Patrol Manual* was published, outlining the basic NSP organizational structure that still exists. The manual also listed the qualifications in emergency care and skiing ability that were required of NSP members, contained the guidelines for organizing a local ski patrol, and described the NSP division structure.

By 1941, the California, Central, Eastern, Intermountain, Northern, Pacific Northwest, and Rocky Mountain Divisions had been established. The NSP had a total of 89 registered ski patrols with more that 1,500 registered patrollers. By the 1942 season, the numbers expanded to 180 registered ski patrols and more than 4,000 patrollers. That year, women were welcomed into the organization for the first time.

The National Ski Patrol began a long and fruitful association with the American Red Cross (ARC) when L.M. Thompson, M.D., of the ARC wrote the first edition of *Ski Safety and First Aid* especially for the NSP. Dr. Thompson, who was the first NSP national medical advisor, wrote the original 1938 edition of the *Winter First Aid Manual*, which became the ski patroller's "bible." It was Dr. Thompson who introduced the concept of having patrollers complete accident reports.

From the beginning, NSP rescue work was not confined to ski slopes—patrollers helped out whenever and wherever accidents occurred. Ski patrols in the West and the southern Rockies helped locate Army Air Corps planes that crashed during training missions. As a result, the NSP was incorporated into the Second and Fourth Air Force groups in Colorado and Washington state and became an official branch of Army Air Corps Search and Rescue.

When the United States entered World War II, Minnie Dole approached the War Department on several occasions about developing a winter warfare group similar to those already in existence in European countries such as Finland and Switzerland. After a great deal of effort and red tape, Dole was able to convince the Chief of Staff, General George C. Marshall, of the value of a winter warfare unit and, in 1942, the 87th Mountain Infantry Regiment was activated at both Mt. Rainier and Fort Lewis, Washington.

The regiment was transferred to Camp Hale, Colorado, in 1943 and expanded to become the U.S. Army's famed Tenth Mountain Division. The War Department contracted the NSP to recruit specialized personnel for the outfit. The NSP, the only civilian agency ever so authorized by the armed forces, recruited 7,000 volunteers.

In 1944, the Tenth was transferred to Italy, where it performed with distinction in combat, capturing mountain strongholds that had been judged impregnable and spearheading the drive to the Po River. General Mark Clark called the Tenth the finest division he had ever seen. An amazing number of well-known patrollers, ski area managers, ski equipment manufacturers, and other ski personalities are veterans of this division. The well-known Riva Ridge ski run at Vail, Colorado, was named in honor of the Tenth's assault on that ridge in Italy.

Meanwhile, the National Ski Patrol was becoming well known throughout the world, and numerous countries were beginning to model their own patrol organizations after the NSP. Specifically, in 1942, delegates from Chile, Bolivia, and Argentina visited the United States to study the NSP organization. Japan, Australia, Canada, and New Zealand eventually were to use the NSP as a model for setting up their own patrols.

After World War II, the sport of skiing resumed its phenomenal growth rate. Thousands of army surplus skis, boots, poles, and ski clothing items were sold at bargain prices. This factor, combined with the country's renewed desire for recreation, encouraged the development of many new ski areas.

The growth of the National Ski Patrol kept pace with the increasing popularity of skiing. By 1948, the tenth anniversary of the founding of the NSP, there were 193 ski patrols and more than 4,500 registered patrollers. The first NSP rust-colored parka, dubbed "Rainier Red," was introduced that year through Harold Hirsch of White Stag Manufacturing Company.

In 1949, in conjunction with the U.S. Forest Service, the NSP commissioned Swiss avalanche expert Andre Roche to devise an avalanche rescue training course. Since then, the NSP has maintained a close association with the Forest Service. The following year, former Olympian Dick Durrance (National Appointment #7) was instrumental in bringing the International Ski Federation (FIS) Alpine Ski Championships to the United States. In Aspen, for the first time, the NSP supplied a ski patrol for a major international meet. Composed of 10 volunteer and eight paid patrollers, the FIS Ski Patrol was headed by William Judd, who some years later became NSP national director.

Edward Taylor— National Director, 1949–1956

Following the Alpine Ski Championships, Minnie Dole asked Rocky Mountain Division patroller Edward F. Taylor, who also had been a member of the FIS Ski Patrol, to accept the job of national director.

Taylor had been instrumental in establishing an Army Air Corps winter search and rescue group of NSP volunteers living around Denver, Colorado, during World War II. Lowry Field in Denver was a major training center for navigators and pilots at that time, and these novices provided several opportunities for the rescue group to demonstrate its value in the nearby mountainous terrain.

Taylor agreed to accept appointment as national director on the condition that the national office be moved from New York City to his hometown of Denver so he could properly attend to NSP affairs without extensive travel. Dole agreed to the terms, and the NSP office was established in Denver in 1949.

Taylor's appointment to the position started a precedent that continues today—every one of the NSP's national chairmen began his NSP affiliation as a patroller who worked his way up the ranks to the top administrative level. This tradition has inspired many NSP members to strive to attain either appointed or elected leadership positions in the organization.

Recognizing the potential value of young patrollers, Taylor established the Junior Program during his term of office. He also saw the value of women patrollers and clearly stated the NSP position on the equality of women in his 1952 edition of *The Ski Patrol Manual*: "All those who can meet NSP standards are entitled to membership and any office for which their talents and experience qualify them, regardless of sex." This statement reconfirmed the 1942 decision to admit women into the organization, a development that preceded current government regulations and the women's movement by more than three decades.

During Taylor's tenure as national director, the NSP re-established its liaison with the U.S. Army by agreeing to help recruit and screen potential candidates for the Army's Mountain and Cold Weather Training Command. The NSP also formed military ski patrols for U.S. Army recreation areas in Europe, an action that foreshadowed the formation of the NSP European Division.

When the Canadian Ski Patrol System (CSPS) came into being in the 1940s, its first manual gave acknowledgment to the NSP for organizational

assistance. The NSP also authorized the use of the rust parka by the CSPS. In 1953, NSP's Alaska Division was formed, and the NSP was incorporated in Colorado. It had first been incorporated in 1947 in New York as a nonprofit, philanthropic organization.

Taylor's final contribution to the NSP was to assemble the first meeting of all division chairmen at Aspen, Colorado, in May 1956. He retired at that meeting, and William Judd became the first elected national director. There were 358 ski patrols and 5,229 NSP members at the close of Taylor's term of office.

William Judd— National Director, 1956–1962

William R. Judd of Rocky Mountain Division served as national director from 1956 to 1962. His experience as a member of the FIS Ski Patrol at Aspen aided in the formation of the NSP Olympic Ski Patrol for the 1960 Winter Games at Squaw Valley, California. Ninety NSP members selected from patrols throughout the country formed the first all-volunteer ski patrol to ever serve at the Winter Olympics. This enthusiastic group celebrated its 30th reunion at Squaw Valley in 1990 and its 35th at Mt. Bachelor, Oregon, in 1995.

By 1958, the NSP had outgrown its function as a committee of the NSA, and so with mutual consent between NSP and NSA it became an affiliate member of the National Ski Areas Association. In the late 1950s and early 1960s, the NSP embarked on its formal classroom and field-teaching avalanche program and issued its first series of instructional slides and an avalanche instructor's outline.

The NSP's traditional emphasis on accident prevention was further stimulated by an invitation from the National Safety Council to present talks on ski safety to the general

public. In 1959, the NSP established national advisory committees on release bindings, ski equipment, and ski safety. In 1960, the organization published the country's first comprehensive report of ski accident statistics, *Sitzmarks or Safety*, written by William Judd and Irvin Hendryson, M.D., national medical advisor. The booklet presented ski safety measures for ski areas as well as advice on preconditioning exercises for skiers. Also in 1960, Arthur E. Ellison, Ph.D., organized the National Skier Research Foundation under NSP auspices to study ski accident causes and prevention methods.

By the close of Judd's term as national director in 1962, the first *NSP Supply and Equipment Catalog* had been issued, and the *Training Film Bibliography* had been printed as the first publication of its kind on winter emergency care and rescue techniques. The Safety on Skis (SOS) program also had been developed to promote ski safety and raise funds.

Charles Schobinger—National Director, 1962–1968

Charles W. Schobinger of Rocky Mountain Division was elected national director in 1962. That year, the NSP firmly established the ski patroller classification. From 1962 to 1968, the NSP experienced unprecedented growth, with the number of registered ski patrols jumping from 370 to 782, and the number of patrollers increasing from 5,527 to 14,149.

Schobinger rewrote the administrative section of *The Ski Patrol Manual* in 1963, and this section was approved as the working constitution and bylaws of the NSP. That year, the NSP European Division was formed. The first meeting of an advisory committee, the National Medical Committee, was held, and the National First Aid Committee was formed to implement the recommendations of the Medical Committee. The National Training and Testing Committee also was formed.

The NSP division directors held their first mid-season meeting in 1963 to discuss issues related to on-the-hill patrolling and the national organiza-

tion. A motion drafted by Schobinger that was introduced at the 1963 United States Ski Association board meeting initiated the formation of the National Ski Study Group, forerunner of the American Ski Federation. Meetings between the Ski Study Group and the NSAA eventually led to the development of the Skier's Responsibility Code (now Your Responsibility Code) and the uniform trail marking system.

The NSP adopted the gold cross as its official emblem in 1964. That same year, the organization introduced *The Toboggan Round-up*, an equipment catalog offering various rescue toboggans. Advanced ski patrol clinics designed primarily for full-time professional patrollers were initiated in 1965 and held annually throughout Schobinger's term. The following year, the NSP developed the auxiliary and certified patroller classifications.

In January 1966, the NSP joined with NSAA, the United States Ski Association, Professional Ski Instructors of America, Ski Industries of America, U.S. Ski Writers Association, and Federal Recreational Services to sponsor a National Ski Week proclaimed by President Lyndon B. Johnson to promote the sport of skiing. Also that year, the NSP Executive Committee, which at that time consisted of the national director and the assistant national directors, was formed specifically to meet the administrative requirements of the growing organization. In 1967, Edward L. Ericson was hired to serve as NSP's first full-time executive administrator.

By the time Schobinger stepped down as national director in 1968, the NSP had the administrative structure it needed to function as a major national education organization. New national advisory committees were created to provide expertise in specialized areas, and administrative procedures had been developed and disseminated through manuals and bylaws. The special needs of the

rapidly emerging professional patroller were being met through the Certified Program and the advanced ski patrol clinics. Eventually, the increasingly complex financial requirements of the NSP led to the need for a national treasurer in 1968.

Harry Pollard Jr.—National Director, 1968–1976

In 1968, Harry G. Pollard of Eastern Division became the NSP's fifth national director. In 1969, the NSP Board of Directors was expanded to include a representative elected by professional ski patrol directors. Peter McNulty from Mt. Tom Ski Area in Holyoke, Massachusetts, was the first person elected to that position. Also that year, the national headquarters in Denver was moved from 828 17th Street to 2901 Sheridan Boulevard.

During this period, the association established the candidate category for NSP members who had finished their emergency care requirements but had not yet completed on-the-hill training. In 1970, the certified patroller category was redefined and reserved mainly for full-time professional patrollers. Also, the NSP publication *National Notes* (which later became the *National Patroller* and is now *Ski Patrol Magazine*) was first published and sent to all registered patrollers.

The largest percentage growth in NSP history occurred in 1971. Along with the addition of two new divisions—the non-voting Far East and the fully-franchised Southern Division—the NSP grew from about 19,000 members to 22,629 members, an 18 percent increase. The following year, the national board voted to change its structure to incorporate proportional voting. Until then, the board had consisted of the 10 division directors; proportional voting meant the addition of 11 members, known as board representatives, to provide greater representation from the larger divisions (Eastern, Central, and Far West).

The first annual Junior Training Seminar took place in 1972 at Bridger Bowl, Montana, under the direction of Jerry Frederickson, national junior advisor. The Edward F. Taylor Outstanding Junior Patroller Award also was created in honor of the second national director. In 1973, the board voted to permit junior patrollers to wear the rust parka, at division option.

Also in 1973, the NSP began accepting the 81-hour Emergency Medical Technician Course developed by the American College of Orthopaedic Surgeons (following the U.S. Department of Transportation curriculum) as a substitute for the American Red Cross Advanced First Aid Course. The NSP still required its members to have supplemental training in Winter First Aid. The organization activated a nationwide pilot program for nordic ski patrols and, in 1974, established the national program under the leadership of David P. Hodgdon, national nordic advisor. The NSP also added a one-hour search and rescue exercise to the on-the-hill refresher.

During the early 1970s the American Red Cross completely revised its first aid courses. The NSP was, and

still is, a consultant to the American Red Cross in this area. In 1974, the NSP adopted the new ARC Standard First Aid and Personal Safety Course and NSP's Winter First Aid Course as the minimum requirement for junior, candidate, and patroller classifications. Senior and certified patrollers were required to take the new Advanced First Aid and Emergency Care Course. The NSP published the *Ski Patrol First Aid Instructors' Guide*, approved by the ARC, which was distributed to all NSP first aid instructors to help them convert to the new ARC courses. In 1975, the NSP Board of Directors voted to modify the NSP emergency care course to better address the needs of patrollers. The board also moved that, beginning in 1977, all members would be required to complete the ARC's cardiopulmonary resuscitation (CPR) course.

With the collaboration of ski area operators and ski lift engineers, the NSP published the first *Lift Evacuation Technical Manual* in 1975. The manual was distributed to all ski patrol directors and area operators.

The same year, Senator Thomas J. McIntyre of New Hampshire and Representative Jack F. Kemp of New York initiated legislation in Congress for a Federal Charter. In 1975 and 1976, two safety films were released: Aetna's "Flight Without Wings" and Safeco's "Skier's Choice." The national binding release program gained increasing acceptance from 1975 on.

Many significant organizational changes occurred within the National Ski Patrol during Pollard's tenure. Most important, the NSP achieved unprecedented recognition among other national ski organizations under his leadership. The NSP played a prime role in 1972 in establishing the American Ski Federation (ASF), an aggregate of member organizations representing the U.S. ski industry. The ASF was composed of the National Ski Patrol; National Ski Areas Association; Ski

Industries of America; United States Ski Association; Cross Country Ski Areas Association; and Professional Ski Instructors of America.

Pollard served as the president of the ASF in 1975. The NSP's association with this organization has provided an opportunity to participate fully in national activities that have affected the development of skiing and ski safety. It also has given clear testimony to NSP's role as the undisputed voice of ski patrolling in the United States.

One of Harry Pollard's most endearing and enduring legacies was the appointment in 1969 of Walter Gregg as national legal counsel. An NSP member since 1965, Gregg served in this position until his death in 1991. During his many years as legal counsel, Gregg wrote the present NSP bylaws; negotiated the joint statement of understanding between NSAA and NSP, which clarified the role of ski patrols at ski areas; worked with National Medical Advisor Warren Bowman and then Assistant National Director John Clair to establish the legal basis for the Winter Emergency Care (now Outdoor Emergency Care) program; and helped structure the purchase of the new national headquarters in Lakewood.

Gregg also established and held biyearly meetings of the National Legal Committee, which resulted in thoughtful advice to the NSP on everything from patents and Roberts Rules of Order to risk management and how best to avoid litigation.

Charles Haskins— National Director, 1976–1978

Charles Haskins of Far West Division was elected the sixth national director in 1976. As the national treasurer since 1969, Haskins had led the organization to a sound financial condition. Under his custodianship, and through the voluntary contributions of thousands of patrollers and friends, the NSP was able to purchase the building that housed the national office on Sheridan Boulevard, mortgage-free.

During his two-year tenure, Haskins made several unprecedented contributions. He broke the gender barrier by appointing Luann Skinner of Utah as the first woman assistant national director and Dodie Krueger of Colorado to the newly-created position of national auxiliary advisor.

While Haskins was director, Pete Austin of Pennsylvania helped form the Alumni Association for retired patrollers. Also, the national medical advisor, Warren D. Bowman Jr., M.D., wrote the second revised edition of the *NSPS Winter First Aid Manual;* the price was $1.25.

Under Haskins' administration, the NSP published a ski patrol physical fitness booklet and publicized openings for the 1980 Olympics Ski Patrol. In 1977, the organization published a revised edition of *The Ski Patroller's Manual.*

Donald Williams— National Director, 1978–1982

Shortly after Donald C. Williams of Central Division took office as national director in 1978, a number of important developments occurred in NSP history. The organization became a charter member of the International Federation of Ski Patrols (Fedération Internationale des Patrouilles de Ski [FIPS]) and participated in the first FIPS international patrolling symposium. The NSP also joined with the Boy Scouts of America Explorer Post Program in an effort to develop ski safety awareness among high school youth and recruit future NSP members.

To establish closer ties with ski area management, the NSP met with NSAA for the first time on a national level to discuss issues of mutual concern and benefit. The result was a formal statement of understanding regarding the relationship between NSP volunteer members and ski areas. This document formalized the agreement between the two organizations that the NSP neither directs nor is responsible for the day-to-day patrolling actions of NSP volunteer members; rather, the NSP's role is to provide membership services to assist patrols in fulfilling their obligations to area management. (The statement of understanding is presented in appendix D.)

In 1979, the National Safety Council honored the NSP with the annual Distinguished Service to Safety Award. As 1980 began, with Olympic fever gripping the nation, the NSP again provided volunteer ski patrol services to cover the jumping, cross-country, and biathlon events. This time, however, both an alpine and nordic patrol participated in the Winter Games—it was the first time a volunteer nordic ski patrol had served at an international meet. Additionally, about 30

NSP members served on a volunteer basis as race stewards, gatekeepers, course judges, and in other official capacities at the XIII Olympic Winter Games in Lake Placid, New York.

On December 2, 1980, after years of concerted lobbying efforts, President Jimmy Carter signed Public Law 96-489: "an act to promote safety and health in skiing and other outdoor winter recreation activities." This legislation, which had been sponsored in the U.S. Senate by Senator Orrin Hatch of Utah and in the U.S. House of Representatives by Congressman Jack Kemp of New York, formally granted a federal charter to the NSP in recognition of its civic contributions. To wit: "Mr. Speaker, by granting this Federal charter we are paying tribute to the spirit of community service and volunteerism in our country. The members of the National Ski Patrol are truly reflective of this spirit and are deserving of the recognition associated with a Federal charter of this kind." The NSP is registered under Section 501 (c)(1) of the Internal Revenue Code as a nonprofit association organized and operated exclusively for educational purposes. All subordinate units are granted exempt status under section 501 (c)(3).

The NSP expanded its international activities as it became more actively involved in FIPS programs. In 1980, Williams appointed Gretchen R. Besser, Ph.D, as NSP's first international liaison. She led an NSP contingent that participated in the FIPS Congress in Australia in 1981, together with patrollers from Australia, Canada, Chile, France, Japan, and New Zealand. Much broader representation was planned for the next international symposium, to be held in Maribel, France, in 1983. Besser instituted a patroller exchange program to foster on-hill patrol experience with other countries, especially South America. Also, National Medical Advisor Bowman represented the NSP at the International Society for Safety in Skiing meeting in Bormeo, Italy.

In 1981, Stephen M. Over of the American Ski Federation was hired as the executive director of the NSP. During this period, the national office operations became fully computerized, including the ever-expanding registration process. NSP membership was approaching 24,000 at this time.

Under the direction of Hans Roder, the national mountaineering advisor, the *Ski Mountaineering Manual* was published in 1980, the culmination of long, patient research and effort. Training advisor William Simonsen supervised revision and publication of the *Lift Evacuation Manual* in 1982. Other ongoing manuals were the *Journal of Winter Emergency Care*, with its up-to-date first aid documentation, and the *Tracks and Banner* journal, which was devoted to avalanche safety and rescue.

Ronald Ricketts— National Chairman, 1982–1986

At the 1982 annual board meeting, Ronald L. Ricketts of Alaska Division, former national treasurer, succeeded Williams as the eighth national direc-

tor. At that same meeting, the NSP Board of Directors changed the title of national director to national chairman.

Ricketts concentrated on implementing skier safety programs, consolidating the position of the professional patroller within the NSP, and setting in motion a broad-based strategic action plan. During Ricketts' four years as national chairman, Executive Director Stephen Over would lead an aggressive campaign to enlist a growing number of commercial sponsors/suppliers for NSP projects that included American Motors, DuPont, Bausch and Lomb, W.L. Gore and Associates, and The North Face, among others.

Ricketts appointed Assistant National Chairman Dale Williamson to coordinate an area management relations committee to strengthen patrol relationships with ski area operators. Also during this time, the board of directors approved a proposal by Hilbert H. Finn of Eastern Division to adopt the rust and blue parka as the official uniform.

On the international scene, the NSP continued its involvement with FIPS and the international ski patrolling community at a meeting in Meribel, France. The International Commission for Alpine Rescue (IKAR) welcomed the NSP—which was repre-

sented by Dr. Warren Bowman, national medical advisor, and Robin Faisant, national avalanche advisor— into its 18-nation membership.

Also in 1983, William Simonsen, assistant national chairman, and Brian McCartney, professional patrol director at Vail, Colorado, devised a plan to create the Professional Division pilot program in the Rocky Mountain Division. That same year, Gretchen Besser, national historian, published a book-length history titled *The National Ski Patrol: Samaritans of the Snow.*

The national executive committee and assistant national chairmen also began to develop a strategic action plan for long-range goals. After careful analysis of both the historical and potential development of the NSP, the planning team drafted a mission statement for the organization: "To serve the ski industry and skiing public through promotion of skiing safety and providing safety services." Some of the objectives for the next five years were to attain NSP representation at 90 percent of the ski areas in the country, raise the level of the endowment fund to $1 million, develop a ski safety program in conjunction with area management, and attain a professional level of ski patrol management proficiency among NSP officers.

With the release of a winter equipment catalog (later replaced with the *NSP Winter Catalog)*, the national office began to warehouse and sell T-shirts, caps, tents, backpacks, medical supplies, and other items to members.

The year 1984 marked the retirement of three NSP publications— *National Patroller*, *Journal of Winter Emergency Care*, and *Tracks and Banner*—and the launching of a glossy, four-color journal—*Ski Patrol Magazine*—that would be published four times a year. National training advisor Lloyd Alexander devised a program to improve skiing skills; the national office published the *NSP*

Officer's Handbook, a patrol directors' manual (now *NSP Policies and Procedures*); and a committee looked into the desirability of a dress code or more standardized uniform to improve patrollers' on-the-hill appearance. As the result of this study, the board approved a simple new patch with the NSP insignia to replace multiple patches on patrol parkas.

It was during this time that one of the most significant developments occurred in the history of the National Ski Patrol. The NSP had always relied on the American Red Cross to provide the first aid training required for NSP membership. While the ARC courses were beneficial, it had become increasingly apparent that they no longer met the specialized training needs of ski patrollers. NSP leaders began to recognize the advantages of a comprehensive, self-directed emergency care program tailored to the outdoor winter setting in which ski patrollers work. In 1985, an ad hoc committee drafted the curriculum for a patrol-oriented emergency care course of EMT level, to be called the Winter Emergency Care (WEC) Course. The course would focus on cold-weather injuries and illnesses and would de-emphasize the topics covered in the ARC courses that are extraneous to ski patrollers (i.e., bites and stings, poisoning, childbirth, and heat injury).

Also during the mid-1980s, to increase public awareness of the importance of skier safety, the NSP joined forces with NSAA, SIA, and PSIA to campaign for skier safety awareness. A new version of the Skier's Responsibility Code, with updated language and graphics, became the cornerstone of a program to educate the public and reduce skier accidents. Representatives of NSP, NSAA, SIA, PSIA, and the U.S. Ski Coaches Association met and devised the slogan "Be Aware—Ski With Care," to appear with a pictogram of a skier inside a yellow diamond. This safety message saturated ski areas, ski shops,

public service ads, and brochures.

The success of the two-year Professional Division pilot program in the Rocky Mountain Division prompted an expansion of the program throughout the country. Ultimately, this national, non-geographic division was to consist of professional patrols directly registered with the NSP national office. The Professional Division director would participate as a full voting member on the NSP Board of Directors. Jack Mason, professional patrol director at Winter Park Resort in Colorado, was elected the first director of the Professional Division.

By the end of the 1985 season, NSP patrollers, both professional and volunteer, were serving 560 out of a reported 650 ski areas. This figure represented an increase of 15 percent since 1983.

Marlen Guell— National Chairman, 1986–1992

Marlen Guell of Pacific Northwest Division, an assistant national chairman and the treasurer of the American Ski Federation, took office as national chairman in June 1986. Guell's immediate objectives were to revise the advisorship program; refine the NSP strategic plan; strengthen ties with other ski industry organizations; establish an education department; and oversee the final implementation phase of the Winter Emergency Care program. Judy Bunce, a 20-year patroller with a background in medical education, was hired as the director of the education department.

The NSP embarked on a course of upgrading its educational materials, beginning with *The Ski Patroller's Manual* (13th edition, 1990) and the *NSP Officer's Handbook* (1990). The NSP board confirmed at its 1993 annual meeting that the *NSP Officer's Handbook*, as amended in 1992, constituted the approved national

policies of the NSP. All other publications were considered to be educational documents. In 1994, the NSP Board of Directors voted to change the name *Officer's Handbook* to *NSP Policies and Procedures* to more accurately reflect the contents of the publication.

Field trials of the new Winter Emergency Care Course became operative at selected fall refreshers in 1986. New on-snow requirements made it mandatory for all patrollers to participate in an annual ski and toboggan refresher with specific objectives.

At the request of the National Avalanche Foundation, the NSP agreed to participate in the day-to-day administration of the Foundation, including operation of the biennial National Avalanche School, coordinated by Frankie Barr, NSP's director of administration. From its inception, NSP patrollers have served on the faculty and staff of this school, which has been described as the oldest, largest, and most prestigious avalanche training program in the world. More than 1,000 people from the ski industry and U.S. Forest Service have attended the school since the NSP began administering this program in 1987.

After diligent searching by the NSP executive director, Stephen Over, and with the help of the national legal counsel, Walter Gregg, the association purchased a new building in 1987, and the national office staff moved from Sheridan Boulevard into a $1-million, 21,000-square-foot building at 133 South Van Gordon Street in Lakewood, Colorado. (The mortgage was burned six years later, in January 1993.)

Also in 1987, the NSP Board adopted Winter Emergency Care as the association's "emergency care standard," meaning that WEC certification became an NSP membership requirement. The board voted to implement the course system-wide and develop a cadre of instructors and instructor trainers to deliver the education program to the local patroller. Warren D. Bowman Jr., M.D., wrote the accompanying textbook, *Outdoor Emergency Care* (1988), as a guideline for devising emergency care for people who become ill or injured at ski areas or in the wilderness. This extensively illustrated textbook (currently being revised for the third-edition release in the fall of 1998) emphasizes anatomy, physiology, in-depth patient assessment, and improvisation of emergency care equipment and techniques. In 1989, only two years after the NSP had implemented WEC on a national basis, the American Society of Association Executives recognized the program as the year's "Best Educational Program Based on the Needs of Industry or Professional Associations."

As an outgrowth of the Leadership Training Program for division officers, a task force co-chaired by Ronald Andrea of Eastern Division and Mike Shellito of Far West Division began developing an instructor training program and manual. The goal was to improve the quality and effectiveness of training in all NSP disciplines, including WEC, skiing and toboggan handling, mountaineering, nordic, certified, and avalanche.

At the 1988 Winter Olympic

Games in Calgary, Alberta, 17 NSP members were among 200 Canadian patrollers selected for the Olympic patrol. They served at the alpine, nordic, jump, and bobsled/luge venues.

In June 1988, 50 years after Minnie Dole had recruited a handful of individuals to form a skier safety organization, more than 340 patrollers, their family members, and friends gathered at the board of directors annual meeting in Boston to celebrate the National Ski Patrol's golden anniversary. The evening's festivities honored Minnie Dole's children, C. Minot "Mint" Dole Jr., and Susan Armstrong, as well as seven 50-year patrollers. Veterans of World War II joined with present-day troops of the reactivated Tenth Mountain Division to celebrate NSP ties to the Tenth.

By its 50th year, the NSP had 625 patrols with more than 24,000 patrollers. These represented 92 percent of the ski areas in the United States and in some parts of Europe and Asia.

Early in 1989, the board of directors adopted the concept for a new Senior Program, following an exhaustive study conducted under Eastern Division Director George Helwig and his Senior Program Committee. The board voted to revise the program to emphasize accident site and problem management rather than memorization and testing.

The NSP education department released its first two training videos, *History and Physical Examination* and *Lower Extremity Injuries* (filmed at California's Mammoth Mountain Ski Area), to supplement WEC instruction with additional skills application and the realistic depiction of emergency situations.

Also in 1989, under the sponsorship of American Express, NSP created a Ski Safety Team, composed of four outstanding patrollers who would visit ski resorts around the country to share ski safety ideas and promote the

excitement and etiquette of skiing. The team's charter members were Jack Mason of Winter Park Resort, Colorado; Brian McCartney of Vail/Beaver Creek, Colorado; Gary Reitman of Mammoth Mountain Ski Area, California; and Pete Wither of Steamboat Ski Area, Colorado.

Paid and volunteer patrollers from all over the country volunteered their services on race patrol and course maintenance crews for the World Alpine Ski Championships at Vail/Beaver Creek—the first time in 40 years this event had been held in the United States. Also in 1989, NSP members helped staff the Fourth International Winter Special Olympics in Reno, Nevada, and Lake Tahoe, California, and the World Junior Ski Championships at Alyeska Resort, Alaska.

That same year the NSP secured liability insurance coverage for patrollers engaged in educational, training, and certification programs, but left to area management the responsibility of insuring patrollers during day-to-day patrolling duties. In May, a contingent of patrollers led by National Chairman Marlen Guell and the NSP/American Express Ski Safety Team attended the seventh FIPS Congress in Riksgransen, Sweden. The NSP education director, Judy Bunce, provided FIPS attendees with an in-depth on-hill presentation on the WEC and accident investigation program—which generated considerable interest, since no other country had implemented a comprehensive, self-directed emergency care program on a national basis.

The Professional Division continued to expand. During the 1989 fiscal year, registrations approached 80 areas, representing more than 1,600 full-time paid patrollers. Several Professional Division members served as instructors for the second annual Institute for Ski Industry Personnel, which was held in selected cities and sponsored by USIA (which, at that time, consisted of the merged associations, NSAA and SIA); NSP; and PSIA. By 1990, this institute was revamped under the new name Institute of Ski Industries Studies (ISIA) to offer seminars on three main aspects of ski area operations: general management principles, liability considerations and skier etiquette, and the effect on operations of the B77 National Standards Committee, a subcommittee of the American National Standards Institute Committee on Aerial Passenger Tramways.

In January 1990, the NSP Board of Directors voted unanimously to consolidate its national office and administrative services with PSIA under the management of the same executive director, an event that National Chairman Marlen Guell likened in magnitude to the birth of the WEC program and the purchase of the NSP building in Lakewood, Colorado. The new relationship with PSIA was expected to have significant consequences in terms of unified marketing and the promotion of ski safety and skiing. Also, it strengthened both organizations' position with other ski industry groups and improved their ability to respond to the ever-changing demands of the ski industry. Each organization would operate independently, with its own board of directors and budgeting processes, while sharing some of the same national office staff. Cost savings realized by both organizations were expected ultimately to mean less frequent and expensive dues increases.

In cooperation with Colorado Ski Country USA, NSP and PSIA developed skier responsibility public service announcements for broadcast stations and cable networks around the country. Additionally, with the assistance of Professional Division delegate Skip King, the NSP and USIA produced a ski safety video, *Flight Log*, which was first shown at the USIA ski trade show and convention in Boston in May 1990.

By the 1991 ski season, every NSP geographic division was field testing one or more of the core requirements of the new Senior Program—WEC, skiing, and toboggan handling. At its 1991 meeting, the board made some modifications based on feedback from these pilot programs: clinics/evaluations would replace testing; seniors would be required to attend a clinic refresher every three years; and age and service requirements would be eliminated. The new program was implemented during the 1992–93 season, under the leadership of Mike Shellito, national training advisor; Dick Rosston, national ski and toboggan advisor; and Jeff Olsen, national WEC supervisor. The national office published an accompanying textbook, the *Senior Manual*.

For the first time in NSP history, at its 1991 annual meeting the board adopted a code of conduct establishing ethical standards for patrollers and defining disciplinary procedures in the event a complaint were to be made against a member. This code went into effect during the 1991–92 season. The board also eliminated the junior classification, recognizing that all members and candidates must be 15 years of age on or before the opening of the ski area, with the same duties, responsibilities, and privileges, subject to applicable federal and state law. The name of the Outstanding Junior Ski Patroller Award was changed to the Outstanding Student Ski Patroller Award, recognizing that any NSP patroller could be nominated for this award through the member's senior year in high school.

NSP continued its role as a participant and leader in international ski patrol forums by sending a delegation to the FIPS meeting in Australia (September 1991). At this symposium, Assistant National Chairman Jack Mason was elected treasurer of the Fedération Internationale des Patrouilles de Ski.

In 1992, the NSP communications department oversaw the redesign of *Ski Patrol Magazine,* resulting in a facelift to the overall format and a new masthead logo. The redesign came on the heels of a formal readership survey, in which 2,000 randomly selected readers provided input about the magazine's content as well as its graphic appearance. The majority of the respondents credited the magazine for helping them become more effective patrollers.

In response to the acquired immunodeficiency syndrome (AIDS) epidemic and OSHA requirements, the NSP revised its emergency care training to include an emphasis on universal precautions. The NSP continues to provide its membership with updates on OSHA's regulations regarding how to reduce exposure to blood-borne pathogens. In 1992 Interagency Liaison John Clair was instrumental in helping individual patrollers and ski areas obtain the Hepatitis B vaccine through a sponsor arrangement with a pharmaceutical company.

Jack Mason— National Chairman, 1992–1996

During the 1992 annual meeting in Chiemsee, Germany—the first annual meeting hosted by the European Division—Jack Mason became the first paid ski patroller elected to the position of national chairman.

Mason's platform reflected a new emphasis on the NSP's role as an education institution first and foremost. During Mason's term of office, the NSP harnessed the knowledge and expertise of the ski patrols and ski schools at the largest ski areas in the country to develop programs such as the Skiing Enhancement Seminar, designed to help patrollers improve their skiing skills, and the Ski Trainer's Workshop, designed to help patrol trainers identify sound skiing technique in others.

One of Mason's priorities as

national chairman was to strengthen the association's strategic planning process. During his term, the board voted that every budget item must relate directly to the strategic plan. He also rearranged the NSP national advisors organizational chart so that "action teams" were charged with developing or implementing specific programs that were identified in the strategic plan.

In November 1992, the National Ski Areas Association (newly reconstituted as an independent association after the USIA merger with SIA was dissolved) signed a lease with NSP to relocate to the third floor of Ski Patrol Building in Lakewood. A close working relationship with ski area management was—and still is—vital, as NSP continues to implement education programs at ski areas. The formal relationship between NSP and NSAA is codified in the Joint Statement of Understanding, initially iterated in 1979 and subsequently amended, most recently in 1993. NSAA's move to the Lakewood facility, following consolidation of NSP and PSIA, helped stabilize costs and services for all three associations and centered the primary ski industry associations under one roof. This arrangement has

allowed for better communication among the associations, resulting in a more unified voice to the rest of the ski and outdoor recreation industry.

Also at this time, NSP and PSIA experienced a "growing pain" as a result of their success in providing top-quality education materials: they began to suffer a lack of space at the warehouse facility they were co-leasing because member demands for materials exceeded the space available to house inventory. In 1994, after investigating various leasing options, the NSP and PSIA together built a 10,000-square-foot warehouse in Lakewood to provide adequate shipping and storage capacity well into the foreseeable future. The associations also leased a small amount of space to NSAA to accommodate its shipping needs.

The NSP's renewed emphasis on education culminated in the inaugural "Powderfall," the national patrolling conference held in April 1993 at Snowbird, Utah. This popular conference offers ski clinics with members of the PSIA demonstration team, sessions on toboggan handling, meetings with national advisors in a variety of disciplines, and opportunities for socializing and networking.

Mason's commitment to NSP's educational focus was rewarded by the enthusiastic acceptance of Powderfall. So successful was the inaugural event that it has become a popular annual gathering, heralded by participants as the one of the most useful and enjoyable education events the NSP has ever offered. Also in 1993, Mason began what would become his annual commitment to personally sign 5,000 letters of thanks to every instructor in the system. That same year, NSP introduced the National Outstanding Instructor Award to recognize those exceptional, dedicated members who share their expertise and love of patrolling with others.

The national Senior Auxiliary Pilot Program had been developed in 1990

in conjunction with the new Senior Program for basic patrollers. After being piloted and critiqued throughout the 1991–93 seasons, the Senior Auxiliary Program was adopted by the board in June 1993. The board also approved the Patroller Enrichment Seminar (PES)—a core component for senior auxiliaries—consisting of four modules: patrol facilities management; administrative policies management; expanded patroller services; and NSP education and leadership opportunities.

In the summer of 1993, the NSP published the second edition of *Outdoor Emergency Care,* written by National Medical Advisor Warren D. Bowman Jr., M.D. The revised textbook reflected changes in emergency care techniques and equipment that had developed since the first edition was released in 1988. Two chapters were devoted to patient assessment in emergency care, and a new section was included on the prevention of AIDS, hepatitis, and other blood-borne infections. The *Winter Emergency Care Instructor's Manual* for course trainers was also released. By this time, WEC held a strong appeal for area management and professional patrollers alike and had been integrated into many wilderness/mountaineering groups.

In 1993, Mason formed the New Paradigm Committee (NPC), whose purpose was to examine the administrative structure and effectiveness of the organization and recommend change so the NSP could more directly move toward its stated mission. The NPC report, delivered to the board in January 1994, revealed dissension within the organization about the NSP's priorities and its plans for the future. The report challenged the board to evaluate the organization's priorities—its reason for existence. The board met at a retreat in October 1994 in Chicago with facilitator Grace McGartland to examine the essential nature and purpose of the NSP. This highly successful two days of reflection led to the development of a new mission statement and strategic plan that encapsulates the ways in which the association operates and how NSP members use the support and training they get from their organization.

In another departure from tradition, the board in January 1994 voted to allow snowboarding patrollers to participate in NSP training. That same year, requirements that snowboard patrollers must meet the same performance objectives as alpine patrollers were published in the *Ski and Toboggan Training Manual.* In approving snowboard training for patrollers, the board emphasized that, as with the application of all NSP programs, the actual use of snowboard patrollers is up to individual areas.

In 1994 the board of directors voted to change the name of the Winter Emergency Care Course to Outdoor Emergency Care to better reflect the expanding scope of NSP training and patrollers' involvement in the recreation industry. In the spring of 1994 the NSP introduced Outdoor First Care, a one-day course designed to train people how to cope with outdoor emergencies until emergency medical personnel arrive. That summer, Outdoor First Care and Outdoor Emergency Care became an important part of an innovative bike patrol program developed by the NSP and the National Off-Road Bicycle Association (NORBA). Program participants would be certified in either Outdoor Emergency Care (for certification as "bike patrollers") or Outdoor First Care (for certification as "bike ambassadors"). The program continues to gain popularity at resorts with mountain biking facilities.

Overall, in the 1980s to the 1990s a gradual but consistent shift in NSP priorities took place. The organization moved from being a "rescue organization" to serving as an "education organization" that provides tools

for patrollers to use while functioning as members of ski patrols. The NSP's programs help prepare patrollers to provide area management with effective services to the skiing public.

Under the guidance of the national education advisors and with the volunteer efforts of each discipline-specific national advisory committee, all existing education programs were reviewed and updated. In many cases the committees developed new texts and accompanying instructor materials, and the instructor development programs for each of NSP education disciplines were completed. *Mountain Travel and Rescue,* a text for both Basic and Advanced Mountaineering courses, was published in 1995. Instructor manuals were compiled for the NSP's mountaineering and avalanche disciplines, and draft instructor manuals were in place for nordic patrollers and the Patroller Enrichment Seminars. In 1995, an NSP instructor newsletter, *Pointers,* was created to address the specific needs of the growing number of NSP instructors, many of them are trained to teach more than one education discipline.

The NSP's home page, developed by the national marketing department, made its debut on the World Wide Web in the summer of 1996, providing another communications tool between the NSP and its members as well as the worldwide outdoor recreation community. A new e-mail address (nsp@nsp.org) and fax-on-demand service also were introduced to support the association's efforts to communicate effectively with the member—a direct tenet of the NSP mission statement.

John Clair— National Chairman, 1996–

The NSP Board elected John J. Clair national chairman in June 1996. Clair, who is from Eastern Division,

pledged to continue to move the association into the information age by utilizing technology to develop and maintain strong member communications. His platform also included strengthening the image and value of volunteer patrollers to their local area management and maintaining the NSP's position of superior and dynamic leadership within the ski and outdoor recreation industry.

Wendy Schrupp

Clair officially reorganized the national advisors into a "national education committee" and renamed them program directors. Additional individuals were named to support positions as part of the national volunteer staff, e.g., national medical director, Alumni Association coordinator, awards coordinator, NSP historian, marketing counsel, and special training projects director.

The National Education Committee consists of the program directors from the Avalanche, Mountaineering, Leadership Development (replacing Auxiliary), Instructor Development, Ski and Toboggan—Alpine (ski/snowboard and nordic), and OEC programs. Additionally, Instructor Development was expanded to a national-level advisory charged with developing a full range of tools and programs for all the NSP instructors. The National Education Committee accepted the challenge to further standardize the teaching of the NSP educational courses, to develop a quality standard for all programs, and to seek ways to simplify the delivery and administration of all the programs.

The board of directors, under Clair's guidance, continues to explore ways to deliver educational programs in the most effective manner and to ensure that every course taught maintains a national standard of excellence. The National Ski Patrol faces many sobering challenges now and in the coming years. It must continue to provide its members with the educational tools that help them meet diverse and increasingly sophisticated needs and expectations. It must maintain its position as a valued resource within an ever-changing outdoor recreation industry. And, it must continue to address a variety of issues—from licensing and pre-hospital care regulations to liability—that have a direct and significant impact on NSP's volunteer heritage.

Summary

As of spring 1997, NSP's membership has grown to 28,000, its annual operating budget is $1,730,000, and the national office staff has grown to more than 20 (many of whom work for both NSP and PSIA). Because of NSP's success as an association, supported by the efforts of the marketing department, it has been able to attract a number of corporate sponsors. The NSP has not had a dues increase since 1990—the longest span without an increase in the history of the association. Income from official sponsors has supplemented dues income, to the extent that dues now account for only 49 percent of NSP's revenue against a long-term average of approximately 66 percent.

Over the years, the NSP has acted as a nationwide conduit of the latest information on outdoor emergency care and patrolling procedures, and it has provided skier safety education for a growing skiing public. Individual members, many of whom belong to ambulance squads, mountain rescue councils, and other lifesaving groups, have been responsible for saving countless lives by applying their skills wherever needed. The NSP contribution to every phase of skiing and snowboarding is evidenced by the significant number of patrollers who have been elected to the National Ski Hall of Fame.

Recognized worldwide for its various education programs, and for the excellent emergency care and rescue services its members provide on management's behalf, the National Ski Patrol is made up of dedicated, talented individuals who optimistically face the challenges presented by the outdoor recreation industry. The organization was endowed with the flexibility and dynamics to meet these challenges through the qualities of its founder, Minnie Dole, who closed an era in American skiing by his death on March 4, 1976.

The early days of ski patrolling.

The National Ski Patrol is an association of 28,500 members who are represented at 99 percent of the ski areas in the United States and in some parts of Europe and Asia.

As described in chapter 1, the history of the NSP is rich and varied, reflecting the dedication of members who are motivated by the love of outdoor recreation and the desire to help those in need. This long tradition of promoting the enjoyment and safety of skiing prompted the United States Congress to grant a federal charter to the NSP in 1980 under Public Law 96-489. The NSP is registered under Section 501 (c)(1) of the Internal Revenue Code as a nonprofit association organized and operated exclusively for educational purposes. All subordinate units are granted exempt status under section 501 (c)(3).

The NSP is dedicated to providing its members with educational programs and materials that will help them fulfill their role within the outdoor recreation community, whether in the context of skiing, snowboarding, or otherwise. Normally, NSP members provide this service under the direction of a ski area operator, a public lands administrator, or the manager of some other kind of outdoor recreation.

NSP's Strategic Plan

The National Ski Patrol has a formal strategic plan that describes succinctly the association's purpose, how the NSP fulfills that purpose, and where it plans to go. The strategic plan helps the board of directors determine how and where to spend the association's time and money.

The strategic plan is vital to the ongoing administration of the NSP because of its role in helping the association's leaders forecast and determine how to respond to issues that may affect NSP members. Consequently, the plan is under constant revision. Each year, the plan is reviewed, updated, and approved by

CHAPTER 2

NSP—An Education Association

the board of directors.

The foundation of the plan is the vision, mission, and strategic intents described in the following sections. The plan itself consists of objectives, strategies, and action plans that describe short-term activity. The association budget supports each action plan. Proposed projects or activities do not receive funding if they do not directly relate to or support an action plan.

NSP's Vision

In October 1994, the NSP Board of Directors went on a retreat to develop a vision statement—the first such statement in the association's history. A vision is a realistic, credible model for the future. The NSP vision describes *why* the association exists in terms of the impact it has in the world and the *difference* the association makes by being in existence. Because the NSP vision is considered valid for four to six years, it is currently called Vision 2000:

We are a leading partner in the ski and outdoor recreation community as an adaptable resource of valuable individuals benefiting this community.

The NSP is a strong, independent component of the outdoor recreation industry, providing unique educational programs not offered elsewhere. At the same time, the association values the strategic alliances it has made with its partners in the recreation industry. These alliances reflect the board of directors' quick response to

the changing dynamics of the industry, and the organization's ongoing commitment to provide excellent educational resources to the benefit of its members and those they serve.

NSP's Mission

The mission is the keystone of the strategic plan. The NSP mission defines *who* the association serves as well as its *primary purposes*. It also provides a foundation for the association's goals and direction.

The mission of an organization often is different from that of its subunits. Further, the association's mission may be different from each member's mission. Similarly, the mission of the National Ski Patrol is to provide its members with educational resources to help them fulfill the duties required of them by area management. However, these specific tasks likely will vary from one local area to another, as will each person's level of involvement in the area's overall operations. What is important is that the mission statements of each are interrelated. The NSP mission statement identifies the concerns of the NSP as an *association*, at the same time expressing a commitment to serve its members in their varied activities.

As defined in the NSP mission statement, the association's goal is to develop high-quality training programs in multiple disciplines and to deliver these programs to the membership in a cost-effective manner. The NSP's subunits—the geographical divisions—carry out the association's mission by delivering education programs, monitoring quality assurance, and providing the national level with feedback on the effectiveness of the programs and methods of delivery. The members, in turn, access these programs to increase their level of expertise as patrollers, thereby increasing their value to those for whom they work and providing a service to the public.

The mission contains strategic intents, which describe the ways in which the association wishes to serve its members, area management, and the public. These intents serve as the association's blueprint for action and drive the association's direction.

The NSP mission statement, as approved by the NSP Board of Directors in January 1995, is as follows:

We are a member-driven association. Our members support and participate in the ski and outdoor recreation community by providing emergency care, rescue, and education services. Our association supports us by surpassing member expectations through the strategic intents:
- *an esprit de corps that inspires members to belong;*
- *exceptional education programs;*
- *dynamic communication;*
- *outstanding membership support services;*
- *energetic interagency relations; and*
- *a strong financial position.*

Benefits of Belonging

During the NSP Board's 1994 retreat to evaluate the organization's priorities, the strategic intents were developed to identify the key benefits NSP members receive when using the support and training they get from their national association. The strategic intents are described in detail in the following sections.

An Esprit de Corps that Inspires Members to Belong

Patrollers devote a great deal of time and effort to the skiing and snowboarding public, area management, and the national association. In return, the National Ski Patrol recognizes this excellence and dedication at all levels through public expressions of appreciation in the form of service awards, certificates of appreci-

Scott Markewitz

ation, and special appointments, among other honors.

This type of recognition among one's peers is a stimulus for continued and improved performance. More important, the awards presented by the National Ski Patrol are sincere expressions of appreciation for accomplishments in the service of the NSP and the skiing and snowboarding public. The NSP recognizes three types of awards or insignia:
- those that recognize meritorious service;
- those that identify patrollers with outstanding ability or special skills; and
- those that are awarded to members or non-members for distinguished service to the NSP and to the sport of skiing and snowboarding.

In addition to providing awards as a membership benefit and performance incentive, the association offers various opportunities for members to enjoy the rewards of interacting with other patrollers. NSP programs encourage the participation of both volunteer and paid

patrollers, so that individuals in these two NSP membership categories can exchange knowledge and strengthen communication. National conferences, seminars, and events are organized to bring members from all divisions together to enjoy fellowship and share information about topics of interest.

Further, the national organization routinely conducts formal surveys to determine whether members are satisfied with the benefits they receive due to their NSP affiliation. It is extremely important to the board of directors, the volunteer staff, and the paid office staff to identify and respond to the needs and desires of the membership.

The most current information about these various forms of recognition and appreciation is available in *NSP Policies and Procedures.*

Exceptional Education Programs

Access to exceptional education programs is important to the success of all NSP members, who must continually update their skills so that area management and the public will have confidence in their ability to provide state-of-the-art emergency care. To this end, national program committees develop and refine educational programs in a variety of areas such as alpine toboggan handling (skiing/snowboarding), avalanche awareness and rescue, outdoor emergency care, nordic toboggan handling, mountain travel and rescue, patroller enrichment, leadership development, and instructor development.

These programs and corresponding educational materials, clinics, courses, and meetings are offered throughout the world. The NSP's goal is to provide the highest quality standards of training and assure that quality through instructor support.

One example of NSP's commitment to provide exceptional education

opportunities is Powderfall, the association's national education conference introduced in 1993. The event was so well-received that first year that the NSP began offering it on an annual basis. The NSP also offers special-interest seminars, such as national instructor training conferences, medical symposiums, and skiing improvement and skiing evaluation clinics in coordination with the Professional Ski Instructors of America. In addition, the national office provides various educational resources through a lending library of videos.

Dynamic Communication

Ski Patrol Magazine, published four times per year, is the definitive publication about what is happening in the world of ski patrolling. It is sent to all registered members and associates of the NSP. The magazine contains information on emergency care techniques and equipment; skiing, snowboarding, and toboggan handling; search and rescue; avalanche awareness; training methods; and association and recreation industry news, among other topics. The summer issue contains the annual OEC *Refresher Study Guide,* which patrollers use to prepare for membership recertification in the fall.

In addition to publishing the magazine, the association sends out periodic mailings, including Patrol Officer Bulletins (POBs) and national memos, which serve as communication links with national and division officers and national program directors. POBs and memos are generally informational but may be used to communicate national policy. A synopsis of the essential mailings is published in *Ski Patrol Magazine*.

A communication link to all NSP instructors is *Pointers*, an instructor newsletter that is published two to three times per year, and the *OEC Instructor's Bulletin*, which accompanies the *OEC Refresher Study Guide* each summer.

Entering into an age of technology along the information highway makes NSP's strategic intent of providing dynamic communication particularly exciting. The national office is now equipped to send and receive electronic mail. The national office address for electronic mail sent through the Internet is nsp@nsp.org. The NSP also is represented on the World Wide Web with a national home page at http://www.nsp.org. The home page provides up-to-date information on what's new, who's who, education programs, national publications, and much more.

Also, the toll-free FAX number, 800-222-ISKI (4754), is available to any NSP member. The national office local FAX number is 303-988-3005. The FAX number can be used to change addresses, make inquiries about course registrations, place catalog orders, etc. The membership is encouraged to use the 800 FAX number whenever possible.

Fax-on-demand also is available to NSP members. The service entails simply dialing 800-825-0997 from a touch-tone phone and inputting the document number from a menu of topics. After the caller hangs up, the service automatically faxes the document to the number requested.

The national office 800-voice line is reserved for officers (patrol directors, section chiefs, region directors, and division directors), division OEC supervisors, and national program directors. This service is extended to these individuals because their NSP duties require them to communicate frequently with the national office.

With the operation of radio systems, ski patrols are required to comply with applicable regulations of the Federal Communications Commission (FCC). In 1987, the FCC determined that ski patrols are subunits of the National Ski Patrol System, Inc., and therefore, radio licenses are issued to NSP and then assigned to each patrol. No ski patrol may operate radio equipment without a valid license issued to ski area management or to the National Ski Patrol System, Inc. The National Ski Patrol has established an internal process to ensure the validity and correction of submitted applications in the name of the National Ski Patrol. Since no two ski areas are alike and the equipment available and the procedures used are generally specific to that area, it is essential that patrollers be well trained to use the types of communications systems and equipment found at their area.

Outstanding Membership Support Services

The NSP national office is the principal administrative unit of the organization. The office is managed by an executive director and is staffed by the personnel required to effectively administer NSP operations. A separate warehouse houses and ships the education materials and other catalog products.

A direct return on member dues is the ability to purchase, at member prices, all the manuals, videos, and

Martin Crabb

The NSP headquarters were purchased in 1987.

Martin Crabb

NSP and PSIA built the warehouse in 1994.

Energetic Interagency Relations

While NSP's excellent education programs benefit the individual member in many ways, they also allow the association to develop partnerships and links with other skiing and outdoor recreation organizations, which helps unify and strengthen the industry overall.

Industry partners include the Professional Ski Instructors of America (PSIA), the National Ski Areas Association (NSAA), the National Ski Retailers Association (NSRA), and SnowSports Industries America (SIA), among others. Further, NSP represents the United States at the Fedération Internationale des Patrouilles de Ski (FIPS), an international group dedicated to ski safety education.

The NSP also establishes and maintains proactive relationships with the outdoor recreation community at-large; with government agencies such as the U.S. Forest Service; with industry standards groups such as the American National Standards Institute, Inc. (ANSI) and the American Society for Testing and Materials (ASTM); and with related organizations such as state emergency medical services groups, the International Mountain Bicycling Association (IMBA) and National Off-Road Bicycle Association (NORBA).

Working on promotional programs with corporate sponsors and other companies, the office staff have negotiated special pricing on automobiles, credit cards, and members' access to insurance programs. In addition, ski manufacturer promotional sales are often available through ski retailers and manufacturers' representatives for NSP members. Each of these programs can be worth many times the cost of annual NSP dues.

NSP negotiates the support of various corporate sponsors to help promote ski patrolling to the public. The association also promotes ski

materials that make up the NSP education program, plus a wide variety of other publications concerning ski patrolling. The *NSP Winter Catalog*, published annually, offers competitive prices on a number of hard-to-find items designed to help ski patrollers do their jobs efficiently and comfortably.

To meet membership needs and provide members with outstanding support, the Member Information and Services Team (MIST) was introduced in 1993. Using the direct phone line (303-988-1646), members can speak with people who are trained to answer questions about individual membership and course registrations, catalog orders, awards, and special events.

The national office periodically surveys the membership to find out if these services are meeting their needs and expectations. Survey topics have included whether NSP should offer association programs to non-members; whether the association should continue to have a ski patrol uniform program; and whether NSP should pursue alternative education programs and offer CD-ROM versions of the association's education materials.

patrolling to ski area management at trade shows and conventions. The NSP has formed a close working relationship with NSAA to address issues common to both ski patrols and ski areas, develop national ski safety programs, co-author lift evacuation technical materials, strengthen government relations, and remain abreast of OSHA regulations. In addition, NSP works closely with PSIA on education programs involving skiing enhancement and ski training for patrollers.

Strong Financial Position

Because the NSP is a nonprofit education association, its revenue comes primarily from member dues. The annual national dues (currently $27) support the programs and services addressed in NSP's mission. At the time of this printing, there has not been a dues increase since 1990, the longest period without an increase in the history of the association. A report of NSP's financial position, as prepared by the national treasurer, is published in each fall issue of *Ski Patrol Magazine*.

Dues income is supplemented by non-dues revenue through merchandising and affinity programs, sponsorships, and advertising revenue. Non-dues revenue allows the association to offer high-quality member education programs at a significantly lower price than if the association were forced to rely solely on member dues.

The National Ski Patrol, like other nonprofit associations, allocates its funds according to established priorities. There are two major categories of expense: (1) fixed expenses, the expected costs of the organization, and (2) variable expenses, the funds that are used for the programs specified by the strategic plan.

The national treasurer and the executive director prepare the budget annually based on the strategic plan. The budget is then presented to the board of directors at the annual meet-

Scott Markewitz

Mt. Bachelor Photo

ing for final approval. The NSP board establishes the national dues with each budget review cycle.

Benefits To Area Management

NSP develops consistent standards of training and quality content for its nationally recognized education programs. These standards of training are identical for paid employees and volunteers (agents of area management).

NSP develops courses and continuing education programs are specifically targeted to the work that area management may require of its patrollers, including outdoor emergency care, avalanche mitigation, on-the-hill patrolling skills, and lift evacuation (in conjunction with NSAA).

National Policy-Making

The national board of directors is the governing body of the National Ski Patrol. The board holds two regular national meetings each year: a business-oriented midwinter meeting and a special convention-type annual meeting in which participation by the general membership is encouraged.

The bylaws of the National Ski Patrol are the governing ordinances for the association and create the framework for guiding national administrative operations. The NSP Board of Directors adopts and amends the bylaws based on national needs. Amendments to the bylaws must be approved by two-thirds of the board at two successive meetings.

Thus, an amendment approved at the annual meeting in June must be approved again at the following midwinter meeting, and vice versa. This provides the membership with sufficient time to carefully review the full implications of an amendment and give input to the board before the amendment is passed. The bylaws are published annually in the *NSP Policies and Procedures* manual and also are available from the national office.

The board's legislative actions are the result of the proposal process. Any patroller may submit a proposal for a change or addition to NSP policies by way of the national chairman, assistant national chairmen, a board member, or a national program director.

Proposals are the means by which the board of directors considers and adopts changes or additions to NSP policies, procedures, or bylaws. Each proposal is prepared on a national office form that requests a descriptive title, references, proposal text, budget information, financial impact, and a statement of explanation or justification of the proposal. Proposals to amend bylaws must comply with the provisions of the NSP Bylaws, Article XIII, and section 5.3.7. of *NSP*

Policies and Procedures.

Proposals are first considered by a committee of board members at the meetings. If the committee determines that the proposal may have some merit for the organization, it brings the proposal before the entire board. At that time, the board considers whether to approve or reject the proposal.

There are two standing committees of the board of directors: the administration committee and the operations committee. The administration committee handles proposals dealing with registration, the national office administration and operation, catalog items and supplies, dues, public relations, awards, classifications, and similar topics. The operations committee handles proposals dealing with outdoor emergency care, avalanche, mountaineering, proficiency, senior, certified, training, and similar topics.

Each committee is made up of one half of the total number of board members attending the meeting, consisting of division directors and board representatives (excepting the national chairman and national treasurer, who do not sit on either committee). To ensure equal representation on the committees, half of the division directors serve on the administration committee, and the other half serve on the operations committee. Division directors representing divisions that have only one board member may express their preference about which committee they wish to serve. Divisions with more than one board member are represented on both committees and may have no more than two members on one committee. The assistant national chairmen chair the administration and operations committees. The assistant national chairmen have no vote.

The chairperson of each committee reports on the proposals considered by the committee, including the voting tabulation of the committee. All proposals brought before the board as seconded motions are open for discussion and approval or rejection by the board. No second is required. No action is taken by the board on any proposal that has been rejected in committee unless a board member moves for adoption of the proposal. Any such motion requires a second. Only board members and the national treasurer may vote on issues that are presented to the board. The national chairman may vote only in the event of a tie.

If the proposal is approved, the national chairman works with the assistant national chairmen and the national office staff to implement the new policy. The *NSP Policies and Procedures* manual, amended annually and published in September, contains the approved national policies of the National Ski Patrol System, Inc. All other publications are educational or informational documents and may not reflect current NSP policies.

The board establishes and the executive director oversees the implementation of national policies. The board has the ability to effect change in the organization as well as maintain continuity of policies and programs through the legislative process. The board's role is to represent the interests of the NSP membership at large rather than focus exclusively on the interests of a specific division, group, or individual.

Membership in the National Ski Patrol means being a part of the largest education association for patrollers in the world. Consequently, every NSP member—regardless of type of service, skill classification, or member level (see table 3.1)—is expected to demonstrate an above-average level of skills and knowledge in emergency response.

Of equal importance is the patroller's responsibility to display integrity, maturity, and good judgment. Additionally, NSP members are expected to display a good attitude toward ski patrolling. A patroller should always be cooperative, constructive, and demonstrate a willingness to accept responsibilities and a desire to improve skills and knowledge.

Type of Service

A patroller is an individual who, whether volunteering or receiving pay for services, works with an established ski or snowboard patrol to provide

mountain resort guests with emergency care and rescue services under the supervision of area management or the public lands administration.

Area management generally delegates the recruitment of volunteer patrollers to the volunteer patrol director, who in turn may appoint a recruitment advisor. By the same token, management usually delegates the recruiting of paid patrollers to the paid patrol director. Local patrols develop recruitment programs appropriate for the ski area, location, and needs, although area management has the final say on the skill types and number of patrollers appropriate for the area.

Volunteer

A *volunteer* patroller is an individual who performs services or assumes obligations, at his or her own free will, under the supervision of area management or the public lands administration.

The Joint Statement of Understanding between the National Ski Patrol and the National Ski Areas Association defines the relationship between ski area management and its volunteer patrols and patrollers (appendix D). Ski area management makes the final decision on how many patrollers the area will have, which patrollers can work or volunteer at the area, and what their responsibilities will entail. NSP provides the ski and outdoor recreation community with education programs for individuals who may wish to apply for patrolling positions at ski areas or in public lands.

The patrol director (acting for area management) as well as the area

Table 3.1 Membership Categories

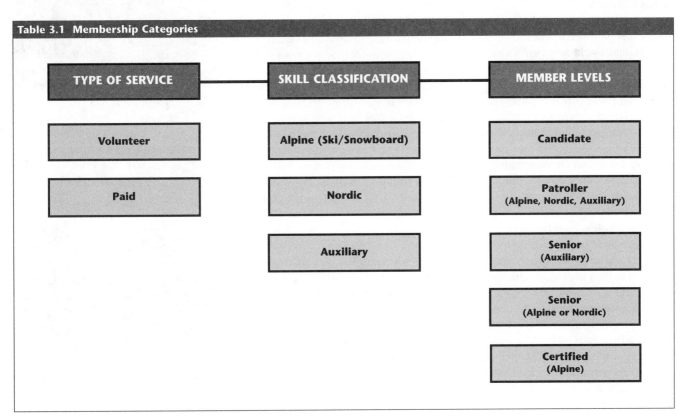

TYPE OF SERVICE	SKILL CLASSIFICATION	MEMBER LEVELS
Volunteer	Alpine (Ski/Snowboard)	Candidate
Paid	Nordic	Patroller (Alpine, Nordic, Auxiliary)
	Auxiliary	Senior (Auxiliary)
		Senior (Alpine or Nordic)
		Certified (Alpine)

manager or public lands administrator, have full discretion to refuse to allow an NSP member to patrol at the area during the season and to re-register any NSP member at the beginning of each season. NSP members who are dropped from the local patrol retain membership in the national organization through the rest of the membership year, meaning, essentially, that they will continue to receive national mailings and may purchase catalog items at member prices for the remainder of the ski season. An NSP member who violates the NSP Code of Conduct is subject to additional disciplinary actions based on the code violation (see appendix A).

Paid

Paid patrollers may be registered in the NSP through the Professional Division or through their geographic division. There are three categories of registration: full-time paid patroller, part-time paid patroller, and professional patroller.

In the Professional Division, a *full-time paid* patroller is an individual who is paid by ski area management to work a full-time schedule during the ski season. In other words, ski patrolling is the patroller's vocation during the ski season. Compensation for paid staff must come in the form of FICA wages. To qualify as a full-time paid patroller for NSP registration purposes, the patroller must be paid the entire time he or she works a regular schedule.

In the Professional Division, a *part-time paid patroller* is an individual who is paid by ski area management to work a part-time schedule during the ski season.

In an NSP geographic division, a *professional patroller* is an individual who is employed by area management and is paid wages subject to federal tax withholding for services that average 16 hours or more per week per ski season.

Skill Classification

The NSP offers various skill classifications that pertain to a person's area of interest and skill proficiency. These skill classifications include alpine (ski/snowboard), nordic, or auxiliary patrolling and are described in the following sections.

Members may register in two skill classifications by meeting the proficiency performance objectives of both classifications. It is not uncommon for patrollers to switch between alpine skis, nordic skis, and snowboards while performing their duties at a ski area. There are many dual-registered NSP members who patrol some of the time on alpine skis and some of the time on a snowboard, or who provide patrolling duties on nordic skis at a cross-country area in addition to patrolling at a downhill ski area. Members of this dual-registration classification may be volunteer or paid.

Alpine (Ski/Snowboard)

NSP members who are registered as alpine patrollers may carry out their on-hill duties—including transporting toboggans—on downhill skis, telemark skis, or a snowboard, depending on their equipment preference and the approval of area management. Alpine patrollers may achieve a more advanced NSP alpine membership classification by completing alpine senior or alpine certified training (see chapters 10, 12, 18 and appendix E).

Nordic

The nordic patroller skis and transports toboggans while using nordic equipment. A nordic patroller transporting a toboggan with telemark or nordic ski equipment at an alpine area must follow NSP's protocol for alpine toboggan handling. A nordic patroller may achieve a more advanced NSP nordic membership classification by completing nordic

senior training (see chapters 16, 18 and appendix F).

Auxiliary

The NSP member who is registered as an auxiliary patroller may provide any services deemed necessary by area management and the patrol, except for transporting loaded toboggans. An auxiliary patroller may achieve a more advanced NSP auxiliary membership classification by completing a senior auxiliary program (see chapter 18 and appendix H).

Member Level

Member levels refer to five categories of registration that pertain to the patroller's level of education achievement: candidate, patroller, senior alpine or nordic, senior auxiliary, and certified.

Candidate

The candidate member category is the entry level of membership in the NSP. A candidate may apply for entry-level membership in the alpine (ski/snowboard), nordic, or auxiliary patroller skill classification.

Many ski areas have an applicant screening day in which prospective candidates are invited to ski with the patrol. The NSP try-out period is limited to two days. The try-out fee is $5, which the patrol director remits to the national office.

The applicant screening program allows prospective candidates to learn more about the workings of the ski patrol—and what is expected of its members—before they commit to the demanding role of care provider. The program also allows the local patrol to evaluate potential candidates before accepting them into the program and beginning the arduous process of on-the-hill training.

All applicants accepted as candidates are required to register and pay

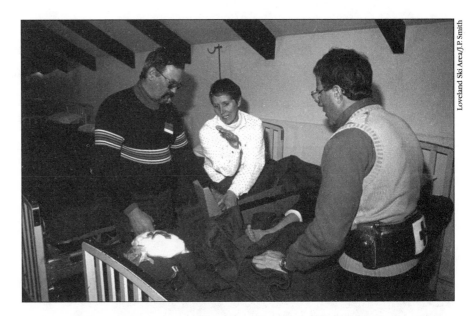

Loveland Ski Area/J.P. Smith

dues as candidates before participating in any on-the-hill training. Membership benefits begin at this level. For example, candidates receive all membership mailings, including *Ski Patrol Magazine,* and may order catalog products at member prices. Candidates must complete certain training before they can advance to NSP patroller status. If they do not advance to patroller status, national dues will not be refunded. (Specific information on the various education and training programs can be found in chapters 9 through 18 in this manual.)

The time required to fulfill all the basic training requirements varies from one patrol to another. Training may take a few weeks or it may be scheduled over the entire ski season. During candidate training, it is area management's discretion whether to allow candidates to wear a patrol uniform, insignia, or some other type of patroller designation.

All NSP candidates must successfully complete the Outdoor Emergency Care Course (either the full course, if they need complete emergency care training, or a challenge, if they have current certification or license in medicine or emergency medical services). Candidate training in the NSP Outdoor Emergency Care

Course is parallel to emergency medical technician basic training; however, OEC is tailored to the special considerations of illness and emergencies that may occur in the outdoor environment. In addition to taking the OEC Course, all candidates must complete professional rescuer cardiopulmonary resuscitation (CPR) training through the American Heart Association, American Red Cross, or National Safety Council, if the candidate's patrol does not offer it as part of OEC training (see chapter 17).

NSP also requires candidates to complete the local patrol's skiing/snowboarding and toboggan-handling training. Most candidates complete this training during the first season. The NSP does not require auxiliary candidates to participate in skiing/snowboarding and toboggan-handling training, although local patrols may require this. Finally, all candidates receive training in local area procedures and policies also.

At the completion of candidate training, the local patrol may conduct a final evaluation of candidates before advancing them to the patroller classification. Evaluations usually take place at the candidate's home area, but occasionally smaller patrols may choose to combine their basic evaluation

Certified

The certified designation is the highest education level of NSP membership. This designation indicates that the individual not only has met the NSP patroller requirements but has taken a series of modules in which he or she demonstrated extensive knowledge of patrol and ski area operation management and strong skill proficiency, leadership, instructional ability, and communication skills. It is recommended that the patroller achieve senior status before entering the certified program. The certified program is designed to meet training objectives for the alpine skill classification.

Other Membership Types

The NSP also offers the following registration categories to identify members with special interests or needs.

Medical

A physician patroller or a medical associate must have a medical doctor (M.D.) or osteopathic doctor (D.O.) degree and either have a current medical license in the state in which the physician will render services or be on active medical duty with a federal agency.

A *physician patroller* must meet the same requirements and fulfill the same patroller training and responsibilities as any other member of the patrol with the same skill level. The physician patroller is entitled to wear a patrol parka but without any insignia that would identify the person as an M.D. or D.O.

A *medical associate* must pay NSP membership dues and also obtain a copy of *Outdoor Emergency Care* and *The Ski Patroller's Manual*. A medical associate is not required to provide emergency care or perform any other on-the hill/trail patroller duties; however, the associate may be asked to

program. Each local area may add to the national criteria to suit local terrain, snow conditions, or other factors.

If the candidate has not met all the national and local requirements, he or she cannot be advanced to a patroller level. The patrol director has the option of either terminating the candidate's membership at the end of the ski season or re-registering the person as a candidate the following season.

By the end of candidate training and before starting actual patrolling, the member must have acquired a uniform conforming to the area policy, a vest or aid belt in which to carry emergency care supplies, and any other items required by the patrol.

Patroller

Once the candidate has met all the membership requirements, the patroller designation is the next level of membership in the NSP. This category indicates that the individual has completed all candidate training and meets all NSP membership requirements in the skill classification(s) of his or her choice—alpine (ski/snowboard), auxiliary, or nordic.

Each season, patrollers must remit NSP membership dues to the patrol

director and must obtain recertification in all the NSP education and training membership requirements. This consists of attending the annual OEC refresher, professional-rescuer CPR refresher, and on-the-hill/trail refresher, which focuses on skiing and toboggan-handling skills and includes a review of local area policies and procedures. Auxiliary patrollers may be exempt from portions of the on-the-hill/trail refresher program, depending on local policy.

Members may achieve a more advanced NSP membership level by completing a senior or certified training program.

Senior

Beyond the patroller category, senior designation is the next level of membership in the NSP. This level indicates that the individual has not only met the NSP patroller requirements but has taken a series of core and elective education programs in which he or she demonstrated expanded patrolling knowledge and skills, leadership, and problem management capabilities. Senior-level programs are available for all three NSP classifications: alpine, auxiliary, and nordic patrolling.

present specific topics for an OEC course or provide other expertise for the OEC programs and, if authorized by area management, provide medical assistance. A medical associate is not required to have an Outdoor Emergency Care card or complete refreshers. It is, however, every member's responsibility to maintain knowledge of on-the-hill/trail practice of emergency care, transportation techniques, and patrol room procedures. The medical associate may not wear the official NSP uniform.

Young Adult (Student)

NSP members and patrol candidates must be 15 years of age on or before the opening of the ski area. Young adult patrollers (age 15 through high school graduation) must meet the same requirements and fulfill the same patroller training and responsibilities as any other member of the patrol with the same skill level.

NSP young adult programs at the local level must be conducted in accordance with applicable federal, state, and local laws; school district policies and procedures; and the ski area's rules and regulations. Division legal counsel should be engaged to help identify and interpret the effects of these regulations on young adult programs. The NSP national association imposes no limitation on young adult patrollers' activities that are not common to all who participate in NSP programs.

Lifetime Members

An NSP member who has served at least one year as a registered member is eligible to become a lifetime member. For the one-time lifetime membership fee, all future annual dues are waived. Divisions may opt to duplicate this waiver by offering their own division lifetime memberships. As of this printing, the one-time membership fee is $400 for an active patroller and $200 if 55 years or older. The one-time alumni membership fee is $200.

Active lifetime members must satisfy the national and local performance objectives in all aspects of training and annual certification to register in the alpine (ski/snowboard), auxiliary, or nordic skill classification. Active lifetime members also must meet the uniform requirements of the area at which they patrol. Alumni lifetime members are not required to maintain any skill qualifications.

Lifetime members receive a gold lifetime membership pin, a walnut-framed lifetime membership certificate, and a lifetime membership registration card. When an active lifetime member is no longer an active patroller, the lifetime membership automatically becomes a lifetime alumni membership. Lifetime membership fees go directly to the NSP endowment fund.

Inactive Members and Reentry of Former Members

An inactive member is someone who was registered as an active member of the NSP (other than as a candidate) but who has temporarily discontinued patrolling. The temporary period should not exceed one or two years. It is the prerogative of the patrol director and area management whether to allow a person to reenter active patrolling status from an inactive position or former member position.

During the inactive registration period, an inactive member must pay the same national, division, region, section, and local dues as an active patroller and comply with any additional division, region, section, and patrol policies. Individuals applying for reentry may be asked for letters of recommendation or the names of former patrol directors who can be contacted as references. An inactive member may not wear the official NSP uniform.

Awards and honorary appointments (merit stars, National Appointments, Leadership Commendation Appointments, etc.) are unaffected by active or inactive status.

To re-qualify for active membership, a person must have a valid OEC card, with successful completion of refreshers since the card was issued; a current CPR-BLS card; and satisfy national proficiency skill performance objectives in all aspects of the desired skill classification. The patrol director is responsible for the reentry evaluation.

If the person seeking reentry no longer holds a valid OEC card with the appropriate refreshers completed, he or she must complete an OEC course or challenge. If the individual no longer holds a valid CPR-BLS card, he or she must complete a professional-rescuer CPR course.

Membership Requirements

All members are required to meet basic national membership requirements and complete annual training, refreshers, and continuing education in the following topics: Outdoor Emergency Care, professional-rescuer CPR, skiing/snowboarding and toboggan handling (may not be required for auxiliary patrollers), and local patrol issues. Some divisions impose additional requirements such as completion of the Basic Avalanche Course. NSP members who transfer from one division to another must meet all of the requirements of the division and the patrol they wish to join.

To maintain national membership in the NSP, a member must log a minimum of 10 patrolling sessions each year. A session consists of a regular day or night duty assignment. Any scheduled session that has been canceled by circumstances beyond the patroller's control counts toward meeting the requirement. The patrol director may make exceptions to this rule.

NSP recommends that members who are elected or appointed to higher office be given credit toward the 10-session patrolling requirement for duty performed in the higher office. Similarly, NSP recommends that members who instruct education courses, serve as evaluators of training programs within the division, or hold education program supervisory positions be given credit toward the 10-session patrolling requirement for duty performed. The local patrol director has the final authority with respect to granting duty credit for NSP membership.

Geographic Division

To maintain membership in a geographic division of the NSP, members must meet the annual continuing education requirements and remit membership dues through the geographic division registration process.

Professional Division

Whereas patrollers register individually in the NSP geographic divisions, entire patrols register in the NSP Professional Division. To be a member of the Professional Division, patrollers must be paid by ski area management to work during the ski season and also must meet the NSP national membership requirements. Because these paid patrollers, including the patrol director, are employees of area management, the area has the ultimate responsibility for the patrol organization. Membership in these patrols is limited to full- or part-time paid patrollers. Individuals registered with the Professional Division receive all the same national member benefits as patrollers registered with a geographic division.

A Professional Division member may join a patrol in a geographic division as a *secondary* registration by paying the required division, region, section, and patrol dues and meeting the local patrol requirements. This enhances access to education services, special events, and communications provided by the geographic division.

Paid patrols registered with a geographic division are associate members of the Professional Division, with the patrol director receiving all mailings and communications routinely directed to patrols registered with the Professional Division.

College Leave

Patrollers may maintain their NSP membership while away at college, as long as they provide the patrol director with a letter of acceptance/continuation from the member's college or university and keep their OEC card current by attending the refreshers. With the approval of the patrol director, students may make up the refreshers at any time during the valid three-year certification period if they cannot attend the regularly scheduled refreshers. Members are not required to fulfill the regular 10-day duty requirement during college leave.

Members should be encouraged to satisfy membership requirements on holidays and school breaks, providing they have met the annual refresher requirements. Members on college leave still must pay all national, division, region, section, and patrol annual dues.

Active Military Duty

At the discretion of the division director, members may have their national dues waived if their duty in defending the United States prevents them from performing their patrolling duties during the normal patrolling season. Upon returning from active military duty, these individuals must take the OEC refreshers required by NSP that they missed during military duty and fulfill any other requirements to resume their pre-service NSP classification.

Registration Process

The NSP geographic divisions and the Professional Division have different registration processes. For further information on the registration process, refer to the most current *NSP Policies and Procedures*, chapter 8.

The patrol director controls the quality and effectiveness of the patrol by registering only those individuals who meet NSP member qualifications and local requirements. Individual members are registered on a calendar-year basis and are recertified annually after completing the refresher programs. A new member registering with the NSP between January 1 and June 30 will be registered until the end of that calendar year. A member joining between July 1 and December 31 will be registered until the end of the second calendar year. This registration process assures that the national and division records are kept up to date and that mailing lists for publications, elections, and other mailings are accurate.

NSP Code of Conduct

NSP membership is a privilege accorded those who meet and maintain the qualifications for membership. Inherent in NSP membership is the obligation to conduct oneself in a civil manner when dealing with others.

In an effort to delineate some of the responsibilities of NSP membership, the board of directors has adopted a code of conduct. The NSP Code of Conduct is intended to let members know what behavior is expected. The code also provides procedures for handling violations of the code. In all cases, the intention is to provide a speedy, fair, and appropriate resolution of disputes without getting bogged down in a bureaucratic or legal morass.

The entire code is set forth in *NSP Policies and Procedures,* chapter 7. A summary of the code's provisions is in appendix A of *The Ski Patroller's Manual*.

Alumni Association

The purpose of the Alumni Association is to provide a communication link for individuals previously registered with the National Ski Patrol. Members of the Alumni Association continue to receive some member benefits such *Ski Patrol Magazine* and may purchase products from the *NSP Winter Catalog*. Alumni Association members also have the opportunity to lend their experience and knowledge to their local patrol and to education programs.

Membership in the Alumni Association is available to any individual who has been registered with the NSP as a patroller for at least one year. The national office handles annual registration in the Alumni Association.

Alumni members are not required to fulfill any refresher requirements except those needed to maintain any instructor certifications they may wish to continue. Any registered alumni who satisfies the continuing requirements for being an instructor may serve in that capacity with the division in which he or she is an alumni. Alumni members serve in an advisory capacity at local, region, division, and national levels of the NSP.

There are alumni pins and patches available through the *NSP Winter Catalog*. Alumni are authorized to wear the official alumni chest patch on their personal parkas. Alumni may purchase and wear a basic I.D. bar with the word "Alumni" under their name; however, they are not authorized to wear the official NSP uniform.

Awards and honorary appointments, e.g., merit stars, the National Appointment and the Leadership Commendation Appointment, will continue to be recognized. Alumni may purchase patches and I.D. bars that indicate these honorary achievements.

If a member of the Alumni Association wishes to return to active NSP membership status, he or she must meet the requirements as set forth in *NSP Policies and Procedures*, chapter 7.

Associate Registration

Associates are individuals who have a need or desire to participate in NSP education programs. The association registration is not a skill classification; however, associates may participate in and be credentialed in any NSP training or education program, paying the designated associate course enrollment fee.

Associates receive *Ski Patrol Magazine* and the *NSP Winter Catalog*. They may not perform any on-the-hill/trail ski patrolling duties with an NSP-member ski patrol and are not authorized to wear the official NSP uniform. These individuals are not members of the National Ski Patrol and have no voting rights, nor are they considered in geographic membership counts.

Affiliate Organizations

The NSP may enter into affiliation education agreements with outside organizations so those groups can coordinate NSP education programs and offer them to their members. Affiliate organization instructors teaching NSP courses must demonstrate the same instructor qualifications as NSP members, complete the same instructor recertification requirements, and each be registered as an NSP associate.

An outside organization desiring access to NSP educational programs for its members may obtain an affiliate application from the NSP national office. The organization submits the completed form to the NSP education director, who evaluates the request in conjunction with the appropriate program director. In evaluating a request for affiliation, the education director and program director consider the following factors in their evaluation of a request for affiliation: the outside organization's objectives in using the NSP program; its ability to deliver education programs in a high-quality manner; how much the organization intends to charge students for the program and how much of that revenue will be returned to the NSP; whether NSP materials will be used in the course, and if not, what other materials will be used; and what procedures the organization will follow in training instructors and providing quality assurance.

Any negotiated agreement must be approved by the NSP Executive Committee before the implementation of the agreement.

A patrol is composed of volunteer and/or paid members who serve area management by providing education programs, emergency care, and rescue services to the skiing and snowboarding public. The patrol performs these services at an organized ski area at the direction of area management or the public lands administration. The patrol usually is administered by a patrol director who is either a paid representative of area management or who volunteers his or her time at the behest of management.

Types of Patrols

The National Ski Patrol has three types of patrols: area, service, and administrative. An area or service patrol consists of a minimum of a patrol director and one or more additional patrollers who are members of the NSP and whose primary registration is with that patrol. In contrast, the administrative patrol's patrol director is the national chairman and additional members' primary registration is with the national association. For example, a national program director may register with the administrative patrol because the increased volunteer responsibilities for a national program may prohibit that individual from completing the annual area patrol's member requirements.

Area Patrols

An area patrol, either alpine or nordic, consisting of volunteer and/or paid patrollers, is a working unit or department of ski area management or the public lands administration. The management group has the full right of approval of the patrol director, other patrol members, and local patrol policy. Every area patrol is under the supervision of area management and must abide by the policies and procedures established by that management.

At the direction of area manage-

ment or the public lands administration, the ski patrol provides emergency care and transportation services to resort guests who are in distress due to illness or injury. The patrol also promotes safety education and supports area management's risk management policies.

Because of the differences between resorts in terms of terrain, snow conditions, equipment, and in the popularity of skiing, the composition and specific objectives of area patrols may vary somewhat; however, the members of all patrols registered with the NSP must meet the established NSP knowledge and skill proficiency requirements in emergency care, skiing/snowboarding, and toboggan handling.

An *alpine patrol* is a patrol whose members use alpine skiing (downhill or telemark) or snowboarding techniques and equipment to carry out their patrolling duties at a specific ski area. Typical activities for an alpine patroller include providing emergency care and rescue services on the slopes, patrolling at the area's alpine racing events, and promoting local safety programs. Auxiliary patrollers also may provide any services deemed necessary at the ski area by the area management or patrol, except for transporting loaded toboggans.

A *nordic patrol* is an area ski patrol or service patrol (see Service Patrols, following section) whose members use nordic skiing techniques and equipment to carry out their patrolling duties. Auxiliary members also may serve on nordic patrols. Typical activities for the nordic patroller include patrolling nordic ski

center trails or public or private lands available for nordic skiing and providing coverage for competitive events such as citizen cross-country races or ski jumping events. The nordic patroller also may accompany a touring group to provide emergency care and evacuation services.

Service Patrols

The service patrol consists of NSP members who are not directly affiliated with a ski area or public lands area but who serve as a unit to provide patrolling services to a particular geographic area or region. The service patrol may be organized on a division, region, or other geographic basis.

An example of a service patrol is a nordic patrol that is responsible for covering various community trail systems or that accompanies touring groups to provide emergency care and evacuation services. The nordic patrol might also provide services such as education, training, and other programs of benefit to a geographic division, a local NSP patrol, and the outdoor recreation community.

Service patrol members must meet the same NSP membership and registration requirements of patrollers registered with area patrols. Members of service patrols, regardless of member level, skill classification, or tenure, may be signed on to duty *only* at the ski area or service location with the concurrence of the area patrol director.

Administrative Patrols

An administrative patrol consists of a group of individuals whose responsibilities of office prevent them from fulfilling their duty requirements at a specific ski area. Administrative patrols exist only at the division and national levels.

Although administrative patrollers are not expected to fulfill duty requirements at an area, they must participate in the Outdoor Emergency Care refresher and the on-the-hill/trail refresher with another non-administrative patrol, and it is their responsibility to sign up for these refreshers. Patrol directors should recognize the need for administrative patrollers to remain unhindered by duty requirements, but they may sign up administrative patrollers for duty days depending on the requirements of the area's management.

The division administrative patrols may consist of division directors, national board representatives, region directors, section chiefs, division supervisors, chairpersons of active committees, or other NSP members whose responsibilities of office prevent them from fulfilling the duty requirements at a specific area. Membership in the division administrative patrol is granted at the discretion of the division director.

The national administrative patrol is referred to as the U.S. Ski Patrol and functions similarly to the division administrative patrol, except that the national chairman is responsible for verifying completion of refresher requirements. Members of the U.S. Ski Patrol may include the national chairman, assistant national chairmen, the national treasurer, executive committee members, national board members, national program directors, and other NSP members in national-level positions.

Ski Patrol Management

A patrol, once established at a given ski area, is under the supervision of the ski area management or public lands administration and must abide by the policies and procedures established by that management. The ski area or public lands management ultimately supervises and controls the patrolling activities of individual NSP members and patrols at each ski area. As such, the ski area or public lands administra-

tion bears legal responsibility for all patrolling activities at the area.

Within the NSP, patrol directors are responsible for verifying with the national office the completion of all their patrollers' NSP membership requirements on an annual basis. It is extremely important to maintain accurate records on all patrollers. This accuracy supports the risk management efforts of ski area managers, who depend on their patrollers being qualified and capable of meeting the standards of training for the ski industry.

Patrol directors also have the privilege of voting for individuals who are running for elected offices within their geographic divisions.

Registering with the NSP

Patrols are registered with the National Ski Patrol on an annual basis that coincides with the NSP fiscal year, July 1 through June 30. All patrols must re-register by July 1 to maintain membership in the national organization. New patrols can join the system at any time during the year.

Guidelines for annual patrol registration or registering a new volunteer or paid patrol are located in *NSP Policies and Procedures,* chapter 8.

Two patrols at the same area may register separately with the NSP, either as a volunteer patrol in the geographic division and a paid patrol in the Professional Division, or as an alpine and a nordic patrol in the same division. Each of these patrols may have a patrol director or there may be one patrol director who leads both the paid and volunteer members, depending on area management's preference.

Like other organizations, the National Ski Patrol is composed of various entities that have different functions and modes of authority. This chapter contains a description of the organizational structure of the NSP—from the national to the division level.

Specific details on the NSP's organizational structure (table 5.1) and job descriptions for the various officers can be found in the NSP Bylaws and in *NSP Policies and Procedures*.

National Officers

These NSP officers are members who have been either elected or appointed to volunteer positions at the national level. In general, these individuals serve the membership by helping to guide the organization along the path set forth by the association's strategic plan.

National Board of Directors

The national board of directors consists of the national chairman, national treasurer, division directors, and division board representatives. Each year, in accordance with the national bylaws, one-half of the national board members are elected to serve a two-year term. Only the division directors, board representatives, and treasurer have voting privileges. The national chairman may cast a vote only to break a tie.

Board Representation

Divisions that register up to 5 percent of the national membership have one division director, who is allowed one board vote. Divisions with 5 to 10 percent of the total membership have one board representative in addition to the division director, each having one vote. Divisions with 10 to 20 percent of the total membership have two board representatives in addition to the division director, each having one vote.

Divisions with more than 20 percent of the total membership have three board representatives in addition to the division director, each having one vote. Alumni registrations are not factored into proportional voting.

The board of directors supports and fosters the NSP mission statement. The board is responsible for creating and carrying out the policies and responsibilities as defined in the *NSP Policies and Procedures* manual.

The board members offer expertise in a variety of technical areas for which the national organization could not afford to pay otherwise. Board members, who are elected to this position, receive no monetary compensation for the substantial time and energy the position requires of them. At the same time, this endeavor provides an unusual opportunity to help build a stronger organization that meets the needs of its membership.

Board members must be thoroughly familiar with the organization's goals, objectives, and programs so they can balance the needs and desires of the NSP membership with the mission and objectives of the overall association.

One of the most important functions of a board member is to facilitate communication between the association membership, ski areas, and the paid staff at the national headquarters. Board members also must accurately and fairly present the current policies, NSP education programs, and activities of the association—even those with which they may personally disagree—to their division officers, members, and ski area management.

National Chairman

The national chairman is the chief elected officer of the NSP. The board elects the chairman for a two-year term in even-numbered years.

The responsibilities in this position include providing leadership and coordination of long-range planning, directing policy-making functions, and overseeing other national activities to assure that all NSP objectives are carried out from initial planning to completion.

The national chairman is responsible to the board of directors and is governed within the limits described by the bylaws or as set forth by the board. The national chairman serves as chairman of the board of directors, chairman of the executive committee, and member ex-officio of all national committees of the NSP. The chairman is responsible for the appointment, direction, and termination of assistant national chairmen, national program directors, and other national positions such as medical director, historian, subcommittee chairmen, and committee chairmen.

An important function of the national chairman is to represent the NSP in a positive, professional manner to the individual member. The chairman also promotes public relations between the NSP and the rest of the outdoor recreation industry, the emergency medical community, and the general public.

National Treasurer

The national treasurer is responsible for monitoring the financial operations of the National Ski Patrol, including the organization's funds, securities, and other assets. The board of directors selects the treasurer by way of the process outlined in the current edition of *NSP Policies and Procedures*. The national treasurer is a voting member of the board of directors and the executive committee.

Table 5.1 National Ski Patrol Organizational Chart

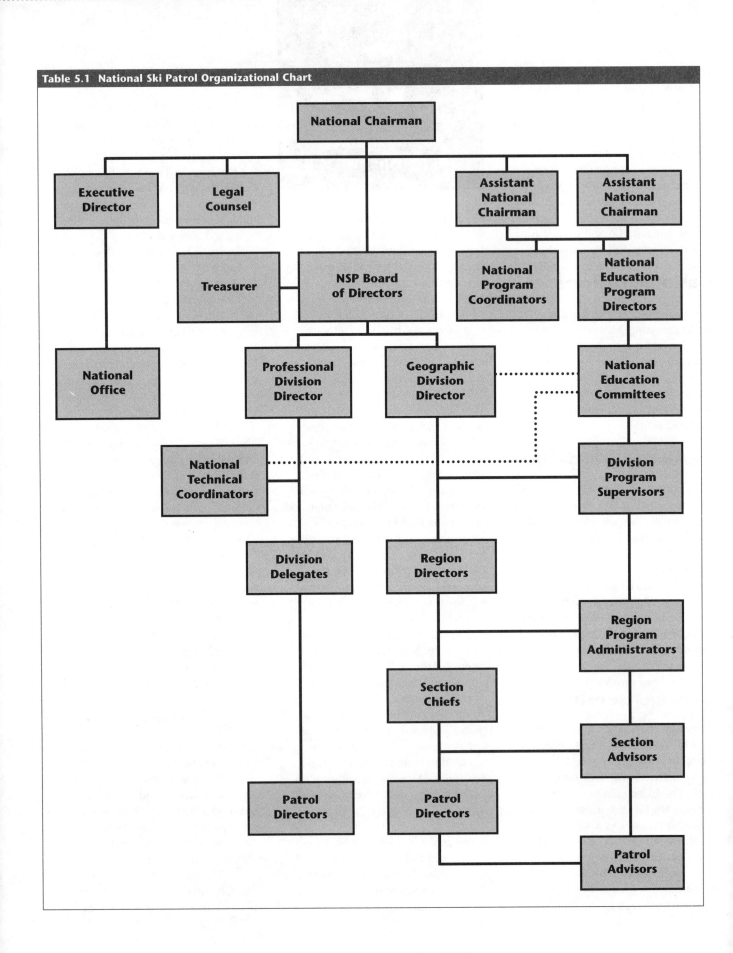

The treasurer prepares financial reports, as necessary, with the assistance of the national office. The treasurer assists the national chairman and board of directors in guiding the executive director to establish sound financial business practices. The treasurer reviews the NSP's cash statements and monthly financial statements, works with the auditors on an annual basis to examine the organization's financial records and help prepare the national budget, and assists in investing the members' equity in appropriate sources, subject to the approval of the board of directors. The treasurer performs all specific financial functions that cannot be delegated and that are approved by law, corporation charter, or bylaws.

Executive Committee

The executive committee consists of the national chairman, the national treasurer, and additional members elected by the board of directors following NSP bylaw provisions. This committee directs the affairs of the NSP when the board of directors is not in session. The executive committee has only interim executive authority in directing the affairs of the National Ski Patrol.

The assistant national chairmen, national legal counsel, and the executive director generally attend the executive committee meetings to be available to provide information on their areas of responsibility, if needed, and also because their positions require that they stay apprised of the proceedings of this group. They do not vote on any policies or decisions.

The executive committee may not always take action on a particular issue but instead makes recommendations to the board for subsequent decisions. Occasionally, the executive committee makes decisions for the board and national office administration between scheduled board meetings. The committee acts on proposals and recommendations submitted by the national chairman and the executive director. The committee also acts as the NSP risk management commission, described as follows.

Risk Management Commission

The risk management commission consists of the voting executive committee members. This group has rule-making authority with respect to the management of risk created by the education and member services programs of the NSP. The committee has the authority to enforce national policies and committee rulings throughout the NSP organization. The committee reports its action(s), if any, to the board of directors at the annual board meeting.

The NSP has a risk management policy to assist in the implementation of programs as determined by the board of directors in the NSP Strategic Plan. The policy has a reactive element to deal with accidents, lawsuits, and other emergencies, and a proactive element to deal with program development and implementation.

National Volunteer Staff

The national volunteer staff consists of the first assistant national chairman, who serves as the chief elected officer in the absence of the national chairman, and any additional assistant national chairmen the national chairman may appoint. The board of directors must approve the national chairman's appointments of the volunteer staff.

Assistant National Chairmen

The assistant national chairmen serve at the direction and prerogative of the national chairman. The assistant national chairmen participate in strategic and budget planning, supervise national program directors and committees for the various NSP disciplines, and serve on a variety of association committees throughout the outdoor recreation industry. At board meetings, they may chair or co-chair a committee to review board proposals. As directed by the national chairman, these individuals may oversee programs and project budgets of national program directors.

National Legal Counsel

The national chairman generally appoints legal counsel to provide expert legal advice to the board of directors, apprise the board of directors of the organization's current risks, and help guide the board in its decision-making processes.

National Program Directors

An individual who is nominated for appointment as a national program director must possess expertise in the program for which he or she is being considered. The board of directors confirms the appointment of national program directors (see table 5.2).

A national program director has primary responsibility for advising the board of directors and the national office on a specific education discipline. The program directors constitute the national education committee, which strives to simplify and standardize the national education delivery system and to provide education programs of exceptional quality.

Serving on this committee are the program directors for the following disciplines: avalanche, instructor development, leadership development, nordic, mountaineering, outdoor emergency care, and ski and toboggan for alpine (ski/snowboard). Other advisory positions may change during various administrations but

Table 5.2 National Program Committees and Volunteer Program Staff

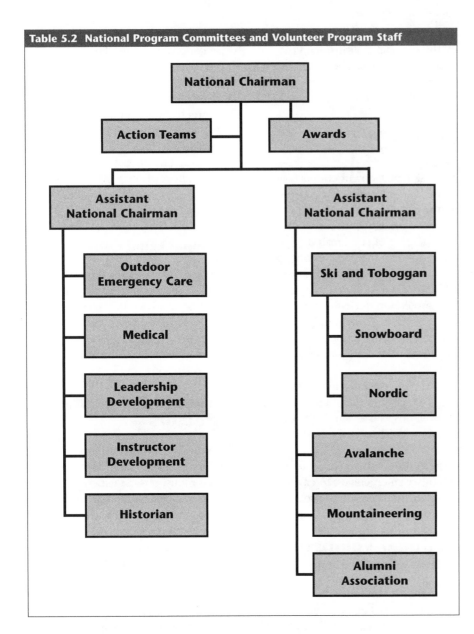

- National Chairman
  - Action Teams
  - Awards
  - Assistant National Chairman
    - Outdoor Emergency Care
    - Medical
    - Leadership Development
    - Instructor Development
    - Historian
  - Assistant National Chairman
    - Ski and Toboggan
      - Snowboard
      - Nordic
    - Avalanche
    - Mountaineering
    - Alumni Association

National Committee Structure

There are three types of committees at the national level: (1) national program committees, consisting of the division program supervisors; (2) ad hoc committees, consisting of board members who the national chairman has assigned to gather specific information; and (3) action teams, board-appointed committees whose members' various areas of expertise enable them to address considerations pertaining to education programs.

National Program Committees

The national program committees consist of the corresponding program supervisors from each geographic division and the Professional Division. The committee is chaired by the national program director for that specific discipline. National program directors, in conjunction with their committee, develop and implement new programs, monitor existing programs, and communicate relevant program information to the membership.

In maintaining close contact with the education and communications national office staff, the national program directors help coordinate the development of all education materials and other projects pertaining to their program. The national education department maintains a production schedule that determines the timeline for the development of these materials. This schedule reflects priorities established by the board of directors.

Ad Hoc Committees

The board at times appoints ad hoc committees when it needs to know more about a particular issue or proposal before it can make an informed decision about the subject. Consisting of members of the national board of directors, these ad hoc committees are

currently include the alumni association coordinator, awards coordinator, medical director, and historian.

The national program directors suggest policy changes relating to their discipline through motions to the national board, but they have no policy-making powers. Annually, the program directors provide a written report that outlines their activities, goals, and plans to the national board of directors. The national program directors also prepare annual budget requests for the coming fiscal year for the national treasurer's review. The

national program directors may be asked to attend the board's annual or midwinter meeting when activity in the discipline-specific program justifies their attendance.

The national program directors, through their national program committees, support and foster the NSP mission statement by promoting the association's education programs nationally. The national program directors help assure the integrity of NSP training standards and are knowledgeable about the procedures and integrity of the program in each division.

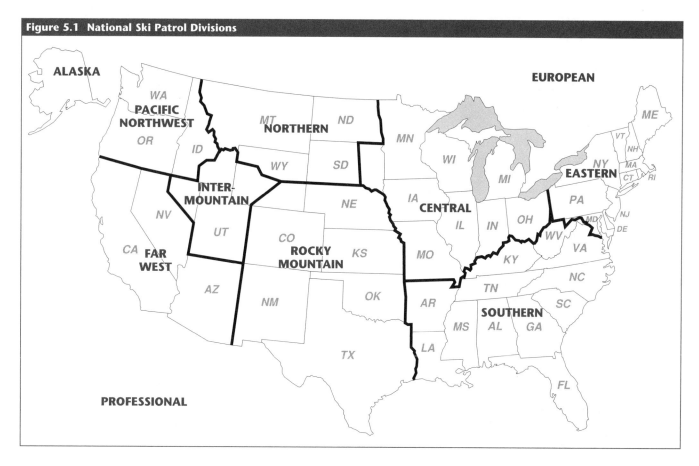

Figure 5.1 National Ski Patrol Divisions

charged with defining the scope of a project and recommending whether it would provide sufficient benefit to the organization or its members.

If the consensus is that the project is not worth pursuing, the committee recommends to the board that the project be eliminated. If the committee identifies potential value in the project, the committee develops the project strategy, then presents that recommendation to the board. Once the work of the committee is complete, it is disbanded. The committees are *not* charged with program development and do not have a programs and projects budget line item.

Action Team Committees

An action team is charged with program development (planning) as defined by the ad hoc committee and approved by the board. Action team committees can include but are not

limited to board members, program directors and supervisors, technical experts, paid staff, and patrol members. The action team is funded through the programs and projects budget line item. This is an ad hoc committee and is disbanded when the task is completed.

Division Structure, Officers, and Supervisors

The National Ski Patrol is organized into 10 geographic divisions and one Professional Division (fig. 5.1). The NSP geographic divisions are Alaska, Central, Eastern, European, Far West, Intermountain, Northern, Pacific Northwest, Rocky Mountain, and Southern. An Asia contingent is registered under the U.S. Administrative Patrol.

Each geographic division may consist of regions, sections, and NSP-registered ski patrols in a specific

geographic area.

The Professional Division has regional boundaries that coincide with the geographic division boundaries, but it may or may not have patrols in all the geographic divisions.

Geographic Divisions

A geographic division has two or more regions and is administered by a division director. A region may be divided into two or more sections and is administered by a region director. A section consists of at least two and usually no more than five registered ski patrols and is administered by a section chief.

The national board of directors determines the boundaries of each division. The division director determines, when appropriate, the boundaries of the regions or sections, unless these perimeters have been specified in the division bylaws.

Each division is responsible for implementing national policies and conducting internal affairs. Methods for conducting division responsibilities are detailed in each division's bylaws, which specify when meetings will be held, how division officers are to be elected or appointed, how the financial affairs of the division will be handled, and other matters of division interest.

The officers of the NSP geographic division are the division director, board representatives, region directors, section chiefs, and patrol directors. The division bylaws specify which of these officers have voting privileges at division meetings. The national board of directors determines the minimum qualifications, responsibilities, and duties of the division officers; however, each division may establish additional requirements.

Division officers are elected in accordance with the procedures established by the national and division bylaws. They take office in accordance with division policy but in no event later than May 1 following a regular election or as soon thereafter as the election is resolved.

Region directors and section chiefs are elected or appointed in accordance with division policy. Patrol directors are elected or appointed in accordance with ski area management policy but serve as voting officers in the division in which their patrol is registered. They take office as soon as possible after the election or appointment.

The transfer of authority from one officer to another should be accomplished as smoothly as possible. The national office should be notified of all officer changes so it can maintain a current mailing list. The officers who are stepping down from the position must meet all their responsibilities and transfer records in a timely manner.

Individuals who wish to serve the NSP as officers should make every effort to gain experience and training in all areas of ski patrolling and patrol management. It is also important to develop a thorough understanding of NSP policies and procedures. Patrollers who are well qualified and eligible for these positions should be considered for candidacy, and those patrollers who desire to hold office should declare themselves for consideration.

Geographic Division Directors

The division director has a dual role as both the chief division officer and a national board member. The division director's responsibilities include promoting NSP education programs within the division, supporting division staff in managing the integrity of NSP training standards, and establishing an atmosphere for the exchange of skills, ideas, proposals, techniques, and information programs between NSP members, ski areas, patrols, regions, and the national association.

Region Directors

Region directors are responsible for the general administration of the region and for promoting NSP education programs within their regions. They may appoint region administrators to help carry out the education and training responsibilities of the region. The region director, in concurrence with the division director, determines the number of region administrators, their qualifications, method of appointment, term of office, and specific duties.

Region directors coordinate region activities and promote uniformity with respect to NSP policies throughout the region. Region directors work with the division director to implement new policies and training programs, and to interact with patrols.

Section Chiefs

A section chief promotes NSP education programs and cooperates with the region director and other NSP officers in maintaining the rules, regulations, and training standards of the NSP. Section chiefs may appoint supervisors, in concurrence with the division and region directors, to help carry out the education and training responsibilities of the section.

Patrol Directors

A patrol director has two lines of responsibility: one to area management or the public lands administration and one to the NSP.

Responsibilities to management include performing in accordance with management policies and maintaining good rapport and communication with area management or the public lands administration. Responsibilities to the National Ski Patrol include serving as an officer within the NSP division in accordance with division bylaws and policies.

Principally, patrol directors must (1) ensure that the patrol members meet the national education requirements; (2) communicate NSP policies to patrol members in a timely and accurate manner; and (3) maintain administrative and financial data and all other records for their patrols.

Division Program Supervisors

The division director appoints division program supervisors to help carry out the education and training responsibilities of the division. The division director determines the number of supervisors, their qualifications, method of appointment, term of office, and specific duties. The division program supervisor titles generally coincide with national program director titles.

Division program supervisors are responsible for helping maintain the integrity and standards of NSP programs by participating actively on the respective national program committee. They evaluate how well the existing program is meeting member needs and communicate with the national office, division and region officers, supervisors, administrators, instructors, instructor trainers, members, and others in an effort to create mutual understanding about NSP programs.

Division program supervisors establish and distribute training schedules of courses in collaboration with division and region staff to meet the needs of instructors and members. They also supervise instructor trainers in the division and administer the quality management of the education programs.

Professional Division

The structure of the NSP Professional Division is different from that of the NSP geographic divisions. Whereas patrollers are members of the geographic divisions, entire patrols register as members of the Professional Division.

The Professional Division is not designed to serve the individual patroller or the small patrol directly. The geographic division serves that purpose, and the Professional Division does not compete with the geographic divisions in this regard. The Professional Division provides paid patrols with access to NSP programs that they may wish to take advantage of as well as affiliation with an organization that is widely respected by ski area management. In turn, the NSP benefits from the expertise of Professional Division members, whose invaluable contributions are reflected in many of the association's education programs. The division also provides a forum for information exchange and input into ski patrol policies and procedures.

The officers of the Professional Division are the division director, national board representative(s), and delegates from different regions that coincide with the NSP geographic division boundaries. Each officer in the Professional Division must be employed by a ski area, direct the ski patrol, and represent the management of that ski area.

Professional Division Director

The Professional Division director is the administrative head of the division and is a member of the NSP Board of Directors.

Professional Division Delegates

Delegates are responsible for assessing the needs of the professional patrol membership within their geographic region and helping meet those needs through the resources of the Professional Division and the National Ski Patrol.

Paid Patrol Directors

A paid patrol director's responsibilities encompass the same guidelines as stated for the patrol director in a geographic division.

Professional Division Technical Experts

The division director or delegates appoint technical experts who are the Professional Division counterparts of the NSP division program supervisors. Professional Division technical coordinators often serve on national program committees with NSP national program directors and geographic program supervisors to assist in NSP education and training program development projects.

Like any active sport, skiing and snowboarding present risks of physical injury. In today's litigious society, skiers or snowboarders who are injured may make claims for compensation against the area operator or others. The potential for claims requires that patrollers be aware of the laws regarding ski and snowboard injury claims.

The public's perception of risk allocation has markedly changed in recent times. Before the 1970s, the vast majority of the skiing public assumed that an injury sustained while skiing was a matter of personal responsibility. Now, injured skiers and snowboarders are increasingly seeking to be compensated by someone else for their injuries. Ski injury litigation has grown substantially with this change.

Many states have enacted statutes listing the inherent risks of skiing and snowboarding. These lists include such things as changing weather conditions; variations or steepness in terrain; snow or ice conditions; surface or subsurface conditions such as bare spots, forest growth, and rocks; obstacles or other structures; and collisions with objects or people. All NSP members, regardless of whether they are registered as ski/snowboard, nordic, or auxillary patrollers, should be familiar with their state laws regarding liability for injuries resulting from skiing and snowboarding.

Because of the increase in litigation and at the direction of area management, patrollers must assist in accident prevention, skier and snowboarder education, and the promotion of ski safety; provide adequate and reasonable care of ill or injured skiers and snowboarders at their respective areas; and carefully document accident situations and the care given.

Nothing can prevent the initiation of a lawsuit by someone intent on doing so. However, many things can be done to deter the filing of a lawsuit and to promote the success of the defense in the event a lawsuit is filed.

Patrol Tasks and Potential Liability

All responsible individuals and companies must explore and implement risk management measures to reduce liability exposure. Each NSP member should assess risk in his or her own situation, and be comfortable with the risks assumed when participating in NSP programs as a service provider subject to the direction and control of area management or the public lands administration.

Patrol Duties

The duties of the ski patrol have expanded substantially in the last 25 years. In former times, most ski patrols were primarily rescue organizations, waiting for and attending to those skiers who injured themselves on the slopes. However, today's patrollers sometimes are asked by management to identify and mark obstacles, participate in the safety education of skiers and snowboarders, and assist in myriad other mountain resort tasks. Patrollers must keep in mind that they do these tasks at the direction of area management, whether performing the historical role of caring for injuries on the slopes or handling markings and skier education.

Dealing with reckless skiers and snowboarders is a part of ski patrolling at most areas. Each area should have a consistent policy that all patrollers understand. Patrollers must follow management's directions in these matters and may assist in the development of the policies.

Unless explicitly trained and assigned to such tasks by area management, patrollers should not operate aerial lifts, use explosives, adjust bindings or other equipment, provide ski instruction, or perform other services that are not part of a ski patroller's responsibility. Every patroller should undertake only those activities for which the patroller has been specifically trained and assigned. By following this advice, patrollers will protect themselves against many areas of potential liability.

When participating in NSP training activities, NSP members are required to follow state laws (including any applicable portions of the state skier safety act), the policies of area management, the NSP program guidelines, and Your Responsibility Code, a behavior standard promulgated by NSAA and endorsed by the NSP (see appendix C).

Personal Risk Management

Patrollers can provide themselves the maximum protection against potential liability by following these general guidelines:

Understanding the Role of a Patroller

Patrollers should have a full understanding of the duties and responsibilities of the ski patrol at their area. Ski area managers often accomplish this by preparing and distributing a job description for patrollers, including volunteer patrollers.

Preparation

NSP members should prepare for the role of patroller by participating actively in training and refresher programs. Continuous training and refreshing is the best way to hone patrolling skills. The NSP offers numerous programs to advance skills vital to patrolling. A good way to maintain and improve skills is to become an NSP instructor in one or more patrolling disciplines.

Limiting Performance to Patrol Tasks

Patrollers should confine their patrolling activities to those that are part of their specific role. If patrollers are not trained to operate a chairlift, insert an intravenous line, or conduct a race, they should not perform these tasks.

Understanding Insurance Coverage

Patrollers should understand and be comfortable with the interaction of NSP, ski area, and personal liability insurance coverage, the Good Samaritan law, and volunteer protection statutes in their state.

Exercising Good Personal Risk Management

Patrollers often participate as emergency care providers in special events such as community foot races, Special Olympics, and other activities or special events. Before such participation, each patroller should be sure the special event sponsor or organizer has a reasonable risk management program, including adequate insurance that provides coverage for the patroller for emergency care errors and omissions.

Rescuing Ill or Injured Persons

One of the primary responsibilities of a patroller is to provide emergency care and transportation to area guests when they become ill or injured.

Duty to Act Reasonably

In general, the law requires every individual to act as a reasonable and

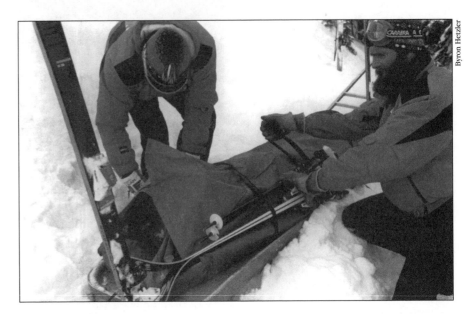

Byron Hetzler

prudent person would under the same or similar circumstances. This general requirement has application to both NSP education programs as well as ski patrol operations. The law imposes duties on NSP and area management in the implementation of their respective mission statements.

For instance, NSP has a duty to provide reasonable training in emergency care as part of its Outdoor Emergency Care Program. NSP discharges this duty through the training and support of credentialed OEC instructors. On the other hand, ski areas have a duty to provide reasonable ski patrol services as part of their mountain operations. State laws provide the standard for the administration of emergency care, and each patroller should strive to provide the appropriate level of care to ill or injured skiers and snowboarders.

Many ski safety acts require that ski areas take appropriate steps to avoid creating artificial dangers on hills or trails. This may include the placement of rope lines, bamboo poles, signs, and other marking. These materials should be set up in accordance with the ski safety act, and so as to not create an unreasonable impediment to normal skiing and snowboarding operations.

Ski safety acts also impose specific duties or responsibilities on skiers and snowboarders. Many acts require that skiers and snowboarders refrain from actions that would create a hazard for themselves and others, such as swinging lift chairs, dropping or throwing objects from a lift, or crossing surface lifts at other than designated points. Some ski safety acts require that skiers and snowboarders involved in a collision leave their name and contact information with others involved in the incident and/or with area management. Some ski safety acts also require skiers and snowboarders to observe and obey slope and trail closures as well as area boundaries.

The purpose of these requirements is to allow all skiers and snowboarders to participate in the sport for the maximum enjoyment while reasonably mitigating risks. Ski patrollers should become familiar with the laws and ordinances applicable to mountain operations at their area.

Duty to Rescue

In most states, the law imposes no duty on a person to rescue an individual from an emergency situation if the potential rescuer did not create the obstacle or the emergency. Some older court cases even allowed a potential rescuer to stand by and do nothing while a person drowned before the observer's eyes. In response to these types of cases, some states (Vermont, Minnesota, and Rhode Island) have imposed a duty to aid an individual in peril where it does not endanger the rescuer to do so.

Most states have not yet imposed the duty to rescue on ordinary individuals. However, patrollers should understand that whenever they don their ski patrol uniform and are providing ski patrol services, they have assumed this duty and must exercise reasonable care in aiding individuals on the slopes, trails, and other facilities. This includes all aspects of a specific rescue, from responding in a timely manner to administering emergency care and evacuating the ill or injured individual.

Consent

A patroller must obtain an injured person's consent before administering any aid. Typically this is done when the patroller greets the person and inquires as to whether the person needs assistance, for example: "Hi! I'm Debbie Etoile with the Sleepy Hollow Ski Patrol. May I help you?" In almost all cases, an affirmative answer is given to that question. Consent has then been obtained and aid may be given to the ill or injured individual.

Some special situations arise concerning the question of consent. An unresponsive or delirious individual obviously cannot give explicit consent to emergency care. The law implies consent to assist those individuals until they regain the mental ability to make a conscious and considered decision whether they wish to continue to receive care. Accordingly, patrollers should provide care in situations where the person's mental state does not permit the individual to make rational decisions regarding his or her condition and emergency care.

Consent for the treatment of children can pose challenges. A parent or guardian who is present has the authority to decide about the child's care. Occasionally, a parent or guardian may initially refuse assistance when the patroller believes assistance is appropriate. In such cases, the patroller should remain at the scene and attempt to persuade the parent or guardian of the need for care. In the absence of a parent or guardian, the patroller should consult with the child and give appropriate care.

Adults who are responsive and otherwise mentally competent to make a reasoned decision are fully capable of declining care in a particular situation. The patroller must respect such a decision, as patrollers do not have the authority to force assistance on any individual who is competent to refuse it. Patrollers should be as persuasive as possible in offering care when their judgment indicates care is appropriate.

If the patroller believes that a skier or snowboarder requires assistance and the person repeatedly refuses, the patroller should present the person with an accident report form and ask the individual to sign the statement indicating the refusal of aid. The patroller should obtain the person's name, address, and telephone number; have bystanders witness the refusal of care; and record their names, addresses, and telephone numbers on the form. If the person refuses to sign the form, the patroller should fill the form out anyway and record any witnesses present. The form should be kept with the other accident report forms.

In all situations where the patroller believes assistance is required, the patroller should remain on the scene and attempt to persuade the ill or injured person (or, in the case of a child, the parent or guardian) regarding the need for care. Occasionally, a skier or snowboarder initially refuses care. Then, after discovering the

extent of the injury or the fact that he or she cannot continue skiing or snowboarding, the person allows patrollers to provide emergency care.

If there is any doubt regarding the issue of consent, it is generally preferable to provide appropriate emergency care.

Duty to Continue Care

Once a patroller has undertaken care of an ill or injured skier or snowboarder, the patroller must not abandon the person. There are limited circumstances under which a patroller may part company and discontinue care for an ill or injured person. These include the following: (1) the person has been declared dead by a competent authority (the persons who have this authority vary from state to state); (2) the patroller must leave to obtain additional assistance; (3) the person has been turned over to competent emergency medical service personnel or medical authority for further treatment; (4) the person is mentally competent to decide to refuse care and has refused care after repeated inquiry by the patroller; or (5) the person is sufficiently healthy to travel alone or with friends and has been advised to seek further medical help.

There are rare occasions when a person sustains injuries that result in serious injury or death on a slope or backcountry trail. This situation is always tragic, but the patroller has an obligation to continue to render aid until the person is either obviously dead (e.g., decapitation), the patroller physically can no longer render care, or the person has been declared dead by a competent authority.

Sometimes a question is raised as to who is a competent medical person to continue medical care. In the alpine situation, the patroller who transports the toboggan generally turns the person over to an aid room attendant or continues care in the aid room. The

aid room attendant may then turn a person over to an ambulance service or medical authority. In nordic situations where there is no aid room, a patroller's obligations may include a duty to summon an ambulance to meet the patroller at a roadside location. When an ill or injured person is turned over to an ambulance crew, the patroller should give a detailed history of the illness or injuries and treatment to the ambulance crew.

Often, the person is sufficiently healthy to travel with friends for further medical care. The patroller should be satisfied that the friends understand the severity of the situation and the necessity for immediate medical assistance. No person should be turned over to individuals who appear to be intoxicated or otherwise mentally impaired, or who do not appreciate the necessity for continuing care.

When the person is turned over to an ambulance crew or sent with friends to a hospital, the patroller should obtain the names of the ambulance attendants or the ill or injured person's friends. The patroller should note on the accident form that the person was turned over to an ambulance service or to friends and advised to proceed directly to the hospital or other definitive medical care.

If appropriate, the patroller should always advise the person to seek further medical care and then note that this was done on the accident form. If the illness or injury is minor and further medical care is unlikely to be needed, the patroller should advise the person of those circumstances under which medical attention should be sought.

The Skier's Equipment

In the typical situation where a person is evacuated by a toboggan or other device, the person entrusts his or her ski equipment or snowboard

to the patroller. The patroller must be cautious in the care of such property and take reasonable steps to assure it is not lost or stolen while in the patrol's custody.

Sometimes an observer at an accident scene volunteers to carry the ill or injured person's equipment to the aid room or trail head, and the patient may even consent to this arrangement; however, this may be a problematic solution. If the individual who carries the equipment falls and gets injured, the individual may make a claim. It is also possible that the person who volunteers to carry the equipment will steal or lose it. Consequently, it is better to load the person's equipment in the toboggan or arrange for a patroller to carry the equipment to the aid room or trail head.

Some Caution Notes

It is important to remember that a patroller is merely an emergency care giver and not a physician. Unless specifically trained and directed by area management, a patroller must not attempt treatment beyond the knowledge and skills taught in the Outdoor Emergency Care Program. A patroller should not offer the person a specific diagnosis of the particular illness or injury, even if the patroller feels certain about what the problem is.

A patroller must not offer an opinion as to the cause of any accident. It is rare indeed that a patroller actually observes the circumstances of an accident and, even in such situations, the patroller may misjudge the cause. If involved in an accident with a ski area guest, a patroller should neither accuse the person of wrongdoing nor accept blame for the accident. Those issues can and will be determined later.

Good Samaritan and Volunteer Protection Laws

In normal circumstances, all individuals are legally responsible for negli-

gent acts that cause damage or injury to another person, even when they volunteer as rescuers. So-called "Good Samaritan" laws and volunteer protection statutes may partially shield volunteer rescuers from such liability.

In the 1950s and 1960s, there was a perception among state legislators that physicians were refusing to assist at accident scenes because of a fear of being sued. The problem was highlighted by a ski accident at a Lake Tahoe, California, resort, where a woman was injured while skiing and several physicians in the vicinity declined to render assistance. In 1959, the California Legislature enacted the first Good Samaritan law.

The purpose of such laws is to remove the threat of liability in an effort to encourage individuals to help those who are in need. The laws vary with respect to the rescuers who are protected and the circumstances in which protection is afforded. These laws differ so much from state to state that it is difficult to generalize about their application. Patrollers should be familiar with the provisions of the Good Samaritan statute in their own state.

There is some question as to whether the Good Samaritan statute provides protection to volunteer members of organized rescue groups. Some courts have held that the Good Samaritan law does not apply to individuals such as police or members of public ambulance crews who have a pre-existing obligation to assist individuals in danger. Ski patrollers may have such a "pre-existing duty" when they don their parkas and hold themselves out as available to assist ill or injured skiers.

Volunteer protection statutes also vary substantially from state to state. Some provide coverage only for directors and officers of charitable organizations, while others provide coverage for volunteers who provide charitable services.

Patrollers who are concerned

about the provisions of the Good Samaritan laws or volunteer protection statutes in their state should consult their attorney or talk to a ski patrol legal counsel.

Ownership of Equipment and Buildings

Some patrols own the patrol building in which they provide care to ill or injured persons, and some patrols own equipment used in providing patrol services, including emergency care to skiers and snowboarders. The NSP strongly recommends that, wherever possible, all such property be owned by the ski area or agency in charge of administering the public lands on which patrol services are provided.

The ownership of buildings and equipment imposes a duty to maintain the property in serviceable condition. Liability can arise from the use of property and equipment in providing emergency services. The owner of such property should obtain adequate insurance to cover the potential liabilities.

Ski areas own property and equipment necessary for the operation of the ski area. Most areas maintain such property and obtain adequate insurance to cover both liability and casualty losses. In virtually every situation, it is more economical for the area to own patrol-related property and equipment and provide maintenance and insurance coverage. In addition, ownership of such property makes the patrol (and its members) potential targets for claims, while ownership by the area does not appreciably increase the area's exposure to liability.

Incident Records

Most ski areas keep some records of the incidents that occur at the ski area. These records vary from area to area. Patrollers should become familiar with the recordkeeping system established at their area.

Incident Report Forms

The goal of every ski area and its patrol is to help prevent ski accidents. However, because of the inherent risks of the sport, injuries will continue to occur in spite of reasonable measures undertaken.

When a patroller gives care to an ill or injured individual, it is very important to accurately and completely fill out an incident report form. The completeness and integrity of the incident report form is critical to maintaining the form as a reliable record of the circumstances of the incident and the care given.

Incident report forms usually are supplied by area management or the area's insurance company. Nordic patrols not associated with a ski area usually devise their own forms.

The patroller has three goals in filling out incident report forms. First, by accurately documenting the care given and the circumstances surrounding the incident, the patroller may help prevent personal liability as well as the area's liability. Second, in the event that litigation is initiated and a claim is made, the report form often is all that will refresh the recollection of the patroller and other involved parties as to the circumstances of the incident. Third, the incident report forms may be used by area management or public lands agencies in making operational decisions.

Patrollers should be aware that attorneys who represent injured skiers or snowboarders invariably obtain the incident report form filled out by the patroller as one of the first steps in preparing their case. It is therefore essential that the form accurately and completely reflects the circumstances of the incident.

The first step is to assure that the form is filled out in a legible manner; above all, the form must be readable. The form also must be completely filled out. The patroller should record the permanent address and tele-

phone number of every person named on the form. This includes the injured person, witnesses, instructors, lift crew, visiting patrollers, etc. Additionally, the full name of the patroller who completes the report should appear at the bottom of the form.

In most cases, there are blanks on the form that are simply not applicable to the situation being reported. In such cases, the patroller should be certain to put "N/A" for "not applicable" in the blank. In cases where the blank may be applicable but the answer is unknown, the patroller should write "N/K" for "not known." As a rule, nothing on the form should be left blank. The location of the incident should be recorded as precisely as possible. The attachment of a trail map or a U.S. Geological Survey (USGS) map with an "X" at the site of the incident often will be of assistance.

With the exception of statements of witnesses and the injured person, all the blanks in the form should be filled out as statements of fact. For example, it is much better practice to say, "I experienced difficulty in removing the person's bindings" than "The person's bindings were cranked down too tight." The first is a report of fact, while the second is an opinion.

The only place for personal opinion is in the block where the injured person describes how the incident occurred and what he or she might have done to prevent it. The patroller should always ask the patient to describe these circumstances in the patient's own words. The patroller should write the statement verbatim, if possible. In the event the statement is verbatim, quotation marks should be used.

The emergency care given the individual on the hill or trail usually includes a complete survey and appropriate care. The patroller should record the fact that a survey was done and also state what emergency care was given. This includes recording what are known as

"negative observations." For example, if the survey reveals nothing other than a sprained knee, the patroller should state, "Remainder of survey unremarkable." This shows that the patroller conducted an appropriate survey and found nothing more.

Some incidents require special handling. If a lift was involved in the incident, area management typically requires the lift operator to prepare a report. If an injury occurs in a ski school class, area management usually requires the instructor to make a report on the incident. If the skis or snowboard were rented from the rental shop at the area, area management often requires the rental shop personnel to inspect the equipment and make a report. Every patroller should know what the area requires and should follow the instructions of area management.

The nordic incident report form generally requires more detailed information concerning the incident, including trail location, expedition members, time started, etc. Nordic patrollers should be certain they understand what is required and how to complete the form.

The discussion on this topic is subject to change or modification by area management, and the patrol should strictly adhere to management's procedures.

Patrollers may believe they have a great memory for detail, but written reports made at the time of an incident are consistently more accurate than human memory. Patrollers can test their memory by reviewing incident report forms they filled out two or three years ago—and will likely be surprised to discover how much detail they have forgotten since the incident occurred.

Incident Investigation

As part of the risk management programs at mountain resorts, ski areas have developed and instituted formal incident investigation (popularly known as "AI" for the previously used term "accident investigation") procedures for the documentation of facts surrounding certain injuries occurring at the area. Patrollers usually act as the investigators, and may also act as the liaison between area management and injured persons, assisting the patients and their families and acting as the eyes and ears of area management. The patroller should know whether the area has an incident investigation procedure and the circumstances under which it is to be initiated.

The National Ski Patrol does not conduct incident investigations. At this time, the NSP does not have an approved incident investigation training program available to all NSP members. The decision to develop and implement an incident investigation program must be undertaken only with the full consent and direction of ski area management.

Investigative efforts are not limited to injuries occurring to skiers and snowboarders. The incident investigation team is often called upon to investigate slip-and-fall incidents on ski area premises, altercations between guests, injuries resulting from the use of resort property (exercise facilities, hotel rooms, restaurant and bar accidents), and even automobile accidents occurring in the parking lot.

The design and implementation of an incident investigation program is a function of area management. Patrollers should participate in such programs under the direction, control, and supervision of area management.

Any inquiries regarding incidents occurring at the ski area should be referred to area management. Patrollers should be cautious in talking about accidents in public places.

Litigation

In very rare circumstances, patrollers may find themselves involved in litigation. It is important to understand how to respond in the event a claim is made or considered by an individual.

Claims are typically made by a demand letter sent by an injured person's attorney to the ski area and/or the ski patroller, demanding payment in a certain sum and threatening litigation if payment is not made. However, litigation can and often is initiated without such a demand letter, and the patroller needs to be wary of any oral demands or threats of suit that are made even without such a demand letter.

Claims Against NSP Members or Patrols

If an NSP member receives a letter setting forth a claim against the patroller or the NSP for the payment of money, or if a member is served with a summons or complaint setting forth such a claim, the member must immediately telephone the NSP executive director at the national office, (303) 988-1111, during business hours (Mountain Time) to inform the executive director of the claim.

If possible, the patroller should transmit the claim letter or summons and complaint by fax to the NSP national office at (303) 988-3005 or (800) 222-4754. Unless otherwise directed by the executive director, the patroller should mail a copy of the letter or summons and complaint to Executive Director, National Ski Patrol System, Inc., 133 South Van Gordon, Suite 100, Lakewood, Colorado 80228-1706.

The patroller also should telephone or personally contact his or her patrol director and the area management or public lands administration to inform them of the claim. The patroller should mail or deliver a copy of the letter or summons and complaint to his or her patrol director and the area management or public lands administration.

Finally, the patroller should notify his or her general liability insurance company (such as a homeowner's or renter's insurance company) of the claim, and follow the insurance company's directions.

The patroller should be very careful about talking to others about the claim. In general, the patroller should refuse to speak to anyone about the claim unless the person is positively identified as an authorized representative of the NSP, the ski area, the public lands administration, the patroller's insurance company, the patroller's attorney, or the ski area's attorney.

Claims Against Ski Areas or Public Lands Agencies

Claims against a ski area or public lands administration are generally made directly to the ski area management or public lands administration. If an NSP member receives a letter setting forth a claim against the ski area or public lands administration, the member should immediately telephone the ski area management or public lands administration and follow their directions. The patroller should mail or deliver a copy of the letter or summons and complaint to the member's patrol director and the area manager or public lands administrator.

As with other claims, the patroller should be very careful about talking to others about the claim. In general, the patroller should refuse to speak to anyone about the claim unless the person is positively identified as an authorized representative of NSP, the ski area, the public lands administration, the patroller's insurance company, the patroller's attorney, or the ski area's attorney.

Claims By Patrollers Against Ski Areas

NSP will not have any role in litigation initiated by an NSP member against a ski area or its management, unless the NSP Executive Committee determines that it is in the best interests of the association to participate in some manner.

Insurance and Other Protection From Liability

One tool of risk management is the transfer of the costs of potential liability through the purchase of liability insurance. Insurance law is voluminous and often highly technical. This discussion is general and is not intended to replace the provisions of the insurance policies discussed. This information is not a complete and wholly accurate rendition of the full terms, conditions, and exclusions of the insurance policy. The summary is provided for general guidance only, and NSP specifically disclaims any liability for any incompleteness or inaccuracy contained in this summary. NSP members with specific questions regarding coverage should submit them in writing to the executive director at the national office.

This discussion is intended simply to prompt investigation and contemplation of the idea of risk relating to NSP instructional programs and ski patrolling. Each NSP member must come to his or her own conclusions regarding personal risk management in the programs in which he or she chooses to participate.

NSP Liability Insurance

The NSP carries a comprehensive general liability policy that provides coverage to the NSP and its members. This insurance is designed to protect NSP members from liability arising from policies and activities that are within the NSP Vision and Mission Statements and approved by the NSP Board of Directors and NSP Executive Committee.

The NSP Vision and Mission Statements (as revised on January 13, 1995) are as follows:

NSP Vision 2000 Statement

We are a leading partner in the ski and outdoor recreation community as an adaptable resource of valuable individuals benefiting this community.

NSP Mission Statement

We are a member-driven association. Our members support and participate in the ski and outdoor recreation community by providing emergency care, rescue, and education services. Our association supports us by surpassing member expectations through an esprit de corps that inspires members to belong, exceptional education programs, dynamic communication, outstanding membership support services, energetic interagency relations, and a strong financial position.

The policies and activities approved by the NSP Board of Directors and NSP Executive Committee are found in the current *NSP Policies and Procedures* manual, as amended by the board. All other NSP publications are educational documents and may or may not reflect current NSP policies.

The NSP has executed a Joint Statement of Understanding with the National Ski Areas Association. The joint statement establishes the proper legal relationship between volunteer patrollers and ski area operators, regardless of whether the ski area is a member of NSAA. The joint statement is reprinted in appendix D. Each fall, a copy of the joint statement is forwarded to all ski areas with NSP-affiliated patrols.

The NSP provides a liability insurance policy but does not provide other forms of insurance (casualty, medical, health, worker's compensation, life insurance, disability, etc.) The NSP liability insurance policy provides liability insurance coverage to NSP national, division, region, section, and

patrol entities, and NSP directors, officers, and members (paid and volunteer), while they are furthering the NSP mission by participating in nationally-authorized NSP activities, such as education or training programs. The policy also covers the NSP and its instructors and instructor trainers against claims that the NSP's education programs and materials are incorrect, inappropriate, or improperly administered, supervised or operated.

If NSP members need certification of insurance for any NSP purpose, they must submit their request in writing to the national office. The request must be for an activity that is directly related to the ongoing programs of the NSP.

The NSP liability insurance policy does not cover a number of activities undertaken by NSP members. The policy does not cover patrollers and patrols (volunteer or paid) while they are providing services to area management or to the public on behalf of area management. The policy does not provide protection to ski areas or special event sponsors or organizers. In addition, the policy does not cover patrollers and patrols (volunteer or paid) while they are providing volunteer or paid services to outside organizations, such as Special Olympics, Walk for Hope, "fun runs," etc. Finally, the policy does not cover the operation of ski swaps or other fund-raising activities.

The NSP does not provide any additional liability insurance coverage, such as first aid errors and omissions insurance for the delivery of emergency care or malpractice insurance for health care providers or other professionals (attorneys, teachers, accountants, etc.) who provide

compensated or free services to the NSP or its divisions, subdivisions, or membership. Patrollers providing emergency services at a ski area should inquire about and be comfortable regarding the insurance that the area provides.

The NSP does not provide any form of health or disability insurance coverage or benefits for its members (volunteer or paid) who are injured while training or patrolling. This includes worker's compensation insurance (which is provided by the ski area to paid patrollers) and medical, health, disability, or life insurance. When engaged in any sport such as skiing or snowboarding, volunteer patrollers should be prepared to fund medical care for their injuries, either through a health/disability insurance policy or through a healthy bank account.

Ski Area Insurance

NSP members, regardless of whether they are volunteer or paid, are representatives of area management when providing patrol services or conducting local patrol training. As such, they are responsible to and are under the direction of area management.

There is no universal requirement that ski areas purchase liability insurance to cover ski operations, including ski patrols and patrollers. Some states may require liability insurance coverage for ski areas, but most do not. In general, most ski areas do purchase such insurance, but the coverage of the insurance policies varies so much from area to area that no general statements can be made.

It is an area operator's prerogative to exceed NSP educational requirements; however, any additional area requirements are outside the auspices of the NSP program insurance and liability coverage.

Patrollers who are concerned about their personal risk as patrollers should ask their area management for information about the ski area's liability insurance.

Public Lands Agency Protection for Volunteers

Most public lands agencies are self-insured through the risk management department of their respective jurisdiction. Often such agencies have programs specifically designed to encourage volunteers to provide beneficial services on public lands. Usually such programs require the patrol to enter into a written agreement with the public agency.

The federal government has at least two laws that provide important advantages to volunteers working within the national forests and national parks: Volunteers in National Parks Act of 1969 and Volunteers in the National Forests Act of 1972. These laws authorize forest supervi-

sors and park superintendents to recognize volunteers who provide services in the forests or parks. The acts provide protection against tort claims arising from the volunteer activities and also provide the equivalent of worker's compensation in the event a patroller suffers injury while volunteering. In addition, the acts allow the forests and parks to fund equipment and uniforms for the volunteers. Both laws require an agreement with the forest supervisor or the park superintendent as a prerequisite for protection.

State and local laws may authorize state and local park agencies to enter into similar agreements with patrols providing coverage on park lands.

Patrols that conduct patrol activities on public lands should ask the agency responsible for administering the land about volunteer programs.

Personal Liability Insurance

Many personal liability policies, such as homeowner's and renter's insurance, provide coverage for volunteer activities. Several national insurance companies offer specific coverage for volunteer activities, either through umbrella policies or volunteer riders. Specific information may be obtained from the patroller's insurance agent.

Subunit or Local Insurance

If liability insurance is purchased by a subunit or at a local level, the name of the National Ski Patrol System, Inc., or any abbreviation thereof, must not be included in any manner, shape, or form as a party additionally insured under the policy. If a particular patrol must be named as a party insured, the patrol should be referred to as the "_____ Ski Patrol" without any reference that might connect the patrol with the NSP.

Patrollers provide essential services to ski areas, agencies governing public lands, and individual skiers.

Claims against patrollers and the NSP have been rare and largely unsuccessful. A recognition of the potential for liability and the methods for reducing such liability will assist the patroller in taking all reasonable steps to prevent accident claims. The patroller should then be certain there is sufficient insurance in place to protect against the risks that cannot be avoided.

Protection of Intellectual Property the NSP Owns

As an education association, the National Ski Patrol designs, develops, and produces many texts and training materials to accompany its national education programs. To protect the originality of the materials and accompanying designs, the NSP trademarks and logos are registered and written materials copyrighted.

Trademarks and Logos

The NSP holds a number of trademarks covering words and images used in connection with the NSP's activities. The national office regulates the NSP's legal rights respecting the use of the NSP trademarks and logos.

The National Ski Patrol holds the following trademark registrations with the Commissioner of Patents, United States Patent and Trademark Office: (1) the words "National Ski Patrol"; (2) the gold cross; (3) the gold cross with blue outline; (4) the blue and gold triangle, with the words "Ski Patrol" and the gold cross; (5) the blue and gold cross, with the words "National Ski Patrol"; (6) the blue and gold six-pointed star, with the words "National Ski Patrol" and the gold cross; (7) the words "U.S. Ski Patrol" and "United States Ski Patrol"; (8) the words "Winter Emergency Care"; (9) the Winter Emergency Care logo; (10) the words "Outdoor Emergency Care"; (11) the words "Ski Patrol Magazine"; (12) the words

"Outdoor First Care"; and (13) the NSP shield logo.

A division or subunit may not arbitrarily use the NSP logo without obtaining approval from the national office. This approval process enables the NSP to be consistent with Internal Revenue Service guidelines, the NSP charter, and the federal laws regarding copyrights and trademarks.

Membership in the National Ski Patrol entitles the different levels of the organization the right to use the logo and copyrighted materials in connection with local membership services. A patrol may use the logos within the patrol, a section may use the logos within the section, a region may use the logos within the region, and a division may use the logos within the division, for non-commercial purposes. Exceptions to this policy will be considered. Such requests must be submitted in writing to the national office.

A patrol is authorized to use the logos for fund-raising purposes, provided (1) the logo is not altered or defaced, (2) all uses are consistent with good taste and common sense, and (3) the fund-raising effort is confined to the specific geographic area of the local patrol.

The NSP logos may not be changed in character or appearance whatsoever. Changes to existing logos or the creation of new logos to symbolize national programs or the national organization without specific approval of the national organization is prohibited.

The national level of the NSP has exclusive rights with respect to use of the NSP logo and copyrighted material for commercial purposes. No NSP subunit may use NSP trademarks to promote commercial interests of any kind.

The NSP vigorously enforces its rights regarding the use of its logos. Through the official supplier and endorsement program, the National Ski Patrol generates significant revenues that supplement dues paid by the association's members.

Copyrights

The NSP holds copyrights in all of NSP's educational products. Copyright privileges assure that the hard work of volunteers and national staff in assembling and producing valuable educational resources will not be copied by others. Without the ability to recoup some of the development and production costs of educational materials through sales and licensing agreements, the NSP would have to rely much more heavily on member dues to support its programs.

Copying or otherwise reproducing NSP copyrighted materials for distribution is prohibited without prior written authorization from the executive director at the national office. The NSP will vigorously enforce its rights with respect to copyrighted materials and other published materials.

Anyone seeking to use the NSP copyrights or trademarks on proposed publications, films, or electronic media must first obtain the approval of the executive director in accordance with the policies and guidelines of the NSP Board of Directors.

All proposed publications, films, or electronic media generated by outside sources that seek to use NSP copyrights or trademarks must have the approval of the NSP executive director in accordance with the policies established by the NSP Board of Directors.

Ski area management or the public lands administration is responsible for the ski patrol staff relative to recruiting, hiring, training, devising work schedules, making work assignments, setting standards of operation, conducting skill performance evaluation, and motivating, disciplining, and terminating employees.

The patrol usually is managed as a unit within the mountain operations department, which also may include such things as lift maintenance, lift operations, grooming, snowmaking, ski school, and ski racing. An efficient ski patrol is a very important component of mountain operations and requires effective direction. Ultimately, the area manager is responsible for the successful integration and operation of all these departments and their functions.

The Ski Patrol's Role

Any NSP member or group of patrollers performing patrol services is subject to the ski area's standards of mountain and patrol operations and must abide by the policies and procedures established by the area's management. Whereas an area's paid patrollers are *employees* of the area, an area's volunteer patrollers are *agents* of that area. Area management or the public lands administration has the final decision on how many patrollers the area will have, which patrollers can work or volunteer at the area, how many patrollers will provide coverage for any particular duty shift, and what their responsibilities will entail.

The role of local ski patrols varies widely throughout the country, depending on geographic considerations, area management or the public lands administration preferences, state and local laws, and numerous other factors. Services might include opening and closing trails, providing guidance and services to guests, administering emergency care, per-

CHAPTER 7

Mountain Resort Management

forming rescue and lift evacuation, and accomplishing hill safety needs such as identifying and marking obstacles, grooming slopes and ramps, and providing avalanche mitigation services.

Area Management Responsibilities

Area management or the public lands administration usually has clearly written descriptions of the duties and responsibilities of the personnel in each department. Management establishes the complete qualifications required of a department head (e.g., patrol director) and individual patrollers. These qualifications become the standard for hiring paid staff and recruiting volunteers.

Area management or the public lands administration provides the department head with the resources needed to perform the job in a professional and effective manner as well as the authority to get the job done

satisfactorily. The National Ski Areas Association (NSAA) and the National Ski Patrol have developed a joint statement of understanding (see appendix D) that defines the areas of responsibility between NSAA and the NSP and its member volunteer patrols and patrollers.

The joint statement is not comprehensive; there are management matters not addressed by the statement, with the recognition that other matters may be mutually addressed in the future. NSAA encourages its member areas to require their patrollers to meet the current NSP training and educational criteria or their equivalent.

Patrol Supervision

Through planning and budgeting, area management or the public lands administration gives its ski patrol the organizational and supervisory support needed to perform patrolling duties in an effective and efficient manner. Area management or the public lands administration tracks the quality of the patrollers' performance in accordance with operation standards, providing effective reviews and details of corrective action needed, when necessary.

In the 1941 edition of *The*

Wilmot Mountain/Earl Essig

National Ski Patrol Manual, the patrol director is described as the "guiding spirit" of every ski patrol. Despite all the changes that have occurred in the structure of the National Ski Patrol and the mountain recreation industry over the past 50 years, this adage holds true.

The director of an NSP-member patrol has two essential roles that are distinct but interrelated. The first role is that of an educational system coordinator, assuring that NSP programs are delivered in a high-quality, timely manner to the entire patrol. The second role is that of an agent of area management or the public lands administration, conducting any additional, non-NSP training that management desires and working with management to provide the best possible ski patrol services at the area.

In these capacities, it is important that the patrol director maintain the best possible relationship with the ski area manager and all area employees. The patrol director should encourage each patrol member to strive to become a valuable part of the area team, by providing emergency care and rescue services and promoting the area whenever possible. Patrollers should never allow the area manager to view the local patrol and its members as a burden.

The manner in which a patrol is supervised generally depends on how the patrol is structured. A common method of patrol organization is to have both a volunteer and a professional patrol, each with its own administration and each with a patrol director who reports to the area manager. Another common structure consists of two separate patrols, with the professional patrol director reporting to the area manager and the volunteer patrol director reporting to the professional patrol director. While both methods offer certain advantages, they often result in unnecessary duplication of effort.

A single patrol may be organized with paid and volunteer members reporting to the professional patrol director. Often a volunteer is appointed as an assistant patrol director who is responsible for administering the duties of the volunteers. This method promotes the most favorable working relationship. Cooperation and rapport between the two groups is highest when both have the same skill requirements and participate in the same training sessions.

Another effective configuration is a single patrol with paid and volunteer members reporting to the volunteer patrol director. This method works well when there are just a few paid patrollers who wish to register with the NSP, or when there are not enough paid patrollers to form an administrative unit and it is more convenient for them to belong to the volunteer unit.

Regardless of the patrol's configuration, a balanced, mutually respectful working relationship between the paid and volunteer members is essential. The volunteer patrollers must work in cooperation with the paid patrollers and maintain a strong, supportive relationship, regardless of whether the paid patrollers belong to the NSP.

Further, the patrol should be structured in the most effective manner to meet the demands of area management or the public lands administration. The particular organizational structure for ski patrol operations is the responsibility of area management or the public lands administration.

Under the direction of area management or the public lands administration, the patrol director is responsible for the patrol's day-to-day contact with the skiing public. The patrol director oversees the training activities of the patrollers, and verifies to management that every patrol member has met the training and education requirements of the NSP as well as any additional training requirements the area has imposed.

Selection of Patrol Director

Area management or the public lands administration determines the patrol director's qualifications, responsibilities, and duties at the area. The NSP Board of Directors determines the patrol director's responsibilities within the national organization.

Most volunteer patrols elect their patrol directors using methods determined by the patrol's bylaws or customs. In other cases, the patrol director is appointed by the outgoing patrol director, a committee, or the local patrol's board of directors, depending on the patrol's bylaws or customs. While it is not common for area management or the public lands administration to appoint a volunteer patrol director, some areas use this method of selection.

Management at all times has the right to approve the selection of the volunteer patrol director. Further, the area manager has the prerogative to appoint a patrol director for as long a term as desired. Areas that have both volunteer and paid patrols often give the professional patrol director the responsibility for directing the volunteer patrol, either directly or through a volunteer patroller appointed as assistant patrol director.

Patroller Training

While NSP does not direct the day-to-day operations of individual patrols, the association does provide education services to help patrols fulfill their obligations to the area. If requested by area management or the public lands administration, the patrol director of any NSP volunteer patrol verifies that all patrollers at that area have completed the training and education requirements set forth by the NSP Board of Directors and have met all Outdoor Emergency Care requirements.

As a practical matter, patrol directors and other patrol officers and supervisors should work closely with area

Tom Stimpson

training, and the selection of equipment to be used in conjunction with such evacuation or training. Area management also specifies, procures, and maintains evacuation equipment.

Lift evacuation training is conducted at the direction of area management and in a manner consistent with the lift evacuation plan. Training should provide the opportunity for each patroller and other participants to review all aspects of the evacuation plan, including their specific role and duties. Each person should review and practice specific techniques and skills to be used in any actual evacuation.

During the 1980s, the NSP undertook a risk management review of rescuer self-evacuation from aerial lifts. The NSP's position is that it is improper to rely upon self-evacuation as part of a lift evacuation plan. NSP does not support or provide training or technical materials for self-evacuation.

Incident Investigation

In the joint statement between NSAA and NSP, both associations agree that incident investigation and documentation is an important element of patrol activity. Area management establishes procedures for collecting, recording, and maintaining documentation that relates to any incident as well as ensuring confidentiality of incident information. Generally, management delegates these procedures to the patrol. Consequently, when performing incident investigation, patrollers do so under the direction and control of area management or the public lands administration.

When performing ski patrol tasks, especially when providing emergency care, patrollers acquire information regarding the nature of the incident, potential causes, and resulting injuries. Since patrollers perform these tasks under the direction and control of area management or the

management or the public lands administration to achieve the goal of a well-trained, effective patrol that operates in harmony with the other mountain operations departments. This should include frequent communications regarding both training and operations.

Lift Evacuation

The NSP, NSAA, and area management recognize the importance of educating any individual who may have a role in lift evacuation as to the appropriate lift evacuation techniques (ground-based and aerial-based) and the specific implementation of the area lift evacuation plan. Area management designates certain individuals to carry out specific duties as defined in the emergency or lift evacuation plan. Patrollers participate in lift evacuation and lift evacuation training only as ski area management directs.

Area management is solely responsible for establishing policies and procedures for lift operations, maintenance, evacuation, lift evacuation public lands administration, any disclosure of information, whether casual or formal, can take place only as directed by area management or the public lands administration. Patrollers should not make any statements about such incidents to anyone, and should refer any inquiries to the area's designated spokesperson.

Volunteer (Non-Employee) Status

NSAA and NSP agree that volunteer patrollers are not "employees" of the ski area for any purpose. Volunteer patrollers are "agents" of area management or the public lands administration when performing ski patrol services and conducting local patrol training at a ski area. As such, in most states, volunteer patrollers are not entitled to worker's compensation benefits if they are injured while performing patrol services or participating in training.

Management has the right to dismiss the volunteer patrol director or any volunteer patroller at any time. Area management or the public lands administration may request the NSP division director to confirm this decision.

Equipment Ownership and Maintenance

Ski patrols use a variety of equipment to provide patrol services. This equipment often includes rescue toboggans; radios; blankets; medical equipment and supplies; all-terrain vehicles; snowmobiles; avalanche probes and shovels; and ropes and slings. The NSP recommends that area management or the public lands administration own all such equipment. Patrol maintenance and use of such equipment is under the direction and control of area management or the public lands administration.

In some states, motorized equip-

ment such as all-terrain vehicles and snowmobiles must be titled or registered. In such states, area management or the public lands administration should be named owner on the title and/or the registration, with the equipment made available for patrol use as appropriate.

Signage on area equipment should reflect the area's ownership and control of such equipment, and should not be identified with the NSP. Aid room and patrol facilities likewise should be owned and maintained by ski area management or the public lands administration.

The NSP recommends that the ownership, maintenance, replacement, and use of all property for ski patrol purposes be reflected in a written agreement entered into between the area and the local patrol.

Uniforms

The dress code for patrollers is subject to the requirements of area management or the public lands administration. NSP members should wear the uniform approved by area management or the public lands administration when on duty.

NSP Responsibilities

The NSP provides the mountain resort and outdoor recreation community with education programs for individuals who may wish to apply for patrolling positions at ski areas or on public lands. These programs are designed to provide patrollers with specific skills applicable to patrolling tasks. All educational programs are approved by the NSP Board of Directors before they are implemented.

The NSP develops state-of-the-art education programs such as Outdoor Emergency Care through ongoing research and development activities. These programs reflect the demand for such training from mountain resorts and individual patrollers and set forth NSP's training standards. In response to local laws or conditions, area management or the public lands administration implements ski patrol protocols that meet its needs.

The NSP develops and distributes educational materials to provide the basis for local training by ski patrols in support of the NSP training standards. The NSP and its divisions develop and conduct education clinics, seminars, and other events to support the local ski patrol training staffs.

The NSP develops and administers credentialing and recordkeeping systems to validate the educational and training programs conducted by local ski area trainers, and to provide a competency and quality standard for the industry.

The NSP supports overall ski industry education efforts through cooperative programs with many organizations. For instance, the NSP and NSAA have formed a ski safety committee to promote safe skiing practices; the NSP and PSIA have developed joint training programs to improve and maintain patroller skiing skills; and the NSP manages the National Avalanche Foundation's biennial avalanche school.

Also, the NSP, the National Off-Road

Bicycling Association, and the International Mountain Bicycling Association have developed a joint program for training and issuing credentials to bike patrollers and ambassadors. The NSP designates a representative to the American National Standards Institute (ANSI) B77 Committee, which sets standards for the construction and operation of aerial lifts. Further, the NSP and NSAA collaborate in writing and publishing *The Lift Evacuation Manual*, the industry's primary reference on this topic. The NSP participates in a number of other joint programs and committees with outside organizations.

There is a clear distinction between the responsibilities of the NSP and those of area management or the public lands administration: The NSP develops and conducts specific education and training programs to prepare patrollers for service to ski areas; area management or the public lands administration directs and controls actual ski patrol operations. In addition, each ski area conducts such additional education and training programs as it deems necessary to meet the conditions of its ski hill.

Even though a clear symbiotic relationship exists, neither NSP nor its individual members have management authority at mountain resorts. In fact, important organizational principles and leadership accountability are compromised if these are turned over to someone other than area management or the public lands administration.

Ski patrol directors are the critical link between patrollers, the ski area, and the various levels of the National Ski Patrol. The importance of understanding the patrol director job description cannot be overstated. In all things, patrol directors must work closely with area management or the public lands administration to integrate effective patrolling with other ski area operations. All patrollers should seek to provide ski patrol services in harmony with other area activities and in a close working relationship with other area managers and staff.

Ski patrollers devote a great deal of time and effort to the skiing public, ski area management, and the national organization. In return, the National Ski Patrol recognizes this excellence and dedication at all levels through public expressions of appreciation in the form of awards.

This type of recognition amongst one's peers is a stimulus to continued and improved performance. More important, the awards presented by the National Ski Patrol are sincere expressions of appreciation for accomplishments in the service of the NSP and the skiing public.

The NSP recognizes three types of awards or insignia:

1. those that recognize meritorious service;
2. those that identify patrollers with outstanding ability or special skills; and
3. those that are awarded to members or non-members for distinguished service to the NSP and to the sport of skiing.

More details on NSP awards are provided in the *NSP Policies and Procedures* manual, which has the most recent information about the association's programs, rules, and regulations.

Meritorious Service Awards

The NSP has a system of awards designed to recognize and reward its members for outstanding service in individual events and for extended service to the association. Meritorious service awards are designed to recognize and reward patrollers who have performed individual acts of merit, lifesaving, heroism, rescue, or exceptional administrative and organizational service.

Great care is taken to consider the nominations of only those patrollers who have indicated a genuine and lasting devotion to the National Ski Patrol and who, by out-

CHAPTER

8

Awards

standing example, have served in leadership and educational roles. Patrollers with a National Appointment or Leadership Commendation Appointment are expected to continue to serve the NSP with exemplary service, representing themselves to the skiing public as selected goodwill ambassadors of the organization.

National Appointment and Leadership Commendation Appointment

Martin Crabb

Receiving a National Appointment or a Leadership Commendation Appointment is not something for which a patroller—volunteer or paid—can work or plan. A patroller does not apply for a National Appointment or Leadership Commendation Appointment or undergo a skills and knowledge evaluation. To obtain this classification, a patroller must be nominated by other patrollers who hold the same appointment for demonstrating exemplary service to the NSP.

A patroller with a National Appointment or Leadership Commendation Appointment is an individual who has demonstrated leadership, good character, diplomacy, a positive attitude, good judgment, unusual qualities of patrolling ability, a genuine desire to serve the skiing

public, and extraordinary service to the National Ski Patrol.

Great care is taken to consider the nominations of only those patrollers who have met all the award criteria. An individual who receives a National Appointment or Leadership Commendation Appointment usually has served as an officer or advisor of the NSP and in the discharge of those duties has exemplified the qualities that typify the characteristics of these appointments.

The appointments should be overdue rather than premature, but tenure alone is never an adequate criterion. Patrollers with appointments are expected to continue to serve the NSP with exemplary service, representing themselves to the skiing public as selected goodwill ambassadors of the organization. A patroller with a National Appointment or Leadership Commendation Appointment may actively participate in the nomination procedure for other National and Leadership Commendation appointments.

These appointments are for life; however if a patroller with an appointment discredits the honor of the NSP, the appointment will be revoked and the individual will be asked to relinquish the award's insignia.

Qualifications that are common to both appointments include the following. Members nominated for either appointment must have

1. served a minimum of eight ski seasons (with a minimum of one year as a senior or senior auxiliary) as an active member of the National Ski Patrol;
2. demonstrated leadership that benefits the NSP by (a) serving beyond the patrol level, or (b) serving two or more ski seasons as a certified instructor in a program that is beneficial to the NSP, or by (c) demonstrating exceptional performance as a patrol director;
3. demonstrated leadership abilities in working with the skiing public

as related to skier safety education; and

4. never received an appointment before.

The National Appointment qualifications stipulate that the nominee must have been an active senior alpine, nordic, or snowboard patroller or certified patroller for at least one year before nomination. The Leadership Commendation Appointment qualifications specify that nominees must have completed the senior auxiliary requirements at least one year before nomination.

Presentation of either of these appointments must be made at a special occasion by the highest officer in attendance (a section chief or higher officer). The recipient of an appointment receives a certificate, card, pin, badge, and appointment acknowledgment card. Upon receiving the card, the appointee must sign it and mail it to the national office for the appointment and number to become valid. The appointment number is not transferable. The recipient also may have his or her national number engraved on the NSP name bar.

Gold Merit Star

The Gold Merit Star is awarded annually to the National Outstanding Alpine Ski Patroller, National Outstanding Nordic Ski Patroller, National Outstanding Student Ski Patroller, National Outstanding Professional Ski Patroller, National Outstanding Auxiliary Patroller, National Chairman's Outstanding Administrative Patroller, National U.S. Ski Patrol Outstanding Administrative Patroller, National Outstanding Instructor, National Outstanding Patrol Director, and the recipient of the Charles Minot "Minnie" Dole Award.

The Gold Merit Star award consists of a certificate with a gold star on parchment paper. The recipient may also have a gold star engraved on the NSP name bar.

Silver Merit Star

The Silver Merit Star is awarded annually to the runner-up to the National Outstanding Alpine Ski Patroller, National Outstanding Nordic Ski Patroller, National Outstanding Student Ski Patroller, National Outstanding Professional Ski Patroller, National Outstanding Auxiliary Patroller, National Chairman's Outstanding Administrative Patroller, National U.S. Ski Patrol Outstanding Administrative Patroller, National Outstanding Instructor, and the National Outstanding Patrol Director.

The Silver Merit Star award consists of a certificate with a silver star on parchment paper. The recipient may also have a silver star engraved on the NSP name bar.

Purple Merit Star

The Purple Merit Star is the highest NSP meritorious service award and is given to members who individually save or are primarily responsible, in conjunction with others, for saving a human life. This may be accomplished by rendering emergency care to someone who has been stricken by a sudden illness or accident (auto, marine, snow, or any other type of accident). The Purple Merit Star may be presented regardless of where the lifesaving act was performed, provided the emergency care was rendered under the sole direction and sole responsibility of patrollers.

The Purple Merit Star should *not* be awarded if the rescue was accomplished by a mixed-rescue party that was not under the direction of the ski patrol or patrollers. Patrollers who are under the direction of another group (e.g., the Civil Defense Corps or American Red Cross) do not qualify for a Purple Merit Star, nor do individuals who perform the lifesaving act in the course of their normal occupation (ambulance attendant, fireman, etc.), unless that occupation is patrolling.

Generally, only one individual is credited with saving a life, and seldom does more than one individual receive a Purple Merit Star for a single lifesaving event. However, from time to time, primary responsibility is shared by more than one person, and more than one Purple Merit Star may be awarded. These situations will be reviewed on a case-by-case basis.

The nomination must be accompanied by a signed statement from an attending physician or, in the physician's absence, any medically knowledgeable witness (preferably a paramedic or nurse) who can substantiate that the patroller's actions primarily contributed to saving a life.

The Purple Merit Star award consists of a certificate with a purple star on parchment paper. The recipient may also have a purple star engraved on the NSP name bar.

Patrollers who had a supporting role in saving a human life may receive a Green Merit Star or Blue Merit Star if warranted.

Blue Merit Star

The Blue Merit Star is awarded to members for outstanding or heroic use of ski patrol skills in an attempt to save a human life but whose efforts have not met the Purple Merit Star criteria. This award also may be presented to members for outstanding service in support roles associated with the Purple Merit Star.

The same documents as those required for the Purple Merit Star and the Green Merit Star must accompany the nomination.

The Blue Merit Star award consists of a certificate with a blue star on parchment paper. The recipient may also have a blue star engraved on the NSP name bar.

Green Merit Star

The Green Merit Star is awarded to members for an outstanding act of heroism that does not meet the life-saving requirements of the Purple Merit Star. It is given for arduous and hazardous rescue work in which the recipient used ski patrol training, and also in air crash, avalanche, and mountain rescue situations, etc. in which the recipient used ski patrol training.

The nomination must be accompanied by a letter of recommendation from the patrol director or higher officer. Supporting material such as newspaper clippings and statements from government offices and from any person who can attest to the patroller's actions also should be included.

The Green Merit Star award consists of a certificate with a green star. The recipient may also have a green star engraved on the NSP name bar.

Yellow Merit Star

The Yellow Merit Star is awarded to members for any outstanding act or service to the National Ski Patrol. This award has a very broad interpretation and serves as a way of honoring deserving members for a variety of outstanding administrative accomplishments and also for outstanding service in support roles associated with the Purple, Blue, or Green Merit Star actions.

A letter of recommendation from the patrol director or higher officer and any appropriate supporting material should accompany the nomination. A member may receive more than one Yellow Merit Star, but each act or administrative duty must be unrelated to any prior receipt of the award and must have an element of *national* relevance. To maintain the value of the Yellow Merit Star, it should not be given too freely.

The Yellow Merit Star is awarded at the NSP Board of Directors annual meeting to the patrol director of the patrol that receives the National Outstanding Ski Patrol Award. The Yellow Merit Star award consists of a certificate with a yellow star on

parchment paper. The recipient may also have one yellow star engraved on the NSP name bar.

Distinguished Service Award

The NSP Distinguished Service Award (DSA) is designed to be given to members who have performed extraordinary service to the National Ski Patrol and the skiing public over a long period, distinguished by exceptional devotion to duty and outstanding performance. The DSA may be used to recognize members who have made excellent contributions to the system regardless of whether they have a National Appointment or a Leadership Commendation Appointment. Generally, a member receives this award only once.

The DSA also may be presented to individuals not affiliated with the National Ski Patrol for outstanding contributions to the organization (e.g., a ski area manager who has strongly supported the NSP for many years and has contributed significantly to the achievement of the association's goals).

Recipients of the DSA who are members of the NSP will be given a plaque and a sweater pin engraved with the DSA insignia. Recipients outside the NSP will be given a certificate and a plaque engraved with the DSA insignia.

National Outstanding Awards

National outstanding awards provide a means to recognize outstanding patrollers and ski patrols on an annual basis. Each ski season the National Ski Patrol may give outstanding awards, described in the following sections, to patrols and individual patrollers whose nominations have been submitted by a division director. A division may submit only one nomination for each award.

All national outstanding awards

are referred to by their descriptive names, and only the trophy carries the name of the past national chairman. The winners and runner-ups are announced at the NSP Board of Directors annual meeting. The national plaques are kept on display at the national office and the winners also receive a trophy.

No winner of a National Outstanding Award will be eligible for an outstanding award the following season.

Outstanding Alpine Ski Patrol Award

This award is presented each year to the Outstanding Alpine Ski Patrol selected from among nominations sent by division directors to the national office and approved by the awards review committee. This award honors the patrol organization developed by the National Ski Patrol founder, Minnie Dole.

The name of the outstanding alpine ski patrol is engraved on the Friends of Minnie Dole plaque, which is on display at the national office. A special Unit Citation Award certificate and a trophy duly inscribed are presented to the patrol director. The patrol director also is awarded a Yellow Merit Star certificate. Each ski patrol nominated for this award receives a Unit Citation Award as the outstanding alpine patrol in its division.

Outstanding Nordic Ski Patrol Award

This award is presented each year to the Outstanding Nordic Ski Patrol selected from among nominations sent by division directors to the national office and approved by the awards review committee. This award honors former National Chairman Ronald Ricketts, during whose term the nordic program attained its greatest growth.

The name of the outstanding nordic patrol is engraved on the Ronald Ricketts Outstanding Nordic Ski Patrol plaque, which is on display in the national office.

A special Unit Citation Award certificate and trophy duly inscribed are presented to the patrol director. The patrol director also is awarded a Yellow Merit Star certificate. Each ski patrol nominated for this award receives a Unit Citation Award from the national office as the outstanding nordic patrol in its division.

Outstanding Alpine Ski Patroller Award

This award is presented each year to the Outstanding Alpine Ski Patroller selected from among nominations sent by the division directors to the national office and approved by the awards review committee. The con-tributions of the recipients of this award typify the excellence in general ski patrolling and ski patrol leadership and training of past National Director William R. Judd.

Any active volunteer alpine patroller is eligible, except students, candidates, auxiliaries, or those who are eligible for either of the outstanding administrative awards or the Outstanding Patrol Director Award, or those who hold offices or positions above the level of patrol director or section advisor.

The winner's name is engraved on the William R. Judd Outstanding Volunteer Alpine Ski Patroller plaque that was presented to the NSP by the Ski Patrol of Chile. The plaque is on display at the national office.

Outstanding Nordic Ski Patroller Award

This award is presented each year to the Outstanding Nordic Ski Patroller selected from among nominations sent by the division directors to the national office and approved by the awards review committee. The contri-butions of the recipients of this award typify the excellence in administration of past National Chairman Donald C. Williams. It was during Williams' term of office that the nordic program was greatly expanded.

Any active volunteer nordic patroller is eligible, except students, candidates, auxiliaries, or those who are eligible for either of the outstanding administrative awards or the Outstanding Patrol Director Award, or those who hold offices above the level of patrol director or section advisor.

The winner's name is engraved on the Donald C. Williams Outstanding Nordic Ski Patroller plaque, which is on display at the national office.

Outstanding Student Ski Patroller Award

This award is presented each year to the Outstanding Student Ski Patroller selected from among nominations sent by the division directors to the national office and approved by the awards review committee. This award honors the late National Director Edward F. Taylor, who established the junior program while he was in office.

Any NSP student patroller may be nominated for a given year through the member's senior year in high school.

The winner's name is engraved on the Edward E. Taylor Outstanding

Junior Ski Patroller plaque, which is on display at the national office.

Outstanding Professional Ski Patroller Award

This award is presented each year to the Outstanding Professional Ski Patroller selected from nominations sent by the division directors to the national office and approved by the awards review committee. The award honors past National Director Harry G. Pollard, during whose term several special programs for professional patrollers were developed.

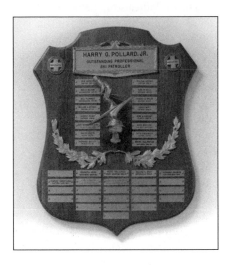

Any member who is registered as paid, is a full-time employee at a ski area, and is paid to patrol is eligible for this award. Those who are eligi-

ble for either of the outstanding administrative awards or those who hold offices or positions above the level of patrol director or section advisor are not eligible for this award.

The winner's name is engraved on the Harry G. Pollard Jr. Outstanding Professional Ski Patroller plaque, which is on display at the national office.

U.S. Ski Patrol Outstanding Administrative Ski Patroller Award

This award is presented each year to the U.S. Ski Patrol Outstanding Administrative Ski Patroller who is selected from nominations of members of (or eligible to be members of) the U.S. Administrative Patrol. This award honors past National Director Charles W. Schobinger, during whose term the current organizational structure of the NSP was developed. Specifically, NSP training and standards programs were established through the creation of national education program committees whose leaders are eligible to be members of the U.S. Ski Patrol (national administrative patrol).

Nominations are submitted by the division directors, national chairman, or assistant national chairmen to the national office. The winner is selected by a majority vote of the executive committee of the NSP Board of

Directors. The national office prepares this ballot (or ballots, should a majority not be obtained on the first ballot) from the nominations received in accordance with the procedures and timetable set forth for all other outstanding awards.

The winner's name is engraved on the Charles W. Schobinger U.S. Ski Patrol Outstanding Administrative Ski Patroller plaque, which is on display at the national office.

National Chairman's Outstanding Administrative Ski Patroller Award

This award is presented each year to a member who has made an outstanding administrative contribution to the NSP beyond the patrol level. This award also honors the national chairman in office at the time the award is presented. The award was established by the NSP Board of Directors to recognize and honor those administrative patrollers who are not eligible for the U.S. Ski Patrol Outstanding Administrative Ski Patroller Award.

The winner is selected from nominations sent by the division directors to the national office and approved by the awards review committee. The nominee may be a section chief, region director, region administrator, or division supervisor. If the individual

is eligible for the U.S. Ski Patrol Outstanding Administrative Award, he or she *may not* be considered for the National Chairman's Outstanding Administrative Ski Patroller Award.

The winner's name is engraved on the National Chairman's Outstanding Administrative Ski Patroller plaque, which is on display at the national office.

Outstanding Auxiliary Patroller Award

This award is presented each year to the Outstanding Auxiliary Patroller selected from among nominations sent by the division director to the national office and approved by the awards review committee. The award honors past National Director Charles C. Haskins, during whose term of office special programs for auxiliary patrollers were developed.

Any active auxiliary patroller is eligible for this award, except those who are eligible for either of the outstanding administrative awards or who hold a position or office above the level of patrol director or section advisor.

The winner's name is engraved on the Charles C. Haskins Outstanding Auxiliary Ski Patroller plaque, which is on display at the national office.

Outstanding Instructor Award

This award is presented each year to a member who has been an NSP

certified instructor in one or more of the NSP educational programs. Only one award is given to cover all NSP instruction disciplines. This award honors Roger Langley, the past chairman of the National Ski Association and National Appointment #1, who encouraged Minnie Dole to establish a national organization that would, in part, develop widespread education and raise the standards and efficiency of ski patrols.

The recipient must have been a certified instructor for at least three ski seasons and actively instructed for the last two seasons. Any NSP member who is a certified instructor is eligible to receive the award.

The winner's name is engraved on the Roger Langley Outstanding Instructor plaque, which is on display at the national office.

Outstanding Patrol Director Award

This award, approved by the NSP Board of Directors in 1996, is issued each year to the Outstanding Patrol Director selected from among those nominations sent by the division director to the national office and approved by the awards review committee. Any active patrol director is eligible for this award.

At this printing, award details are being finalized by the national awards committee. A plaque will be on display at the national office.

Outstanding Avalanche Award

The Montgomery M. Atwater avalanche award is given periodically when outstanding NSP members or non-members have made outstanding or continuing superlative contributions to the avalanche program.

Nominations for the award must be forwarded to the national avalanche program director, who will select a committee of three nationally respected avalanche specialists (including the avalanche program director) and at least one non-NSP member. The award recommendation goes to the NSP national chairman for approval.

A Montgomery M. Atwater plaque will be on display at the national office.

Charles Minot "Minnie" Dole Award

This award recognizes those exceptional few members who, over the years, have closely exemplified the long-term dedication, devotion, and self-sacrifice of the founder of the NSP, Charles Minot "Minnie" Dole. The winner of this award must be an NSP member who has at least 25 years of active patrolling service, is registered as an active member at the time of nomination, has provided continuous leadership for more than 10 years in offices from ski patrol director through national levels, and has designed and implemented programs, projects, procedures, and equipment that have positively affected the entire National Ski Patrol.

A nomination must be made in the form of a letter that has been signed by 10 or more currently registered NSP members with National Appointments. The nomination must receive the executive committee's unanimous approval to be awarded. This award may not be presented to the person who receives an outstanding patroller award that year.

The recipient of the Minnie Dole Award will be announced at the NSP Board of Directors annual meeting. The recipient will receive an engraved plaque, and his or her name will be added to the Minnie Dole memorial plaque on display at the national office. The recipient also may have a Gold Merit Star engraved on the NSP name bar.

National Recognition Awards

Many patrols and individuals deserve national recognition for their dedication and distinguished service to NSP programs and projects. The following methods of recognition are designed for this purpose.

Unit Citation Award

A Unit Citation Award certificate may be presented by the national chairman, upon the recommendation of a division director, to any NSP-registered ski patrol that has performed in any outstanding manner in the NSP, the ski industry, or in other areas of winter

recreation or rescue, and when it is not possible to single out specific people. Nominations for Unit Citations are made in letters to the national awards advisor through appropriate local and division channels. The Unit Citation Award certificate is given automatically to each ski patrol nominated by its division for the National Outstanding Ski Patrol Award.

National Certificate of Appreciation

The National Certificate of Appreciation may be awarded by the national chairman, upon the recommendation of an NSP officer, to individuals or groups for service to or support of the NSP that does not fall within the scope of the other award categories. Members as well as non-NSP members or groups are eligible for this award.

Service Recognition Award

The Service Recognition Award may be used to recognize members who have served the NSP for 10 years or longer. (This award should be given when years of service add up to an increment of five years.) Patrol directors or awards advisors may order service recognition certificates from the national office. The service of elected members of the NSP Board of Directors (i.e., division directors and board representatives) is recognized in a manner similar to that currently used for staff and advisors upon leaving the positions.

Honorary Awards

Honorary awards are used to recognize outstanding individuals and supporters of NSP programs.

Honorary National Appointment

The Honorary National Appointment is awarded at rare intervals to individu-

als who have performed unusual or highly useful service of national significance to the National Ski Patrol. The recipient is not required to meet the skiing, emergency care, or other requirements of registered NSP members, nor is the recipient required or expected to perform the duties of a patroller. The recipients of this award may not wear the official NSP uniform unless they become NSP members. NSP members or retired members are not eligible to receive this award.

This honorary award must be submitted to the national chairman for approval, with the concurrence of the NSP Board of Directors. The presentation of an Honorary National Appointment must be made at a special occasion by the highest officer in attendance (national chairman or designee).

Angel Pin

The NSP Angel Pin may be awarded, upon the approval of the division director or designate, to non-members of NSP who have provided valuable contributions to the NSP.

Division or Region Certificates of Appreciation

The division or region Certificate of Appreciation may be awarded, upon the recommendation of an NSP officer, to individuals or groups that have provided service to or support of the NSP that does not fall within the scope of the other awards categories. This certificate may be awarded to non-members or non-patrol groups for valued contributions in furthering the goals of the NSP.

Administration of Awards

Recognition of deserving individuals and groups must be tempered by careful selection of recipients so that the integrity and credibility of the awards program is maintained.

If the national chairman chooses to appoint a national awards coordinator, the appointment will not extend beyond the tenure of the national chairman; the awards coordinator may be re-appointed by a newly elected chairman. The appointee must be a registered patroller with a National Appointment and have some experience with the NSP awards program.

The national chairman also may delegate some or all of the awards program responsibilities to the national office staff or other national officers, staff members, or assistants. The national awards coordinator or other designees review and approve or reject all awards nominations and requests. For the national outstanding awards, a national outstanding awards review committee is appointed on an annual basis.

Division directors are responsible for administering the national as well as the division awards programs at the division level. Division directors generally delegate some or all of their responsibilities for awards administration to other division officers or staff. However, such delegation does not relieve the division director of the final responsibility for the approval of fully qualified and deserving candidates. All division officers, especially ski patrol directors, should understand how the awards program is administered and who is responsible for the program.

Award Nominations

Current forms for awards nominations can be found in the *NSP Policies and Procedures* manual as well as from division awards coordinators.

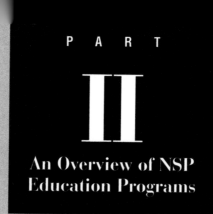

PART

II

An Overview of NSP
Education Programs

In keeping with NSP's strategic intent to provide exceptional education programs, the association's leaders strive to incorporate a consistent philosophy among all national education programs. The association does this by developing performance expectations and quality assurance procedures for each program.

The performance objectives identify what patrollers need to know or demonstrate in order to satisfy NSP education requirements. These objectives emphasize the knowledge and skills all patrollers must have, including the ability to build on the knowledge and skills learned, long after the controlled learning setting comes to an end.

The quality assurance guidelines of NSP programs provide instructors with ways to maintain a learning environment most conducive to learning. Divisions approve the registration of only those patrols whose members satisfy the knowledge and skill requirements established by the NSP Board of Directors.

As national program committees update programs and develop new curriculums, they identify the essential content for each national program in a standard training outline. NSP programs are designed as competency (performance)-based training programs. This philosophy incorporates objectives for each student to fulfill to be considered competent in that discipline.

It is very important that instructors of NSP education programs be flexible. There is no lock-step rigidity on *how* or *when* to teach any program as long as each course meets the training needs of the students and area management. This flexibility allows the instructors to vary their teaching methods to accommodate patrol schedules. The NSP education philosophy encourages training programs that are characterized by activity, variety, and direction based on current practices in adult education.

Program Design

The NSP membership generates many ideas for the association's programs. When an idea for a new program is presented to the NSP Board of Directors, the national chairman appoints an ad hoc committee to investigate program specifics such as applicability to the NSP mission, field tests and pilots, time commitments for development, and possible budget requirements. This appointment is usually made following a board proposal with a directive from the national chairman for a committee report at the next board meeting.

Depending on the results of the committee's review, the committee recommends that the board either proceed with the program or end discussion on the topic.

If the board agrees to proceed with a new program, the national chairman appoints an action team to more specifically outline the program's objectives and parameters, define budget and time projections, and draft a proposal for board consideration. After the board approves the proposal, the program becomes part of the strategic plan with a specific action item and a budget line. The national program committee, headed by the appropriate national education program director, then takes responsibility for the program. When the program is completed, it is submitted to the board for approval. If the program is approved, the production of the program's education materials is then incorporated into the national office production schedule.

Program Development

The national program director for a specific education discipline facilitates development of the program by submitting a budget request to the board of directors. If the board approves the budget (based on the strategic plan and need), the program development process begins with the national program committee meeting.

Experts on the specific education discipline (usually division supervisors with appropriate expertise) develop program content, refine program goals into learning objectives, organize the curriculum, and review materials. Task committees are frequently created from within the national program committee to work on various aspects of the program.

Field work, pilots, and program committee review are integral parts of program development. The committees and task groups work closely with the national education department to follow an established production schedule for the development of materials that accompany the program (i.e., drafts and content reviews), including editing, graphic design, production, and determining inventory needs. All education and training materials must conform to NSP copyrights, policies, and regulations.

Program Delivery

The National Ski Patrol has an instructor development program for individuals who are interested in teaching NSP education courses to members and other interested individuals or groups. Phase I and Phase II instructor development programs provide the necessary training and structure to certify NSP instructors.

Everyone who is involved in delivering NSP education programs must share the objective of providing a positive, effective learning experience for the member. The division, region, section, and patrol officers; the program supervisors and administrators; and the instructor trainers and instructors themselves—all must work cooperatively to maintain the integrity and usefulness of the program.

If NSP education programs are to be recognized as valid programs by the ski industry, outdoor recreation community, and affiliate members, they must be of high quality and meet the immediate needs of these groups. But the programs are truly valuable only through practical application. Every NSP member is expected to demonstrate an above-average level of knowledge in emergency response and other patroller skills. Of equal importance is the patroller's responsibility to display integrity, maturity, and good judgment when providing rescue services for area management. The NSP expects every instructor to have up-to-date knowledge and skills and to be accountable as a quality trainer for the NSP, the ski industry, and the outdoor recreation community.

Program Administration

The NSP's education department relies on instructors, officers, and supervisors to complete all administrative duties and paperwork in a proper and timely manner and to maintain personal teaching records.

Initially, every NSP education course needs to be pre-registered with the national office to receive a course number. Course logs are mailed periodically to national program directors and division supervisors to help them keep track of NSP education courses in their respective disciplines. In addition, members can obtain course information through the fax-on-demand program and via the NSP Website home page. As courses are completed and the instructor of record sends the records to the national office, the office updates the member records in the organizational database. Patrol officers and instructors are asked to verify national office records on an annual basis.

Details for program administration are part of instructor development training and can be found in the instructor manual for each discipline. Updates on administrative procedures are included in *Pointers*, the NSP instructor newsletter published periodically each ski season.

The following chapters, which are not presented in any particular order of importance or development, examine each of the NSP's education programs in detail. Publications and materials that supplement NSP education courses are available through the *Winter Catalog*. Additional information may be obtained from the national education department and the respective national program directors or division supervisors.

The goal of the National Ski Patrol is to provide area management with the services of uniformly trained patrollers whose skiing (downhill and telemark), snowboarding, and toboggan-handling skills are annually evaluated and refreshed. The National Alpine (skiing/snowboarding) Committee has developed training objectives to help patrollers maintain these basic patrolling skills and perform their duties competently and efficiently.

Patrollers are expected to demonstrate an above-average level of skiing/snowboarding ability with emphasis on stability, control, and the use of sound skiing/snowboarding techniques. This level of ability creates a favorable public relations image and gives the public confidence in the abilities of the local patrollers. Strong skiing/snowboarding skills also provide the basis for competent toboggan handling in the transportation of injured skiers.

Basic Alpine Patrolling Skills

The NSP's course for alpine toboggan handling is designed to help patrollers develop the skiing/snowboarding skills and knowledge to fulfill tasks required by area management. Table 10.1 on the following page contains a list of skiing maneuvers and corresponding snowboarding maneuvers.

Toboggan Handling

The basic alpine toboggan-handling course is designed to provide coaching in skiing/snowboarding proficiency, general toboggan-handling proficiency, and general on-hill operations pertaining to toboggan use.

Prerequisites

- Acceptance by patrol for candidate training
- NSP member dues paid
- At least 15 years of age

CHAPTER

10

Alpine Ski and Toboggan Program

Time Commitment

- One to two years

Fees

- National—none
- Division—varies
- Course—varies
- Cost of materials

Credential

- NSP Certificate of Achievement (distributed by instructor)

Continuing Education/ Refresher

- Annual on-the-hill refresher focusing on local skill requirements
- Attendance records kept at the local patrol level; no formal credential

Instructor of Record

- Local ski and toboggan trainers
- Division ski and toboggan supervisors
- Alpine toboggan instructors

Required Text

- *The Ski Patroller's Manual*, National Ski Patrol, 14th edition

References

- NSP *Ski and Toboggan Training Manual,* National Ski Patrol, 1994
- *NSP Policies and Procedures*, National Ski Patrol, current edition
- PSIA American Teaching System

materials, Professional Ski Instructors of America Education Foundation, 1996

Course Objectives

The learner will address the categories that follow to fulfill the course objectives.

Equipment

Toboggans and Toboggan Construction

- Identify the types of toboggans used at the local area.
- Describe how each toboggan component contributes to effective operation.

Rescue Packs

- Demonstrate the proper preparation of a rescue pack for storage in a toboggan.

Toboggan Storage, Inspection, and Setup Procedures

- Inspect a toboggan stored on the mountain using a systematic check of its components for safety and function.
- Position the toboggan on the hill using appropriate anchoring and setup procedures and giving consideration to the environment.

Skiing Maneuvers for Toboggan Operation

- Demonstrate the following skiing maneuvers essential to toboggan operation in a stable, controlled manner.
  - Kick turn without poles on a moderately steep, packed slope
  - Kick turn without poles in moguls
  - Uphill sidestep on steep terrain
  - Downhill sidestep on difficult terrain
  - Herringbone ascent on moderate terrain

Table 10.1 Skiing Maneuvers and Corresponding Snowboarding Maneuvers

Skiing	Snowboarding
Skiing Maneuvers	**Snowboarding Maneuvers**
Wedge	N/A
Wedge turn	Skidded turns
Stem turn	Skidded turns
Sideslip	Sideslip, toe-side and heel-side
Falling leaf	Falling leaf, toe-side and heel-side
Moving direction changes	Moving direction changes
Skating	Skating (rear foot out of binding)
Parallel turns, skidded and carved	Skidded and carved turns
Traverse, both sides	Traverse, toe-side and heel-side
Herringbone, sidestep (up and down)	Climbing
Static direction changes (kick turn)	Static direction changes (fakie)
Unloaded Toboggan	**Unloaded Toboggan**
Quick check/setup	Quick check/setup
Route selection	Route selection
Traversing	Traversing
Descent	Descent
Moving direction changes	Moving direction changes
Static direction changes	Reverse (fakie)
Emergency stop	Emergency stop
Wheelbarrow	Wheelbarrow
Rear run (four-handled toboggan)	Rear run (four-handled toboggan)
Incident Site Management	**Incident Site Management**
Approach	Approach
	Securing the toboggan
	Securing the toboggan (using special measures such as cut-off ski poles, the patient's skis, or another patroller's skis)
Anchoring the skis	Anchoring the board (to the toboggan or in the snow)
Loading the patient	Loading the patient
Loaded Toboggan	**Loaded Toboggan**
Route selection	Route selection
Traversing	Traversing
Descending the fall line	Descending the fall line
Moving direction changes	Moving direction changes
Turns	Turns
Wedge	Skidded
Step	Skidded
Parallel, skidded and carved	Skidded and carved
Sideslip	Sideslip
Falling leaf	Falling leaf
Static direction changes	Reverse (fakie)
Emergency stops	Emergency stops
Tail Rope	**Tail Rope***
Descending	Descending
Traversing	Traversing
Moving direction changes	Moving direction changes
Sideslip to wedge turn	Sideslip to skidded turns
Falling leaf to diagonal	Falling leaf to diagonal
Static belay	Static belay
Four-handled Toboggan	**Four-handled Toboggan**
Route selection	Route selection
Descending and traversing	Descending and traversing
Moving direction changes	Moving direction changes
Static direction changes	Static direction changes
Emergency stops	Emergency stops
Uphill Transportation	**Uphill Transportation**
Lift carry	Lift carry

The NSP recommends snowboard patrollers run heel-side when operating the tail rope.

- Demonstrate the following skiing maneuvers with a toboggan by combining balance, edge, rotary, and pressure-control movements to maintain a stable position and controlled speed on the varied terrain and snow conditions of the local area.
  - Fall-line traverse
  - Traverse with varying leg width, lift uphill ski
  - Fall-line sideslip (poles held at mid-shaft)
  - Falling leaf sideslip (poles held at mid-shaft)
  - Wedge
  - Wedge transitions (wedge to sideslip and back)
  - Gliding wedge turn
  - Stem/step turn from wedge
  - Parallel turns (skidded and carved)
  - Sideslip transition
  - Moving direction changes (wedge, sideslip, parallel)
  - Skating
  - Transitions
  - Hockey stops

Snowboarding Maneuvers for Toboggan Operation

- Demonstrate the following snowboard maneuvers essential to toboggan operation in a stable, controlled manner.
  - Fall-line sideslip (toe-side and heel-side) using a consistent down-the-fall-line approach with edging and balance.

    Edge pressure should be combined with subtle steering and weight shifting to cause the rider to move forward and backward on the board while controlling his or her speed and maintaining fluid momentum down the fall line.
  - Falling leaf sideslip, toe-side and heel-side
  - Skidded and carved turns
  - Emergency stop (hockey stop), toe-side and heel-side

  - Traverse, toe-side and heel-side
- Demonstrate the following snowboarding maneuvers with a toboggan by combining balance, edge, rotary, and pressure-control movements to maintain a stable position and controlled speed on the varied terrain and snow conditions of the local ski area.
  - Traverse
  - Fall-line sideslip, toe-side and heel-side
  - Falling leaf sideslip, toe-side and heel-side
  - Transitions, from sideslip to skidded turns and back to sideslip
  - Skidded and carved turns
  - Moving direction changes
    - Forward, toe-side and heel-side
    - Reverse (fakie)
    - Skating (rear foot out of binding)
  - Emergency stop (hockey stop), toe-side and heel-side

Operating an Unloaded Toboggan

Quick Check and Initial Setup

- Use the quick-check procedures to inspect the toboggan and prepare it for safe, unloaded transportation from a standby toboggan location.

Position In Control Handles

- Demonstrate the proper positioning in the control handles when operating an unloaded toboggan.

Route Selection

- Identify and/or demonstrate the most appropriate route to follow when approaching an ill or injured patient based on the incident scene.

Descending the Fall Line and Turning

- Demonstrate how to operate the front of an unloaded toboggan while descending the fall line on varied terrain and snow conditions.
- Demonstrate how to make turns and transitions between wedge, sideslip, and parallel ski-running positions while operating the front of an unloaded toboggan on varied terrain and snow conditions. Different types of equipment will necessitate different methods for performing turns and transitions.

Traversing

- Demonstrate a smooth, confident traverse and descent of the fall line with an unloaded toboggan using stability, control, and a combination of turns, transitions, and operating positions on the following snow conditions and terrain at the local area.
    - Packed slope
    - Moguls
    - Powder, crud, or ice

Static Direction Changes

- Perform a balanced and stable kick turn while maintaining contact with the toboggan handles on steep terrain or in moguls. (The kick turn requirement applies to alpine skiers only since snowboard patrollers run toboggans using forward and/or reverse—fakie—maneuvers.)

Incident Site Management

Approaching the Incident Site and Securing the Toboggan

- Explain and demonstrate how to approach an incident site safely with an unloaded toboggan, and how to secure the toboggan properly before loading a patient.
- Define effective incident site man-

agement as it relates to the efficient use of all available resources (e.g., time, personnel, and equipment).

Positioning the Patient in the Toboggan and Preparing for Transport

- Describe the significance of patient positioning in the toboggan based on the nature and extent of the injury, the patient's mobility, the number of people able to assist, the terrain, snow conditions, and the type of toboggan.
- Approach a simulated incident site on a more difficult slope with an empty toboggan, secure the toboggan in an appropriate position for the patient, lift the patient into the toboggan, and secure the patient for transport.
- Prepare the toboggan for transport.

Operating the Front of a Loaded Two-Handled Toboggan

General Principles

- Identify the general principles of operating the front of a loaded toboggan for a safe, smooth, and controlled descent.

Route Selection

- Identify appropriate routes to follow with a loaded toboggan on various trails and at many locations throughout the local area to provide the safest and smoothest ride for the patient.

Traversing

- Traverse a loaded toboggan in a stable and controlled manner with minimal lateral slippage on the following conditions.
    - Steepest packed slope at the local area
    - Moguls
    - Powder, crud, or ice

Descending the Fall Line

- Show stability and control while descending the fall line with a loaded toboggan. Combine direction changes, transitions, and braking techniques to ensure the patient a safe and smooth ride on the following conditions.
    - Steep packed slope
    - Moguls
    - Powder, crud, or ice

Moving Direction Changes, Front Operator

- Perform the following maneuvers with a loaded toboggan on a packed slope, in moguls, and on powder, crud, or ice.
  - Skiing Maneuvers
    - Wedge and sideslip transitions
    - Wedge turn
    - Step/stem turn
    - Parallel turn (skidded and/or carved)
    - Falling leaf sideslip
  - Snowboarding Maneuvers
    - Skidded turns
    - Skidded turns to sideslip transitions
    - Falling leaf sideslip

Static Direction Changes, Front Operator

Skiing Maneuvers

- Demonstrate a stable and controlled kick turn without moving the toboggan.

Snowboarding Maneuvers

- Stop to allow a stable and controlled kick turn without moving the toboggan.
- Change directions by moving in the opposite direction on the board, either forward or reverse (fakie).

Toboggan Maneuvers In Varying Conditions, Front Operator

- Descend the fall line with stability and control, combining toboggan maneuvers to ensure the patient a safe and smooth ride on the following conditions.
  - Steep packed slope
  - Moguls
  - Powder, crud, or ice
  - Relatively flat terrain

Operating the Tail Rope of a Loaded Two-Handled Toboggan

General Principles, Tail Rope Operator

- Identify the principles of operating the tail rope of a loaded toboggan to ensure the patient a safe, smooth, and controlled descent.

Descending and Traversing the Fall Line

- Operate the tail rope of a loaded toboggan to demonstrate stability and control while maintaining an appropriate position and rope tension to assist the front operator on the following conditions.
  - Moderate to steep packed slope

  - Moguls
  - Powder, crud, or ice

Moving Direction Changes

- Perform the following maneuvers with stability and control while descending the fall line.
  - Sideslip to wedge (ski patrollers) or skidded (snowboard patrollers) transitions
  - Sideslip direction changes
  - Wedge turns, right and left (ski patrollers)
  - Skidded turns, right and left (snowboard patrollers)
  - Step turns, right and left (ski patrollers)
  - Falling leaf sideslip
  - Diagonal fall-line descent

Operating Loaded Four-Handled Toboggans (General Principles)

- Identify the general principles of operating the front and back of a loaded four-handled toboggan to ensure the patient a safe, smooth, and controlled descent as terrain, snow, and weather conditions dictate.

Traversing Off the Fall Line

- Traverse a loaded toboggan in a stable and controlled manner with minimal lateral slippage on the following conditions.
  - Steepest packed slope at the local area
  - Moguls
  - Powder, crud, or ice

Descending the Slope On or Near the Fall Line

- Descend the fall line with a loaded four-handled toboggan.
- Use sideslip, transition, and braking techniques to demonstrate stability and control.
- Ensure the rider a safe and smooth ride on the following conditions.
  - Steepest packed slope at the local area
  - Moguls
  - Powder, crud, or ice
- Perform the following maneuvers with a loaded toboggan on a packed slope, in moguls, and on powder, crud, or ice.
  - Falling leaf with left and right transitions
  - Fall-line sideslip with left and right transitions

Moving Direction Changes

- Perform the following maneuvers from the traverse and the fall line with a loaded toboggan on a packed slope, in moguls, and on powder, crud, or ice.
  - Wedge maneuvers (ski

patrollers)
  - Skidded maneuvers (snow-board patrollers)
  - Step maneuvers (ski patrollers)
  - Parallel turns, skidded and/or carved (ski patrollers)
  - Turns, skidded and carved (snowboard patrollers)

Static Direction Changes

- Demonstrate a kick turn from the traverse and on the fall line on the following conditions.
  - Steepest packed slope at the local area
  - Moguls
  - Powder, crud, or ice

Power Stops and Parking

- Demonstrate the power stop and the park maneuver in the following conditions.
  - Steeper packed slope
  - Moguls
  - Powder, crud, or ice

Adapting to Terrain and Snow Conditions

- Perform all the maneuvers of transitions, sideslips, moving direction changes, stopping, and terrain

drops in the following conditions.
  - Breakable crust or crud
  - Wet snow
  - Deep powder
  - Ice
- Perform the terrain lift on a relatively flat slope.
- Perform the terrain drop maneuver as conditions dictate.

Operator Position Change

- Demonstrate exchanging operator positions on a variety of terrain and snow conditions.

Static Belay Techniques

- Demonstrate a static belay from the tail-rope position to control the descent of a loaded toboggan down a difficult section of slope at the local area.

Mechanical Transport of Toboggans

Transporting Empty Toboggans

- Demonstrate how to transport an empty toboggan uphill on a chairlift or surface lift using the established method(s) for the local area.

Using Over-the-Snow Vehicles for Transport

The National Ski Patrol does not create training standards for or advise patrollers concerning the use of motorized over-the-snow vehicles (snow cats, snowmobiles, all-terrain vehicles, etc.). The substantial variations in equipment, regulatory requirements, and expected use by area management make it impracticable for the NSP to develop a training component in this area.

Although this equipment may be useful at ski areas, it is area management's prerogative whether to incorporate such equipment into daily operations.

The use and maintenance of motorized over-the-snow vehicles, along with training of personnel, is the responsibility of area management. Employees who operate such vehicles should follow the manufacturer's recommendations and area management's training and operating procedures.

Using Chairlifts to Transport Loaded Toboggans

- Transport a loaded toboggan up or down a chairlift (using an apparatus designed for that purpose) at the local area in a manner that will least impact lift operations and that is consistent with local area policies. (Objectives will vary depending on whether loading apparatus is used.)

Helicopter Rescue

The National Ski Patrol does not create training standards for or advise patrollers concerning the coordination of evacuation and medical care with helicopter services. Area management should determine whether helicopter rescue is necessary and appropriate and establish protocols for determining when such assistance will be requested.

If a patrol identifies a need to evacuate patients by helicopter, the patrol should require each member to participate in a helicopter orientation course (and subsequent refreshers) conducted by the helicopter service in coordination with area management. All patrollers who interact with helicopter rescue services should follow the protocols and operating procedures established by area management and the helicopter service.

Evacuating Toboggans from Aerial Tramways

By agreement with the National Ski Areas Association, NSP members participate in lift evacuation and lift evacuation training (including the evacuation of toboggans from aerial tramways) only when ski area management directs them to do so. Ski area management assumes the sole responsibility for establishing necessary policies and procedures for lift evacuation, arranging lift evacuation training, and selecting equipment for use in conjunction with such evacuation or training.

Area management's lift evacuation plan should incorporate the appropriate procedures for the evacuation of loaded toboggans from the lift. Patrollers conduct lift evacuation training and actual evacuations as agents of area management. Evacuating toboggans from aerial tramways involves the use of equipment and skills that are beyond the scope of a toboggan training course. These activities are more appropriately covered as part of lift evacuation training.

On-the-Hill Refresher

Although area management policies often determine patroller training and skill requirements, the ski patrol director is usually responsible for organizing or delegating the task of coordinating the annual on-the-hill refreshers.

Refresher Training Considerations

The following suggested refreshers may be incorporated into the local patrol refresher schedule but are not limited to the areas mentioned.

Skiing/Snowboarding Proficiency Refresher

- Perform a run on moderate to difficult terrain, making large- and small-radius turns while showing the effective use of edging, turning, pressure control, and rotation skills.
- Perform a run on steep terrain or in moguls while demonstrating stability and control.
- Perform an equipment-carry run in adverse conditions and on varying terrain.
- Perform a controlled run incorporating wedge (ski patrollers) or skidded (snowboard patrollers) turns, sideslipping, transitions, and emergency stop maneuvers.

Alpine (Skiing/Snowboarding) Toboggan Handling Refresher

- Transport the toboggan to a simulated accident site.
- Practice straight running, turning, sideslipping, approaching the injured skier, emergency stopping, and positioning the unloaded toboggan at the accident site.
- Run a loaded toboggan while demonstrating control, smoothness, and appropriate route selection on the area's moderate to difficult terrain.
- Demonstrate skiing/snowboarding skills in the front and back of a loaded toboggan. Include sideslip (forward, backward, and straight down), wedge, and transition maneuvers; straight running; and fall-line, traverse, and braking techniques.

Local Patrol Policies Refresher

The patrollers will refresh the following items.

- The location, degree of difficulty, length, and names of all alpine runs at the area patrolled.
- The location of the area's toboggan stations.
- The procedures for restocking toboggans and returning them to their stations.
- The ability to operate the communications system.
- The review of ski patrol and ski area management operations procedures, including sign-on, assignments, rotations, relief, and sweep.

Skiing Enhancement Seminar (Alpine)

The NSP division ski and toboggan supervisor and the PSIA National Education Committee division representative coordinate the Skiing Enhancement Seminar to provide NSP members with professionally organized ski instruction. The seminar is designed to improve the skiing/snowboarding skills of NSP members and to improve the patroller image within the ski industry and in the public's view.

Prerequisites

- Current NSP membership

Time Commitment

- One day

Fee

- National—none
- PSIA division clinic charges (course and instructor)
- NSP division—varies
- Lift tickets

Credential

- NSP Certificate of Achievement (distributed by instructor)

Scott Markewitz

- Attendance becomes part of member record in national database

Continuing Education/ Refresher

- None

Instructor of Record

- PSIA division clinic leaders
- Qualified and screened PSIA Certified Level III instructors

Required Text

- None

Course Objectives

The learner will address the categories that follow to fulfill the course objectives.

- Identify personal skiing/snowboarding strengths and weaknesses.
- Identify good balance and alignment in self and peers.
- Ski/snowboard with improved efficiency (turn shape and speed control).
- Work with the PSIA seminar instructor to develop exercises for continued improvement.
- Identify opportunities for continued learning.

Ski Trainer's Workshop (Alpine)

This workshop is designed for NSP ski and toboggan trainers and evaluators. The workshop emphasizes a partnership and cooperative effort between PSIA ski instructors and NSP ski and toboggan trainers. The purpose of the workshop is to help NSP trainers use observational clues to hone their eyes for assessing patrollers' abilities and limitations.

Prerequisites

- NSP member
- Instructor Development: Phase I
- PSIA level 7 skier

Recommended Prerequisite

- Skiing Enhancement Seminar, PSIA instructor, or other approved option (to be determined)

Time Commitment

- One to two days

Fee

- National—none
- PSIA division clinic charges (course and instructor)
- NSP division—varies
- Lift tickets

Credential

- NSP Certificate of Achievement (distributed by instructor)

Continuing Education/ Refresher

- None

Instructor of Record

- PSIA division clinic leaders/examiners selected by PSIA division coordinator

Scott Markewitz

Required Text

- None

Course Objectives

The learner will address the categories that follow to fulfill the course objectives.

- Identify the skills necessary for effective toboggan handling.
- Use the NSP evaluation criteria to accurately assess and provide feedback to patrollers regarding skiing/snowboarding skills.
- Explain and demonstrate specific exercises and drills to improve skills necessary for effective toboggan handling and free skiing.
- Recognize NSP training limitations and identify PSIA clinics and other training opportunities to expand or enhance patroller knowledge and skills.

Although an abundance of spectacular images and widespread publicity often imply that most avalanches occur in Utah and Colorado, avalanche potential exists wherever snow falls onto steep slopes. Statistics consistently indicate that the West Coast reports more avalanches per year than the Rocky Mountains. And while skiers from the eastern United States rarely think of avalanche danger as a life-threatening element of outdoor activity, New Hampshire's Mt. Washington has claimed its share of recreationists and Taber, New York, will never forget the two children who lost their lives in the city park.

The truth is that avalanche occurrences are widespread in both geog-

CHAPTER
11
Avalanche Program

raphy and degree of severity. Fortunately, many avalanches and the casualties they often result in can be avoided through public awareness and preparedness. To help instructors educate the public about the dangers of avalanches, the National Avalanche Committee has established several areas of avalanche training, described as follows.

Basic Avalanche Course

The purpose of the Basic Avalanche Course is to provide participants with a general knowledge of and skills for avalanche awareness. This course covers how to increase personal safety in avalanche terrain and how to be an effective member of an avalanche rescue team.

A written exam determines if the student has performed all the minimum reading requirements and has gained the necessary knowledge of all required subject material. Students are evaluated on their skills during their participation in the field exercises.

Prerequisites

- None

Time Commitment

- Six hours in the classroom
- Four to six hours of field work
- Total course time varies with class size and the amount of preparatory work required.

Fees

- National—none
- Division—varies
- Course—varies
- Cost of materials

Credential

- NSP Certificate of Achievement (distributed by instructor)

Continuing Education/ Refresher

- The Basic Avalanche Course refresher is usually incorporated with each patrol's annual on-the-hill refresher.
- Patrollers should devote approximately three hours to the Basic Avalanche Course refresher. This requirement may be satisfied by spending one hour each year reviewing course content or by taking a three-hour session once every three years. Patrollers who are active avalanche instructors need not take the refresher.

Instructor of Record

- NSP Basic or Advanced Avalanche instructor

Required Texts

- *Avalanche Rescue Quick Guide,* National Ski Patrol, 1996
- *The ABC of Avalanche Safety,* E.R. LaChapelle, 1985, or *Snow Sense,* Jill A. Fredston and Doug Fesler, 1994

Course Objectives

The learner will address the categories that follow to fulfill the course objectives.

General Avalanche Awareness

- Identify problems encountered during an avalanche burial.
- Define and explain avalanche-related terms.
- List the avalanche types and know how they relate to avalanche danger.
- Describe how weather contributes to avalanche formation.
- Recognize how the snowpack factors relate to avalanche stability and instability, and be able to explain what it takes to make the snowpack slide.
- Identify terrain factors that contribute to avalanche formation.

Personal Safety

- Identify factors and conditions that influence route selection and safety.
- Demonstrate self-rescue techniques.
- Explain the importance of the human element.
- Define what influences the decision to alter the trip plan.
- List the precautions to take when it is necessary to cross a potentially unstable slope.

Avalanche Rescue Teamwork

- Explain how important it is for each patroller, regardless of his or her role, to follow directions in order to accomplish an efficient avalanche rescue.
- Recognize the objectives of the three stages of the general avalanche rescue plan.
- Describe the local area's specific rescue plan and procedures.
- Define the job description of each

of the avalanche rescue leadership positions.
- List rescue equipment.
- Demonstrate the basic functions of avalanche transceivers.
- Recognize incompatible frequencies and noise interference.
- Practice the basic search patterns.
- Demonstrate the skills required to be a member of a probe line.
- Identify the skills necessary to participate in an immediate (hasty) search.

Field Sessions

The field sessions will vary depending on the available terrain and snow cover. Participants should be able to meet the following criteria.

- Demonstrate and practice performing as a member of an avalanche rescue team in a simulated rescue environment.
- Demonstrate and practice the use of avalanche rescue transceivers.
- Demonstrate and practice probe line procedures.
- Observe a Rutschblock test and the hasty pit technique for testing and observing the snowpack.
- Practice proper route selection and terrain appreciation. Observe the weather and how it affects avalanche hazard.

Basic Avalanche Refresher

The objective of the refresher is to renew and update each patroller's knowledge of avalanche rescue. Specifically, each patroller plays an active role in a simulated mini-rescue and practices with the local ski area's avalanche rescue plan. The Basic Avalanche refresher is generally incorporated with the annual on-the-hill/trail refresher. Recordkeeping for Basic Avalanche refreshers is done at the patrol level and in some divisions at the division level.

contribute to avalanche formation)
- Terrain, safe travel, and self-rescue techniques
- Avalanche fundamentals and snowpack characteristics

Advanced Avalanche Course

The purpose of the Advanced Avalanche Course is to provide students with the knowledge and skills necessary to assume leadership roles in avalanche rescue, the ability to support avalanche rescue operations, and the competence to make ancillary rescue decisions. Students must pass a written examination and prepare a comprehensive report that discusses rescue activities. In addition, experience and recurrent training will be necessary to hone the knowledge and skills learned into true avalanche rescue expertise.

During actual rescue operations, several factors determine who ultimately assumes leadership positions. These factors emanate from the specific circumstances of each event, and include location, availability, willingness, physical and mental status, clothing and personal gear, relative levels of skill and experience, and the other competing needs of a ski resort.

Course Risks

The Advanced Avalanche Course involves extensive field work in alpine winter conditions. Students will encounter risks and dangers inherent to skiing, as well as the additional risks of skiing and working both alone and with a group on steep and difficult slopes. Because the course may be held in part on or near active avalanche paths, it involves the risk of being caught in avalanches. Field studies may be conducted beyond ski area closure boundaries and may involve locations from which the evacuation of injured participants would be long and difficult. The

Refresher Training Considerations

The following suggested refreshers may be incorporated with the Basic Avalanche refresher but are not limited to the areas mentioned.

Area Rescue Plan Refresher

- Review the entire plan.
- Emphasize any changes or additions.
- Describe the locations of in-area and local out-of-area hazards.
- Note the locations and contents of rescue caches.
- Review the communications and alarm system.

- Recognize the available local resources (i.e., county sheriff, state police, other ski patrols, search and rescue teams) and know the protocol for their involvement.

Rescue Techniques Review

The NSP suggests reviewing the following avalanche rescue topics.
- Immediate (hasty) search
- Probing and shoveling techniques
- Transceiver use

Rotating Topic Review

The NSP also suggests reviewing the following topics on a rotating basis.
- Weather (name 10 factors that may

expected to perform in various snow conditions (including deep snow), hike moderate distances, climb moderate to steep slopes, and traverse steep slopes, on skis and/or on foot. It is not the responsibility of NSP instructors to evaluate prospective students' level of conditioning or skiing ability. Rather, the prospective student must determine whether he or she possesses the physical and mental stamina and strength to complete the course. At his or her sole discretion, the instructor may restrict participation in the field sessions if it appears a student will hinder the class. This discretion will be exercised on behalf of the course and is not intended as a protective measure for the student.

Time Commitment

- The time commitment for the Advanced Avalanche Course averages 13 hours of classroom instruction and three days of practical field work, plus homework assignments and report preparation.
- Total course time varies with class size and the amount of preparatory work required.

Fees

- National—none
- Division—varies
- Course—varies
- Cost of materials

Credential

- NSP Certificate of Achievement (distributed by instructor)

Continuing Education/ Refresher

- Students may satisfy the Advanced Avalanche Course refresher requirements by attending portions of an Advanced Avalanche

student must accept the risks associated with the field study of avalanches.

Prerequisites

- Basic Avalanche Course (course knowledge must be current, i.e., taken within the last three years or refreshed before the Advanced Avalanche Course starting date). Non-NSP avalanche training that equals or exceeds the course content for the NSP Basic Avalanche

Course may be substituted upon approval by the division avalanche supervisor.
- Two years active patrol duty experience, not including the candidate year, before the starting date of the Advanced Avalanche Course (unless waived by the division avalanche supervisor).
- Excellent physical condition, strenuous physical exertion, and upper-intermediate to advanced skiing skills. Students are generally

Course. Refresher students should attend two to three classroom sessions specifically aimed at addressing the material in Units 1 and 3. They also must attend one of the field sessions, preferably the final simulated rescue.

- Patrollers attending a separate refresher course should plan to devote about six hours to classroom work and one day to field sessions.

Instructor of Record

- NSP Advanced Avalanche instructor

Required Texts

- *Avalanche Safety for Skiers and Climbers,* Tony Daffern, 1992
- *Avalanche Rescue Fundamentals,* Bill Hotchkiss, Dale Atkins, and Lin Ballard, 1996
- *Avalanche Rescue Quick Guide,* National Ski Patrol, 1996

Optional Texts

- *The Snowy Torrents,* Knox Williams and Betsy Armstrong, 1984
- *The Snowy Torrents,* Nick Logan and Dale Atkins, 1996

Course Objectives

The learner will address the categories that follow to fulfill the course objectives.

Avalanche Rescue Procedures

- Describe or reconstruct an avalanche rescue using the three-stage organization.
- Recognize the leadership positions and define the duties associated with each position.

Avalanche Rescue Decision-Making

- Explain how weather factors and patterns affect the snowpack and avalanche formation.
- Analyze the effects that past, present, and future weather conditions may have on avalanche danger.
- Explain the methods of compiling weather data and the value of weather documentation.
- Describe the process of metamorphism in the snowpack.
- Demonstrate an understanding of the data-gathering procedures necessary to evaluate immediate and long-term snowpack stability.

- Demonstrate knowledge of snowpack mechanics.
- Use knowledge of stability analysis to perform terrain analysis and route selection.
- Describe various avalanche control methods as they relate to a rescue situation.
- Complete a snow pit recording form.
- Demonstrate snow pit collection techniques in the field.

Avalanche Rescue Leadership

- Describe leader/follower group dynamics.
- Explain overall rescue coordination and how the leadership positions interrelate.
- Describe the similarities and differences between a ski patrol rescue leadership system and an Incident Command System (ICS), according to your division's standards.
- Demonstrate the skills necessary to perform as an immediate action team (hasty search) leader.

Effectiveness in Search Procedures

- Skillfully occupy any position of a probe line.
- Demonstrate the basic functions of avalanche transceivers.
- Recognize incompatible frequencies and noise interference.
- Practice the basic search patterns.
- Recognize how to incorporate rescue dogs into a search.
- Explain the special considerations for emergency care of an avalanche victim.
- Write or update an avalanche rescue plan.
- Participate in an avalanche rescue simulation.

Field Sessions

Field work varies considerably with the terrain and snow cover available and the type of students in the class. If all the students are alpine patrollers, the field sessions may address ski area avalanche danger. If the students are nordic patrollers, the sessions may address backcountry avalanche danger. If the class is a mixture of alpine and nordic patrollers, the field sessions should incorporate both rescue systems.

Every student and instructor should carry a shovel during all field sessions. If possible, every participant should wear an avalanche rescue transceiver, also. Before leaving the staging area or parking lot, the transceivers should be tested for receiving and transmitting and then placed in the transmitting mode.

Participants should be able to meet the following criteria.
- Recognize the local terrain features and explain how they relate to avalanche hazard and safe travel to an avalanche accident site.
- Practice transmitting and receiving with transceivers.
- Practice backcountry immediate (hasty) search.
- Practice probe line leadership.
- Practice transceiver searches with deep burials, multiple burials, and burials in different orientations.
- Demonstrate an understanding of snowpack analysis techniques by observing storm charts and recording instruments (where available) and by investigating a snow pit.
- Determine the current and potential change in snowpack stability by plotting the snowpack profile and testing the snowpack.
- Demonstrate transceiver search proficiency by locating a transceiver buried approximately two feet deep in less than two minutes after picking up the initial signal.
- Practice an immediate (hasty) search as part of a formal in-area rescue.
- Participate in an avalanche rescue simulation under conditions closely approximating an actual rescue.

- Observe a rescue dog demonstration (if available).
- Observe avalanche control (if practical).

Advanced Avalanche Refresher

The objective of the refresher is to renew and update each patroller's knowledge of avalanche rescue. Specifically, each patroller reviews general rescue organization methods, practices on-site rescue techniques stipulated by the local area's avalanche rescue plan, and participates in a simulated rescue. Refresher requirements can be met in one of the following ways.
- Help teach the annual on-the-hill/trail avalanche refresher.
- Help teach an avalanche course every two years as an instructor's assistant or as a group leader in the field.
- Attend an Advanced Avalanche refresher every three years.

- Attend a formal avalanche workshop or school, or a university accredited class every three years.
- Be an active avalanche instructor or an active advanced avalanche instructor.

The above efforts should include both classroom and field work concentrating in the areas of rescue organization and search techniques. Recordkeeping for Advanced Avalanche refreshers is done at the patrol and division level.

Refresher Training Considerations

The following suggested refreshers may be incorporated with the Advanced Avalanche refresher but are not limited to the areas mentioned.
- Avalanche Rescue Procedures
- Avalanche Rescue Leadership and Effectiveness in Search Procedures
- Field Work
  - Probing
  - Immediate (hasty) search
  - Transceiver search
  - Simulated rescue exercise

National Avalanche School

The NSP national office administers the National Avalanche School for the National Avalanche Foundation. The school is held every two years (during odd-numbered years) at a location approved by the National Avalanche Foundation Board. This school provides introductory avalanche education for ski industry and government agencies that are involved with avalanches in their day-to-day work.

The school consists of a multiple-day classroom course as well as scheduled field sessions. If the classroom and field sessions are completed, the course credential may count as a senior elective.

The Certified Program enables patrollers to build on those experiences gained while patrolling and through other NSP programs, e.g., Senior, Outdoor Emergency Care, Avalanche, and Instructor Development: Phase I. The purpose of the Certified Program is to help patrollers identify and supplement training resources and to provide training clinics as skill checkpoints and verification of personal progress.

The Certified Program consists of six modules: (1) area operations and risk management, (2) avalanche management, (3) emergency care, (4) rope rescue and lift evacuation, (5) skiing/snowboarding, and (6) toboggan handling. The program requires independent training and advanced research, and participants must complete all modules to receive certification.

Certified candidates must possess highly developed teamwork skills, because those who advance to the certified classification must be able to direct other patrollers during day-to-day services as well as multiple-casualty incidents. More important, they must have the attitude and ability to subordinate themselves to other leaders and be team players. The National Certified Committee strongly recommends that all patrollers complete the Senior Program before entering the Certified Program.

Certified candidates should possess extensive knowledge of patrol and ski area operations. The program requires candidates to demonstrate physical dexterity and skills in leadership, instruction, problem management, decision-making, and interpersonal communication. They also must have the ability, experience, and knowledge to develop various plans and programs that the patrol or area management may need.

The information in this program may not be applicable to all situations that arise in the daily operations of a given ski area or center. NSP education programs and membership requirements should never conflict

Scott Markewitz

with or take priority over area management's standard operating procedures and requirements for daily patrolling activities.

The materials in this chapter, new as of the 1996-97 ski season, are subject to change. Always check with the division ski and toboggan or certified program supervisor to obtain the most current information about the program. Tables 12.1 through 12.6 contain the essential content and performance criteria for each certified module.

Certified Certification

Prerequisites

- Participation in a division-authorized orientation or safety clinic on terrain and conditions approved for a certified clinic Must obtain a recommendation signature from division certified supervisor or designee
- Completion of the NSP senior skiing component or a division-approved equivalent

Recommended Prerequisites

- Completion of the NSP Advanced Avalanche Course or an equivalent training curriculum comparable to lesson guides in the NSP *Avalanche Instructor's Manual*
- Completion of the NSP senior OEC component or a division-approved equivalent
- Completion of the emergency care study guide (obtainable from the division certified program supervisor)

Fees

- National—none
- Division—varies
- Course—varies
- Cost of materials

Credential

- Certified Completion Form (verified and signed by the instructor of record for each module)
- NSP Certificate of Achievement for each module (distributed by the instructor)

Continuing Education/ Refresher

Certified Skiing and Toboggan Skills Recertification

(Administered within division)
- Completion of an evaluation of skiing skills at the certified performance level on a certified-rated hill once every three years
- Completion of an evaluation of toboggan skills at the certified performance level on a certified-rated hill once every three years

Instructor of Record

- Division certified program supervisor (or delegate)

Area Operations and Risk Management Module

Resources

- Local area policies and procedures, i.e., patrol, grooming, snowmaking, lift operations and evacuation, etc.
- ANSI B77 Codes (The most current codes should be followed where they have been adopted, on a state-by-state basis.)
- Your Responsibility Code, National Ski Areas Association
- Current NSP and NSAA catalogs for videos and publications
- *The Ski Patroller's Manual,* National Ski Patrol, 14th edition

Course Objectives

The learner will address the categories that follow to fulfill the course objectives.

Management Policies, Procedures, and General Daily Operations

- Explain local area plans, policies, and procedures for the following topics.
  - Slopes and trails (closures, signage, and hazard-marking)
  - Over-the-snow vehicle operations
  - Snowmaking
  - Lift operations (codes, design criteria, components, power sources)
  - Interfacing with area operations, departments, and management

Existing Local Area Planning Documents

- Explain the local area management planning process, written plans, implementation, and risk management issues for the following topics.

  - Search and rescue
  - Avalanche
  - Multiple-casualty/disaster
  - Emergency vehicle access and evacuation
  - Operations guidelines (EMS, fire, security, alcohol and drug, lift maintenance)

General Risk Management Issues

- Demonstrate a global understanding of ski industry risk management issues.
  - Define the term *risk management*, giving examples of *pre-* and *post*-loss goals
  - Discuss how trail design and maintenance can minimize the risks presented to skiers. (Cite examples from actual ski areas.)
  - Describe the types of safety and risk management training available to various ski area departments.
- Demonstrate an understanding of ski industry insurance issues.
  - List the ski area's insurance carriers and the types of lift inspections the area has.
  - List the different types of insurance losses that your ski area may incur with the public and with employees. Types of losses may include non-skiing exposures to risk (e.g., slipping, sliding, and falling), daycare exposures, instructional exposures, food and beverage exposures (e.g., liquor liability), property loss exposures, workers' compensation (employee safety) exposures
  - Discuss budgeting considerations of running a ski area and their implication to risk management.

Incident Investigation

- Explain what signifies "red flag" incidents.

- Describe an incident investigation kit and the documentation of what goes into a "red flag" incident report (incident investigation procedure), using examples.
- Discuss different types of liability releases and when each is used.

Compliance Issues

- List the laws governing skier/snowboarder behavior at the local area and in the county and state.
- Discuss the compliance issues the local area management deals with, e.g., Americans With Disabilities Act (ADA), OSHA, U.S. Forest Service, etc.

Evaluation

Criteria for acceptable performance will be determined based on written and/or oral assessments of the program components. The topics include management planning, general daily operations, incident investigation, compliance issues, lift operations, grooming, and snowmaking. Components of management and daily operations involve slopes and trails; over-the-snow vehicle operations; interaction with area operations, departments, and management; and risk management issues.

Incident investigation knowledge should include details regarding "red flag" incidents, photographs and diagrams, reporting procedures, and the implications for the area's risk management. The certified candidate should understand compliance issues that consist of the regulatory environment (ADA, OSHA, U.S. Forest Service, etc.) and risk management concerns. Knowledge of lift operations must include ANSI B77 codes, design criteria, lift components, and auxiliary power sources. For grooming and snowmaking, the certified candidate must demonstrate a basic understanding of procedures, equipment and uses, and risk management issues.

Table 12.1 Area Operations and Risk Management Module

Essential Content	Components	Criteria for Acceptable Performance
Home area management policies, procedures, and general daily operations	• Slopes and trails • Over-the-snow vehicle operations • Snowmaking • Lift operations • Interface with area operations/departments/management	Basic knowledge of components based on written/oral assessment(s)
Existing written planning documents	• Search and rescue • Avalanche • Mass casualty • Lift evacuation • Emergency vehicle access • Operations guidelines	Basic knowledge of components based on written/oral assessment(s)
General risk management issues	• Ski industry/area management goals • Trail design • Insurance • Safety and risk management training	Basic knowledge of components based on written/oral assessment(s)
Incident investigation	• "Red flag" types of incidents • Investigation kits • Incident report procedures • Implications for area's risk management	Basic knowledge of components based on written/oral assessment(s)
Compliance issues	• Regulatory environment • Lift operations— ANSI B77 • ADA • OSHA • Forest Service • Risk management issues	Basic knowledge of components based on written/oral assessment(s)

Avalanche Management Module

Resources

- *Avalanche Safety for Skiers and Climbers*, Tony Daffern, 1992
- *The ABC of Avalanche Safety*, E.R. LaChapelle, 1985
- *Avalanche Rescue Quick Guide*, National Ski Patrol, 1996
- *Snow Sense*, Jill A. Fredston and Doug Fesler, 1994
- *Avalanche Instructor's Manual*, National Ski Patrol, 1995
- *Field Guide to Snow Crystals*, E.R. LaChapelle, 1969
- Transceiver manufacturers' product information
- Local ski area policies and procedures for handling explosives and for artillery control
- *Blaster's Handbook*, DuPont
- ATF—Explosives Regulations, current edition
- OSHA Explosives Safety Orders, current state regulations
- *The Snowy Torrents*, Knox Williams and Betsy Armstrong, 1984
- *The Snowy Torrents*, Nick Logan and Dale Atkins, 1996
- *Agricultural Handbook No. 489*, USDA Forest Service, 1978 (out of print)

Course Objectives

The learner will address the categories that follow to fulfill the course objectives.

National Requirement

- Demonstrate a thorough knowledge and understanding of the Basic Avalanche Course curriculum during an interview process or group discussion.
- Demonstrate the application of transceivers in a search environment.

Division Option

- Demonstrate a thorough knowledge and understanding of avalanche mitigation techniques and procedures.
- Discuss explosives/artillery equipment and the proper use of, storage of, and safety procedures for in a written and/or oral assessment.

Evaluation

Demonstrate an understanding of avalanche leadership and management abilities by conducting a

Table 12.2 Avalanche Management Module		
Essential Content	**Components**	**Criteria for Acceptable Performance**
Avalanche Program content	• Avalanche awareness • Personal safety • Avalanche rescue teamwork • Avalanche rescue procedures • Rescue decision making • Leadership and effectiveness in search procedures	Demonstration of knowledge in a written/oral examination and/or interview
Avalanche mitigation	• Compaction • Slope and cornice control • Explosives	Demonstration of knowledge in a written/oral examination and/or interview
Transceiver search	• Application	Search exercise as defined by division

transceiver search in a rescue environment. (The specific requirement should be defined according to division needs.) A possible option is to locate one transceiver buried at a depth of two feet in two minutes and/or locate two transceivers buried at a depth of two feet in five minutes. In both cases, timing starts with the first audio contact.

Criteria for acceptable performance will be determined based on written and/or oral assessments of the avalanche response. The avalanche program content will consist of avalanche awareness, personal safety, rescue decision-making, and leadership and effectiveness during search procedures. Avalanche components will include snowpack evaluation, slope and cornice control, and explosives use. The transceiver search application will be conducted in a search exercise defined by the division.

Emergency Care Module

Resources

- *Outdoor Emergency Care,* National Ski Patrol, current edition
- Certified emergency care study guide
- OEC videos
- *The Ski Patroller's Manual,* National Ski Patrol, 14th edition
- Local EMT/ambulance squads
- Continuing education OEC sessions at local areas

Course Objectives

The learner will address the categories that follow to fulfill the course objectives.
- Demonstrate the knowledge and ability to instruct and direct others.
- Demonstrate leadership, problem management, decision-making, and resource management capabilities and an awareness of area operational issues by serving as both an

incident leader and a team member. The simulated incident should involve multiple injuries and illnesses on difficult terrain under challenging conditions.
- Demonstrate the ability to address written emergency care problems by developing a written or oral plan of response (using the study guide).

Evaluation

Candidates will undergo a written evaluation as well as various hands-on scenarios. Candidates are expected to answer two or more emergency care essay questions with comprehensive responses and a description of how their answers would apply to the general area policies and procedures response plan.

During the hands-on scenarios, candidates will participate in a rotation of practical problems posed by simulated incident scenarios that involve one or more patients and multiple injuries and illnesses. Candidates will be evaluated in both the leader and helper roles while directing a team of patrollers that is responding to a multiple-injury/illness incident involving one or more patients using untrained bystander(s) as the only additional available resource.

Table 12.3 Emergency Care Module

Essential Content	Components	Criteria for Acceptable Performance
Decision-making	• Problem assessment	• Use an appropriate approach and situation evaluation; determine all essential issues and safety needs.
	• Patient assessment	• Conduct primary survey and secondary survey; consider trauma, medical, and patient's condition during interview.
	• Appropriate positioning	• Determine whether to rush individual cases; perform triage in multiple-patient incidents.
	• Safety considerations	• Take necessary actions to identify, protect, mark, and move patient.
Problem management	• Plan of action	• Manage problem flow without repetitive actions; suggest follow-through measures for patient condition; monitor the time used.
	• Anticipation	• Plan ahead, avoid common problems, duplication, unnecessary movement of the patient.
	• OEC skills	• Direct or apply care according to the patient's need and in accordance with OEC skill performance objectives.
	• Transportation	• Use preplanned method using appropriate equipment; position patient in toboggan; determine whether rush case or not; enlist an adequate number of helpers.
Resource management	• People	• Request, use, and direct resources appropriately; keep them busy serving as part of a team.
	• Equipment	• Request and use appropriately; ensure patrollers apply correctly.
	• Response plan	• Apply study guide exercises to resource management.
Leadership	• Communication with the patient, trained helpers, and bystanders	• Inform patient of what is happening; give instructions to helpers; direct bystanders to avoid confusion.
	• Attitude	• Maintain positive and reassuring attitude.
	• Ability to direct	• Be assertive, not helper-directed; use resources; provide clear direction and instructions to helpers.
	• Confidence	• Be self-assured; know what to do and how to do it.
	• Team interaction	• Build and use team approach; control but also delegate.

Rope Rescue and Lift Evacuation Module

Resources

- Candidates must bring their own evacuation equipment to the event.
- *Ski and Toboggan Training Manual*, National Ski Patrol, 1994
- *The Lift Evacuation Technical Manual*, National Ski Patrol, 1990

Course Objectives

The learner will address the categories that follow to fulfill course objectives.

- Demonstrate a clear understanding of area management, NSP, and patroller roles in practical applications of evacuation, by practical, written, and/or oral examination.
  - Aerial rescue, e.g., lifts, trams
  - Ground rescue, e.g., toboggan, cliff, off-trail
- Demonstrate a smooth, confident, and fluid technique when tying knots, handling rope, and using evacuation equipment, in common as well as complicated situations. *(Note: In accordance with NSP policy in the interest of risk management, the NSP lift evacuation component will not include the actual lowering of people.)*
- Demonstrate proper belay techniques.

Evaluation

Candidates may demonstrate their lift evacuation planning knowledge during an interview, group discussion, or written format. Performance involves the demonstration of practical skills and knowledge specifically required in evacuation. It is essential that each candidate demonstrate smooth, confident, and fluid technique

Table 12.4 Rope Rescue and Lift Evacuation Module

Essential Content	Components	Criteria for Acceptable Performance
Lift operations	• Design and codes • Lift components • Auxiliary power sources • Risk management issues	• Demonstrate knowledge in a written and/or oral assessment.
Evacuation planning	• Advanced preparation • Specific procedures	• Demonstrate ability to develop evacuation plans. • Safely and efficiently evacuate aerial tramways used at the area. • Is familiar with area procedures for planning and implementing a rope rescue during aerial and ground rescues.
Implementation	• Use of the plan • Appropriate equipment • Rope handling • Belay techniques	• Serve as an evacuation leader at the local area. • Demonstrate knowledge of rope, knots, associated equipment, and techniques. • Demonstrate ability to handle lift evacuation equipment. • Demonstrate rope-handling skills on the hill in a simulated, non-threatening environment. • Use a belay technique to control the descent of a loaded toboggan down a difficult section of slope.
Post-evacuation activities	• Equipment care • Reports • Information release • Critique	• Demonstrate knowledge of how to store, inspect, and maintain the equipment. • Demonstrate knowledge of local area reports. • Describe local area policies/procedures. • Discuss key components of a post-evacuation critique.

with knots, rope handling, and evacuation equipment in both common and complicated situations.

Skiing Module

Resources

- *Ski and Toboggan Training Manual*, National Ski Patrol, 1994
- Skiing Enhancement Seminar materials
- Ski Trainer's Workshop materials
- PSIA American Teaching System materials, Professional Ski Instructors of America Education Foundation, 1996

Course Objective

The learner will demonstrate various technical skiing skills on specific terrain (in crud snow, on groomed slopes, in moguls, on steep terrain, and in local conditions).

Evaluation

All certified skiing events will be held on expert terrain, subject to area management approval. Whenever recent weather patterns or grooming procedures result in the lack of bumps, crud, or other less-than-ideal conditions, it may be necessary to hold some or all of the ski events during subsequent exams. The division certified program supervisor must evaluate the terrain and conditions available on exam day.

Toboggan Handling Module

Resources

- *Ski and Toboggan Training Manual*, National Ski Patrol, 1994
- Skiing Enhancement Seminar materials
- Ski Trainer's Workshop materials
- PSIA American Teaching System materials, Professional Ski Instructors of America Education Foundation, 1996

Course Objectives

The learner will demonstrate various toboggan-handling skills on specific

Table 12.5 Skiing Module

Essential Content	Components	Criteria for Acceptable Performance
Crud skiing	• Most difficult terrain	• Demonstrate balance, stability, and control. • Perform linked, parallel turns. • Demonstrate a moderate, safe speed appropriate for ability level.
Groomed skiing	• Most difficult terrain	• Demonstrate rounded turn shape. • Demonstrate an efficient mix of long-, medium-, and short-radius turns. • Perform parallel turns. • Demonstrate constant, controlled speed. • Demonstrate weight transfer to the outside ski. • Demonstrate turn completion during carved turns. • Keep the upper body moving toward the inside of the turn. • Demonstrate a balanced, fluid stance. • Demonstrate stability. • Demonstrate fluid vertical motion. • Perform turns as connected arcs without traverses. • Absorb moguls smoothly (between turns). • Adapt to changing terrain.
Mogul skiing	• Most difficult terrain	• Perform a fall-line descent with minimum traverse and sideslipping. • Demonstrate an effective combination of turn size, shape, and technique. • Demonstrate consistent, controlled speed. • Demonstrate the effective use of edges. • Make sure the upper body faces downhill during fall-line turns. • Demonstrate balance and stability. • Ski with the lower body in almost continuous motion while the upper body remains relatively quiet. • Demonstrate appropriate independent and simultaneous leg action. • Use edges and pressure to complete turns. • Perform controlled direction changes. • Adapt to changing terrain.
Steep skiing	• Most difficult terrain	• Perform a fall-line descent with minimum traverse and sideslipping. • Demonstrate an effective combination of turn size, shape, and technique. • Demonstrate consistent, controlled speed. • Perform carved turns with skidding. • Make sure the upper body faces downhill during fall-line turns. • Demonstrate balance.
Skill emphasis for local conditions	• Most difficult terrain	• Demonstrate balance, stability, and control.

terrain to fulfill the course objectives.
- Unloaded toboggan skills
- Loaded toboggan—front operator skills
- Loaded toboggan—tail rope skills (division option)

Evaluation

All certified toboggan events will be held on expert terrain, subject to area management approval. Whenever recent weather patterns or grooming procedures result in the lack of bumps, crud, or less-than-ideal conditions, it may be necessary to hold some or all of the toboggan events during subsequent exams. The division certified program supervisor must evaluate the terrain and conditions available on exam day.

If a certified candidate wants to use a particular type of toboggan for the clinic or evaluation, it is the candidate's responsibility to have that toboggan on the hill and available for his or her use. The candidate should coordinate this effort with the person responsible for running the clinic and evaluation. If no such effort is made, candidates must use whatever toboggan is available at the time of the clinic and evaluation.

Table 12.6 Toboggan Handling Module		
Essential Content	**Components**	**Criteria for Acceptable Performance**
Unloaded toboggan skills	• Most difficult mogul terrain	• Select appropriate route. • Operate at efficient, safe, and controlled speed that is appropriate to terrain and skier traffic, yet reach accident site quickly. • Perform smooth, parallel turns as needed. • Maintain proper body position. • Perform transitions. • Perform sideslips. • Ensure minimal bouncing or slipping of the toboggan. • Perform emergency stops. • Demonstrate at least one recovery technique. • Demonstrate static belay techniques.
Loaded toboggan— Front operator skills	• Most difficult mogul terrain	• Select appropriate route. • Control speed and ski safely and expediently. • Provide a smooth, safe, and comfortable ride for the patient. • Ski in a balanced and stable position. • Control descent with wedge or sideslip. • Control direction with turns and falling leaf. • Brake the toboggan as needed. • Communicate as necessary with patient and with tail rope operator. • Perform effective wedge, sideslip, and transitions with stability and control. • Avoid slipping during traverses.
Loaded toboggan— Front operator skills	• More to most difficult terrain, in moguls and on smooth slopes	• Select appropriate route. • Control speed and ski safely and expediently. • Provide smooth, safe, and comfortable ride for the patient. • Ski in a balanced and stable position. • Control descent with wedge or sideslip. • Control direction with turns, falling leaf. • Brake toboggan as needed. • Communicate as necessary with patient and with tail rope operator. • Perform effective wedge, sideslip, and transitions with stability and control. • Avoid slipping during traverses.

Because the quality of training a patroller receives directly contributes to the individual's growth, development, and professionalism within the association, the National Instructor Development Committee designed the Instructor Development Program to help patrollers develop and fine-tune their teaching skills.

To become an NSP instructor, an individual must complete the following steps (see table 13.1):

1. Instructor Development: Phase I
2. Instructor Development: Phase II
   - Global Management Module
   - Advanced Instructional Skills Module (specific discipline)
3. Instructor Internship

The Instructor Development Program provides training in instructional and course management skills. The program consists of two courses and an internship. The courses are Phase I, which covers general NSP teaching principles, and Phase II, which teaches the application of these principles to specific NSP disciplines. The internship rounds out the program by providing participants with an actual teaching experience. This chapter outlines the general curriculum for all instructor development courses.

The Phase I Course is applicable to all of the instructional disciplines and needs to be completed only once for entry to any or all of the Phase II courses. Instructor Development: Phase II is made up of two modules—Global Management and Advanced Instructional Skills (discipline specific). Many NSP instructors have credentials to teach multiple disciplines. The national education committee has reorganized the content in existing Phase II programs into a modular approach to save time and to avoid repeating information shared by the disciplines.

Specifically, all new instructors must learn certain details of course management, including procedures for record-keeping, instructor

CHAPTER

13

Instructor Development Program

approval and recertification, quality assurance, and lesson planning and practice teaching as well as how to use instructional materials. However, these areas, which compose the global instructional module, need only be completed once because they are common to all NSP programs. The Global Management module is usually taught by a Phase II discipline-specific instructor trainer (IT) but may also be taught by a Phase I instructor to allow additional flexibility in course scheduling. The module can include students from multiple disciplines and can be taught concurrently with Phase I.

The Advanced Instructional Skills module concentrates on how to teach the content and assess student knowledge and skills in a specific discipline. Some disciplines require instructor candidates to demonstrate the skills they are expected to teach. This module must be completed for every discipline in which an instructor candidate wishes to become an instructor.

When instructor candidates complete the Phase I, Phase II: Global Management and Advanced Instructional Skills modules, they become "intern instructors." During the intern period, an individual is required to teach lessons during two separate courses while being mentored and monitored by an instructor trainer (Phase I or discipline-specific). The intern instructor must follow complete and effective lesson plans to demonstrate instructional methods.

Intern instructors may continue to be mentored in real teaching situations until they demonstrate mastery of instructional skills and the discipline-specific course content. The instructor trainer must notify the national office that instructor status has been granted to an intern instructor before an instructor status is activated.

Once a patroller becomes an instructor in a specific NSP discipline, he or she retains that instructor status for three years. Instructor status may then be renewed by completing specific continuing education requirements, undergoing a mentoring review with an instructor trainer as defined by division policies, and actively teaching courses, refreshers, and local continuing education programs.

Instructors can strive for continued development by participating in a division- or national-sponsored instructor conference, seminar, or clinic at least once every three years. Also, the NSP encourages instructors to stay abreast of developments in their discipline by reading related articles in *Ski Patrol Magazine* and in *Pointers,* a newsletter for NSP instructors.

Instructor Development: Phase I

Participants in the Instructor Development: Phase I Course learn the seven areas (referred to as "strands") of instructor responsibilities and how instructors can apply them to create a positive learning experience for their students. This program builds a strong foundation of educational knowledge for use when planning lessons with the six-pack format, a lesson model for applying all instructional skills into a workable teaching format. The general information covered in Phase I is applicable for all potential NSP instructors, regardless of patrolling specialty.

Prerequisites

- None

Time Commitment

- One day

Fees

- National—none
- Division—varies
- Course—varies
- Cost of materials

Credential

- NSP Certificate of Achievement (distributed by instructor)

Continuing Education/ Refresher

- None

Instructor of Record

- NSP Instructor Development: Phase I instructors

Required Text

- *Training Patrollers Effectively*, National Ski Patrol, 1995

Course Objectives

The learner will address the categories that follow to fulfill the course objectives.

Knowledge of Subject Matter

- Explain that knowledge of discipline-specific course content and the ability to teach that content are assessed within the Instructor Development: Phase II courses developed for the specific disciplines.

Knowledge of Adult Learners

- Summarize the characteristics of adult learners.
- List the different learning styles and discuss how instruction might be modified to accommodate each style.
- *Optional objective*: List and explain the stages of learning as they apply to ski patrol skills.

Human Relations and Communication

- Explain the qualities of human relations necessary for effective instruction.
- List and explain effective listening skills.
- Explain the categories of non-verbal communication.
- Identify and explain positive feedback techniques.

Instructional Management

- Explain the importance of instructional management tasks and list specific examples of how they relate to organization, quality management, and safety.

Knowledge of Curriculum Structure

- Explain the learning levels of information, comprehension, and application, and list student activities for each level.
- Explain the use of key verbs at the beginning of concluding objectives to indicate learning level and specify appropriate activity for that level.
- Describe the difference between the *what* and the *how* of teaching.
- Identify the parts of an objective and explain how an objective guides lesson planning.
- Identify the parts of a lesson guide and list other instructional materials needed for planning an NSP lesson.
- *Optional objective*: List the six levels of learning and distinguish between lower and higher thinking levels.

Instructional Strategies and Methods

- Explain that strategies and methods include both instructor presentation and student practice.

- Compare and contrast various instructional strategies.

Monitoring and Evaluation

- Define the purpose and characteristics of monitoring students on an ongoing basis.
- Define the purpose and characteristics of evaluating students at the conclusion of a course.
- Distinguish between knowledge and performance evaluations.

The Six-Pack: Applying Instructional Skills

- Identify, plan, and list the importance of the six-pack lesson plan.
- Develop a sample lesson plan using the six-pack format.
- Select approach methods for each six-pack step.
- *Highly recommended objective*: Teach a lesson following the six-pack format.

The Six-Pack Format

- Set
  - Compare the various instructional strategies and methods appropriate for a set.
- Concluding Objectives
  - Paraphrase concluding objectives to provide motivation and purpose to the lesson.
- Input: New Information
  - Plan and demonstrate selected strategies and methods for input.
- Output: Learning Activities
  - Explain the role of guided and independent practice during the learning process.
  - Plan and demonstrate selected strategies and methods for students to interact with the lesson materials.
- Student Summary
  - Explain the steps in generating a student lesson summary.
  - Explain the summary's importance to learning.

Table 13.1 Guidelines for Becoming an NSP Instructor							
	Alpine Toboggan	**Avalanche**	**Instructor Develop-ment**	**Mountain-eering**	**Nordic Toboggan**	**Outdoor Emergency Care**	**Leadership Development PES**
Course Completion	Ski Trainer's Workshop (recommended)	Advanced Avalanche	n/a	Basic A Basic M Advanced Mountaineering (recommended)	Advanced Mountaineering Ski Trainer's Workshop (recommended)	Outdoor Emergency Care	Patroller Enrichment Seminar
Phase I	Yes	Yes	Yes	Yes	Yes	Yes	Yes
Phase II: Global Management Module (one time)	Yes	Yes Strong emphasis on safety guide-lines	Yes	Yes Strong emphasis on safety guide-lines	Yes	Yes	Yes
Phase II: Advanced Instructional Skills (Discipline-specific) Module (skill objectives for each instructor discipline)	•Review evaluations, measurements, and documen-tation proce-dures. •Develop and demonstrate specific instructional strategies and drills. •Demonstrate specific com-munication skills and safety issues in outdoor environment. •Skill validation of toboggan handling.	n/a	n/a	n/a	•Demonstrate specific communica-tion skills, time, safety, improv-isation issues in outdoor environment. •Demonstrate ski (winter travel) and toboggan skills (moving and static belays). •Review equipment. •Demonstrate subject-survival skills. •Practice dynamic error recognition.	•Demonstrate working knowledge of instructor manual using specific instructional strategies and safety issues. •Review evalu-ation tools and techniques (skill perform-ance guide-lines, CPIs, scenario devel-opment and evaluation, test bank, etc.). •Identify differences between basic, challenge, senior certified. (All of the above are currently under review by committee.)	•Demonstrate successful classroom techniques. •Demonstrate working know-ledge of *NSP Policies and Procedures.* •Review and be familiar with area/ mountain needs.
Intern Instruction (In real teaching situations)	Yes	Yes—Reinforce specific safety guidelines	Yes	Yes—Reinforce safety/survival guidelines	Yes	Yes	Yes

- Ongoing Monitoring and Evaluations
  - Explain how to monitor and evaluate the student's mastery of skills and knowledge on an ongoing basis.

Instructor Development: Phase II

Participants in the Instructor Development: Phase II Course will learn to prepare instructor candidates to manage and teach NSP discipline-specific programs. One module concentrates on course management, and the other module focuses on the advanced instructional level of how to teach and assess the course objectives and essential content. Course objectives provide the instructor with an outline of what the students should learn (*what to teach*) and what behavior or desired performance the instructor should expect from the students. The program also explains *how to teach* by educating instructor candidates on how to write training sequences and present lessons.

Instructor Development: Phase II courses are available for the following education disciplines:
- Alpine Toboggan
- Avalanche
- Mountaineering
- Nordic Toboggan
- Outdoor Emergency Care
- Patroller Enrichment Seminar

Prerequisites

- Specific discipline course(s) as designated
- Instructor Development: Phase I

Time Commitment

- The time commitment varies depending on class size, clinic requirements, and the amount of homework assigned.

Fees

- National—none
- Division—varies
- Course—varies
- Cost of materials

Credential

- NSP Certificate of Achievement (distributed by instructor)

Continuing Education/Refresher

- None

Instructor of Record

- Global Management module taught by discipline-specific instructor trainers and/or Phase I instructors
- Advanced Instructional Skills (discipline-specific) module taught by discipline-specific instructor trainers

Required Text

- *Training Patrollers Effectively*, National Ski Patrol, 1995
- Discipline-specific instructor's manuals

Course Objectives—Phase II: Global Management Module

The learner will address the categories that follow to fulfill the course objectives.

Instructional Materials

- Explain the purpose of the NSP's education mission.
- Be familiar with various resources available for discipline-specific courses (national and division).
- Review and select appropriate resources and activities for field and classroom lessons.

- Discuss the use of a test bank blueprint and booklet (or disk).

Record-keeping and Administration

- Describe the procedures required by the national office for course registration, administration, course finances, and ordering course materials.
- Describe division administrative requirements (when applicable).

Instructor Approval and Recertification

- Describe the instructor application, training, and mentoring process.
- Explain the job descriptions and instructor requirements within the discipline-specific program.
- Describe the instructor certification and recertification policies and procedures.
- List the functions of the region administrators and division program supervisors for the specific discipline.

Quality Management

- Describe the NSP quality management program.
- Identify national risk management concerns within patrols, sections, regions, and divisions.
- Explain the safety guidelines for the program, which are detailed in the corresponding instructor's manual.
- Use planning documents and record-keeping forms to create an instructional management plan for a course.

Phase I Review

- Review how the instructional strands learned in Instructor Development: Phase I may be applied when presenting a course.

- Explain the structure and requirements of the instructional units (lesson guides) for the course.

Lesson Planning and Practice Teaching

- Define a lesson planning exercise using a logical teaching progression of key skills and NSP performance objectives.
- Use Phase I principles to prepare a model lesson that will meet a course objective.
- Teach the prepared model lesson.
- Develop alternative plans for lesson preparation and course scheduling.
- Demonstrate the processes of giving and receiving positive feedback to improve individual presentations.
- Critique the evaluation criteria developed by each instructor candidate.

Course Objectives—Phase II: Advanced Instructional Skills Module (Discipline-Specific)

The learner will address the requirements that follow to fulfill the course objectives.
- Develop instructional strategies for NSP courses and their objectives.
- Review the purpose of evaluations and identify techniques to evaluate knowledge and skills.
- Explain the purpose, measurement, and documentation procedures for quality course evaluation.
- Outline the different course objectives in the programs, i.e., basic and advanced courses, course challenges, refreshers, continuing education requirements, and senior and certified patroller status.

Instructor Status

The initial instructor approval process requires the completion of

Instructor Development: Phase I, Instructor Development: Phase II modules (two or three, depending on the discipline), and *two* mentored teaching experiences.

To become an instructor in subsequent disciplines requires taking only the Phase II: Advanced Instructional Skills module and intern instructor teaching in two separate courses. Each discipline (Outdoor Emergency Care, Toboggan Handling [alpine skiing/snowboarding or nordic], Avalanche, Mountaineering, and PES) has defined instructional modules. Each discipline-specific advanced instructional skills module addresses specific skill checks and pertinent skills and knowledge activities.

Again, the instructor trainer must notify the national office that an additional instructor status has been granted to an intern instructor before the instructor status is activated.

Continuing Instructor Development

To maintain active status, an instructor must teach content designated by the specific discipline, refreshers, or continuing education. In addition, an instructor must participate in a division or national training program (clinic, seminar, conference) once every three years.

Instructors will review new program objectives, curriculum content, program administration, and instructional development components. Instructors will have many opportunities to learn additional advanced content and apply their instructional skills in actual situations.

The National Leadership Development Committee (formerly National Auxiliary Committee) has developed training objectives to help patrollers enrich their leadership skills and perform their patroller duties in a competent, efficient manner.

The Patroller Enrichment Seminar is a course on developing leadership ability and expanding the NSP's role at the participant's home area. The Patroller Enrichment Seminar (PES), open to any NSP member, encourages patrollers to increase their knowledge of education and leadership opportunities within the patrolling environment and to provide more effective services for area management. This course provides practical information for any patroller who endeavors to attain a leadership role in the NSP, but it is also a core requirement for those seeking senior auxiliary status.

This national education course offers a goal-oriented, objective-based, interactive clinic that can be modified to address local patrolling responsibilities. The goals of the course are as follows.

- Give patrollers an opportunity to develop, improve, and demonstrate advanced skills in managing patrol facilities, carrying out organizational and administrative duties, and expanding the services provided by patrollers.
- Foster a desire to assume leadership roles within the NSP.
- Offer a local training program in which positive role models work with patrollers to help them develop specialized organizational and administrative skills.

The PES consists of four modules: Patrol Facilities Management, Administrative Policies Management, Expanded Patroller Services to Ski Areas, and NSP Education and Leadership Opportunities. These modules may be completed in one full day or partial days. Modules may be taught in various sequences using interactive discussions, presentations, small group assignments, and activities. Evaluation will be continuous throughout each module and will be based on performance objectives.

Patroller Enrichment Seminar

Prerequisite

- Preparatory work of study activities

Time Commitment

- Each of the four clinic modules takes approximately two hours

Fees

- National—none
- Division—varies
- Course—varies
- Cost of materials

Credential

- NSP Certificate of Achievement (distributed by instructor of record)

Continuing Education/ Refresher

A patroller who completes the Senior Auxiliary Program is certified at that level for three years. To maintain senior auxiliary status, the patroller must meet one of the following requirements during each three-year cycle after completing the Senior Auxiliary Program.

- Hold a leadership position at the region level or above (or the patrol level at the discretion of the division auxiliary supervisor).
- Complete a project—approved by the division auxiliary supervisor—that demonstrates leadership abilities. Such projects could include being a member of the patrol bylaws committee, creating forms to be used by the patrol, or organizing an activity that has major impact on the patrol, region, etc.)
- Hold current teaching credential in any NSP discipline.
- Retake the Patroller Enrichment Seminar.

Instructor of Record

- PES instructor

Required Texts

- *The Ski Patroller's Manual*, National Ski Patrol, 14th edition
- *NSP Policies and Procedures*, National Ski Patrol, current edition

Course Objectives

The learner will address the categories that follow to fulfill the course objectives.

Patrol Facilities Management Module

- Describe a variety of patrol facility responsibilities (to be carried out by any member of an individual patrol).
- Upon considering the layout of a familiar patrol facility, explain the strengths and weaknesses of the overall use of space and placement of equipment.
- Describe what a patroller must do when reporting and investigating an incident.

Administrative Policies Management Module

- Use the appropriate administrative guidelines to complete patrol forms and describe the paper-flow process for the completed forms.

- Demonstrate how to plan and develop patrol policies and procedures for a specific emergency situation.

Expanded Patroller Services to Ski Areas Module

- Discuss various opportunities to expand patroller services within the ski industry and outdoor recreation community.
- Identify various training programs and resources that may be necessary to effectively expand patroller services.

NSP Education and Leadership Opportunities Module

- Identify quality leadership skills and describe the effects that each skill has on effective leadership.
- Identify an appropriate path to pursue when seeking an educational or leadership role within a patrol, region, and division.
- Outline the steps and training required to achieve advanced opportunities in a selected role.

National Ski Patrol members often are exposed to severe winter conditions while engaged in their patrolling activities. Exposure to such conditions may occur during regular alpine or nordic patrolling duties or during a search for a missing skier—either within or outside the area boundaries. To help instructors educate the public about mountaineering and search and rescue, the National Mountaineering Committee has established several areas of mountaineering training.

The primary goal of the NSP Basic and Advanced Mountaineering courses is to equip patrollers with the knowledge that will enable them to cope successfully with winter emergencies and to take care of themselves and other individuals in the most adverse winter conditions typical of the area patrolled.

The secondary goal is to provide the patroller with the skills necessary to function as an effective support person on a winter search and rescue team.

The NSP Basic and Advanced Mountaineering courses are designed to help patrollers function proficiently in the mountaineering environment. (The necessary skills and knowledge are detailed in *Mountain Travel and Rescue.*)

All patrol operations, including mountaineering-related activities, are under the direction and control of ski area management or other authorized agencies.

Basic Mountaineering Course

The purpose of the Basic Mountaineering Course is to provide patrollers the knowledge and skills to travel in reasonable comfort and safety in the mountains and to assist in search and rescue. The course is taught primarily in a classroom environment with opportunities to demonstrate proficiency in an outdoor setting.

CHAPTER 15
Mountaineering Program

Prerequisites

- None

Time Commitment

- One day, including field time

Fees

- National—none
- Division—varies
- Course—varies
- Cost of materials

Credential

- NSP Certificate of Achievement (distributed by instructor)

Continuing Education/ Refresher

- None

Instructor of Record

- NSP mountaineering instructor

Required Text

- *Mountain Travel and Rescue,* National Ski Patrol, 1995

Course Objectives

The learner will address the categories that follow to fulfill the course objectives.

Personal Survival

Body Warmth

- List, describe, and give examples of how the body produces and loses heat.

- Explain the consequences of heat imbalance.
- Recognize personal requirements for temperature control.

Water

- List three ways the body loses water.
- Describe symptoms and effects of dehydration and proper hydration.
- Describe hydration needs for different activity levels and climatic conditions.
- Compare benefits and detriments of drinking fluids other than water.
- Describe safe sources of water in the winter environment and how to obtain water safely.
- Describe how to purify water.
- Describe how to store and transport water in the outdoor winter environment.

Nutrition and Food

- Describe the symptoms of insufficient nutrition.
- Describe how activity levels and climatic conditions affect nutritional needs.
- Provide examples of and describe the proper types, amounts, and proportions of food needed for winter travel and in emergency situations.
- Explain the importance of planning and re-packaging food before a trip.

Clothing

- Compare materials commonly used for layered clothing.
- Explain differences in clothing construction and features.
- Explain the purpose and techniques of layering, venting, and other strategies of dressing for the elements.
- Explain the basics of proper footwear and foot care.
- Describe proper dress for a variety of field conditions and climatic regions.

- Demonstrate how to dress appropriately and stay reasonably comfortable during outdoor exercises.

Additional Equipment

- Identify and explain the purpose of additional equipment relative to trip objective, length, conditions, and party needs.
- Explain the importance and methods of selecting and checking equipment before a trip, including equipment for search and rescue.
- Understand the difference between personal equipment (such as skis, which the owner uses) and group equipment (such as tents, which can be shared).

Emergency Shelters

- Describe the purpose of emergency shelters and the features that distinguish them from camping shelters. Discuss their use for a lone rescuer, for a rescuer and victim, and for potential length of stay.
- List and explain equipment, materials, and techniques for building shelters in a variety of environmental settings.
- Construct at least one type of emergency shelter during an outdoor exercise.
- Identify appropriate and inappropriate site selection with respect to safety and efficiency.

Travel

Equipment

- List different types of equipment used to travel on snow (e.g., cross-country skis and snowshoes), including selection criteria, price range, waxes, skins, etc.
- Compare advantages and disadvantages of equipment relative to a variety of terrain and conditions.
- Describe how to size, adjust, and

maintain equipment for comfort and safety before a trip.
- Describe how to use travel equipment.
- Compare different styles of packs, and describe how to select a pack appropriate for the style of travel and trip length.
- Identify commonly needed field repairs and describe the equipment needed and methods used to make such repairs.

Navigation

- Demonstrate the ability to navigate in ungroomed, local terrain—uphill and downhill—during an outdoor exercise.
- Explain the different types of maps available, their applicability to backcountry navigation, and where they can be purchased.
- Estimate the distance between points on a map using a map scale.
- Identify and describe specific features and symbols on a contour map.
- Estimate elevation on a contour map.
- Describe some of the difficulties that can be associated with contour maps.

- Describe an absolute position using a variety of grid systems.
- Orient and correlate a map with features in the field.
- Describe and compare basic features of various compass types.
- Explain the proper care and use of a compass, including effects of other materials, e.g., metal, magnets, extreme cold, electricity, and declination changes with time.
- Explain how to determine and adjust local magnetic declination (maps may be outdated) selecting one or more methods (settable compass, calculated adjustment, marked compass, or marked map).

Route Selection

- Orient and correlate a map with features in the field, and correct for declination.
- Use a map and compass to determine direction of travel between points and to follow a direction.
- Use a compass to determine the direction to a sighted point in the field.
- Recognize the importance of route planning in terms of safety, hazard avoidance, equipment and travel concerns, and time and effort expectations.
- Describe procedures for traveling through hazardous terrain.
- Demonstrate the ability to travel safely along a selected route during an outdoor exercise.

Backcountry Considerations

Camping and Environmental Concerns

- Describe ways to minimize negative effects on the environment by using proper trail etiquette (e.g., "pack it out," prevent animal encounters, and build wood fires only when and where appropriate).
- List different types of shelter that can be obtained for overnight emergencies.

- Describe various ways of obtaining external heat.
- Describe various accepted methods of waste disposal for all seasons.
- Explain the impacts of improper waste disposal.
- Understand and obey local regulations designed to protect the environment.

Teamwork and Group Dynamics

- Discuss the importance of teamwork in achieving safety and objectives.
- Describe methods and techniques of communication.
- Discuss the effects of stress on group dynamics.
- Recognize the importance of personal strengths and weaknesses.
- Describe the importance of handling different roles effectively.

Medical

- Describe the cause, prevention, symptoms, and general treatment of backcountry medical emergencies (HAPE, HACE, snowblindness, frostbite, hypothermia).
- List the minimum emergency care items that should be carried on a trip.
- Discuss various improvisation techniques for emergency care.

Search and Rescue

Overview

- Recognize different types of search procedures and their application.
- Identify the major elements of a search plan and their sequence (e.g., the importance of the lost person profile; when to coordinate with other rescue and regulatory agencies and with whom, specifically).
- Demonstrate how to be an effective member of a search and rescue team.

Emergency Rescue Techniques

- Describe general techniques that might be used during a rescue.
- Identify rescue equipment and its proper care.
- Demonstrate proper ways to assist leaders during rescue activities.

Advanced Mountaineering Course

The purpose of the Advanced Mountaineering Course is to provide students with the knowledge and skills to plan and conduct a successful multi-day trip into a winter environment and to be effective leaders in search and rescue situations. This course offers hands-on experience in route finding, emergency bivouac, and problems that arise in search and rescue situations. Participation in a mock search and rescue exercise is required.

Prerequisites

- Basic Mountaineering Course
- Basic Avalanche Course

Time Commitment

- Two full days and one overnight with adequate travel
- Recommended: three full days, two nights

Note: Many divisions have found it beneficial to have a practice session several weeks before the actual advanced course. By having participants camp out in a "protected" winter environment (e.g., at a ski area where shelter is available if necessary), instructors can check out individual and group equipment, become acquainted with the needs of the participants, observe participants' abilities to travel over winter terrain, and coordinate any other logistical problems that become apparent.

Fees

- National—none
- Division—varies
- Course—varies
- Cost of materials
- Permit fees (if applicable)

Credential

- NSP Certificate of Achievement (distributed by instructor)

Continuing Education/ Refresher

- Local search and rescue—optional

Instructor of Record

- NSP mountaineering instructor as assigned and approved by the division mountaineering supervisor.

Required Text

- *Mountain Travel and Rescue*, National Ski Patrol, 1995

Course Objectives

The learner will address the categories that follow to fulfill the course objectives.

Personal Survival

Body Warmth and Water: Adapting to the Mountaineering Environment

- Review concluding objectives from the Basic Mountaineering Course.
- Demonstrate the ability to have potable water.
- Demonstrate the ability to maintain body temperature.

Nutrition and Food

- Explain various functions of fats, proteins, and carbohydrates.

- Explain the effects of altitude on food preparation.
- Describe ways to properly store and transport food.
- Discuss additional considerations and planning needed for multi-day trips.
- Remain hydrated and fed during a multi-day trip.

Clothing

- Explain how to repair, care for, and maintain personal clothing.
- Discuss additional clothing needs and considerations for multi-day trips.
- Dress appropriately and stay reasonably comfortable during an outdoor exercise.
- Discuss and demonstrate techniques for staying dry and/or drying out during a multi-day trip.

Additional Equipment

- Assemble and pack the items needed for a trip.
- Identify additional equipment appropriate for multi-day trips.
- Identify necessary equipment care, repair, and maintenance before, during, and after a multi-day trip.

Sleeping Gear

- Compare the different materials used in sleeping bags and discuss various types of construction.
- Compare the different materials and construction of sleeping pads and discuss various accessories.
- Select and use an appropriate bag, pad, and possible accessories on a multi-day trip.

Emergency Shelters

- Construct a functional shelter in an appropriate site and spend at least one night in it.

Travel

Travel Equipment

- Differentiate between individual and shared group equipment.
- Discuss ways to determine the amount and distribution of shared equipment.
- Discuss selection, packing tech-

niques, and travel techniques of packs for multi-day trips.
- Discuss other ways to transport equipment.
- Demonstrate the ability to navigate in ungroomed, typical local terrain—uphill and downhill—during an outdoor exercise.
- Assemble and pack the items needed for a trip.

Roped Travel

- Compare different types of ropes and webbing and describe their various uses.
- Discuss the storage, care, and inspection of ropes and webbing.
- Describe knots used for various applications.
- Demonstrate how to select and put on a harness.
- List additional hardware and its use.
- Describe and demonstrate various ways to set up anchor systems.
- Describe various ways to ensure safety in hazardous terrain.
- Demonstrate the correct use of an ice axe.
- Demonstrate the correct use of crampons.

Navigation

- Resect a position on a map from two lines of direction.
- Adjust and read an altimeter and explain its uses.
- Discuss other equipment that might be useful for navigation.
- Demonstrate some navigation techniques when visibility is limited.
- Demonstrate effective map use during a multi-day trip.

Route Selection

- List route selection criteria based on the trip objective, conditions, terrain, and ability and equipment of the party.
- Identify terrain and conditions that may affect route safety and selection.
- Demonstrate various ways to plan and follow a safe route.

Backcountry Considerations

Camping and Environmental Concerns

- Review the concluding objectives of the Basic Mountaineering Course.

- List different types of shelters suitable for winter camping and the advantages and disadvantages of each. Identify appropriate and inappropriate site selection with respect to safety and efficiency.
- Discuss considerations for suitable multi-day camping sites with respect to conditions, safety, party needs, and minimum environmental impact.
- Describe the equipment needed to prepare hot food and to melt water.
- Discuss low-impact camping techniques for groups on multi-day trips, including the need to consider latrines, proper disposal of wastewater, and camp sanitation.
- Describe ways to properly store and transport food.
- Understand and obey all local regulations designed to protect the environment.
- Demonstrate effective camping techniques during a multi-day trip.

Weather

- Explain the characteristics of weather patterns.
- Describe the significance of cloud formations in forecasting weather,

recognizing cloud types, and using cloud formations as indicators of high and low pressure systems.
- Describe other indicators of changing weather, such as wind, using altimeters as barometers.
- Discuss the influences of local topography on weather.
- List sources of current weather forecasts for the intended trip area.
- Recognize the impact of weather on trip planning, execution, and on search and rescue, taking into consideration seasonable variability.
- Demonstrate the ability to monitor and respond to local weather before and during a multi-day trip.

Teamwork, Group Dynamics, and Leadership

- Describe the essential characteristics of leadership.
- Help organize and implement a search and rescue scenario.

Medical

- Describe different treatment and complications of illness or injury caused by winter conditions.
- Discuss the considerations for

necessary supplies and equipment for extended care and transport in backcountry situations.
- Discuss various improvisational emergency care techniques.

Search and Rescue

Typical Search and Rescue Organization

- Review the concluding objectives of the Basic Mountaineering Course.
- Explain the duties and responsibilities of each job during a search and rescue.
- Describe the concept and importance of chain of command in rescue operations, including the various channels of communication. Discuss how patrollers fit into a larger rescue scheme involving local, state, and other rescue organizations, and how the chain of command functions within the area's rescue plan.
- Discuss the importance and methods of written documentation of formal search and rescue.
- Discuss appropriate ways to deal with the media.
- Differentiate between a formal search and rescue and a small party rescue.
- Recognize the roles of mental preparation and attitude in survival.
- List strategies to enhance survival and rescue.
- List ways of alerting patrollers for a rescue.
- If applicable, review own area search and rescue plan and discuss its adequacy.
- Simulate an emergency situation during the outdoor exercise to practice rescue skills.
- Help organize and implement a search and rescue scenario.

Emergency Rescue Techniques

- Describe emergency extrication

techniques such as lowering and hauling.
- Discuss techniques for providing emergency transportation in the backcountry.
- Describe the higher demands of rescue work compared with roped travel, including different knots, knowledge of the more complicated systems of hauling and lowering, patient care, and more equipment.
- Discuss the differences between in-area and backcountry rescues, including equipment, techniques, timeline, communication, etc.
- Demonstrate effective rescue techniques and transportation of a patient during a mock exercise.

Search and Rescue Refreshers

Often patrols hold search and rescue refreshers that are specific to the needs of the local area and the backcountry. These refreshers, normally part of the local on-the-hill/trail refresher, may include a review of the ski area out-of-area search plan, a review of the governing state's search regulations, maintenance or stocking of rescue caches, and even a mock search.

These activities are done in conjunction with the local authorities responsible for the search and rescue. If a patroller becomes part of a search and rescue team that goes beyond ski area boundaries, then he or she is serving under the direction and authorization of that governing agency, not the National Ski Patrol.

The NSP Nordic Program is designed to help patrollers develop and refine the skills and knowledge that ski area management or governing agencies require of patrollers who carry out their patrol duty on nordic equipment. To help instructors train nordic members, the national nordic committee has established several areas of nordic training.

The program is designed to help NSP members become proficient in all on-the-hill/trail operations pertaining to Outdoor Emergency Care, nordic toboggan handling, and mountain travel and rescue techniques. To this end, the NSP offers instruction and training in Outdoor Emergency Care, mountaineering, nordic ski and toboggan skills, and, depending on the patroller's location, avalanche awareness.

For instance, nordic training encourages candidates and patrollers to participate in a variety of exercises that demonstrate basic nordic skiing proficiency and the use of commercial and improvised toboggans. Candidates also must complete an NSP Basic Mountaineering Course that introduces them to such topics as route selection, orienteering, toboggan fabrication, shelter building, and personal survival skills.

Other training, such as the NSP's Basic and/or Advanced Avalanche courses and non-NSP coursework, may be required to meet the needs of the local area.

Nordic patrollers who combine backcountry savvy with strong skiing ability, toboggan-handling skill, and solid emergency care acumen can provide an important measure of safety in whatever environment they work—be it the backcountry, a nordic ski center, or a lift-served ski area.

Moreover, patrollers who have these qualifications create a favorable image to the general public and also boost the confidence that winter recreationists may have in the abilities of local patrollers.

CHAPTER

16

Nordic Ski and Toboggan Program

Basic Nordic Patrolling Skills

The general goal of the National Ski Patrol with regard to its Nordic Program is to provide area management the services of uniformly trained patrollers whose nordic skiing and toboggan-handling skills are annually evaluated and refreshed. The NSP has developed specific training goals and objectives to help patrollers maintain strong patrolling skills and perform their duties in a competent and efficient manner.

Patrollers must demonstrate an above-average level of skiing ability with emphasis on stability, control, and the use of sound skiing technique. They must be able to ski the most advanced slope or trail at their area in a strong and competent manner. Strong skiing skills also provide the foundation for competent toboggan handling when transporting ill or injured snow sports enthusiasts.

Just like its alpine cousin, the Nordic Program is designed to provide patrollers with the knowledge necessary to perform the various tasks and responsibilities required of them by area management or whoever has jurisdiction over the area they patrol. Table 16.1 on the following page contains a list of nordic skiing and toboggan-handling skills and equivalent alpine skills.

Toboggan Handling

Like their colleagues on alpine skis and snowboards, patrollers on nordic equipment must be proficient in Outdoor Emergency Care, but they must

also be well-versed in the many different types of toboggans used by ski patrols and local backcountry rescue organizations. In addition, they must be skilled at fabricating an emergency toboggan from items carried in their duty pack. The basic training program is designed to cover these nuances of nordic patrolling and provide coaching in nordic skiing, general toboggan-handling, and various other on-the-hill/trail and backcountry operations.

Prerequisites

- Acceptance by patrol for candidate training
- NSP member dues paid
- 15 years of age
- Basic Mountaineering Course
- Overnight bivouac
- Skiing evaluation (while wearing area-approved duty pack)

Time Commitment

- One to two years

Fee

- National—none
- Division—varies
- Course—varies
- Cost of materials

Credential

- NSP Certificate of Achievement (distributed by instructor)

Continuing Education/ Refresher

- Annual on-the-hill/trail refresher on local skill requirements
- Attendance records kept at the local level; no formal credential

Instructor of Record

- Local ski and toboggan trainer
- Division ski and toboggan supervisor
- Alpine toboggan instructor

Required Text

- *The Ski Patroller's Manual,* National Ski Patrol, 14th edition

References

- *Nordic Training Manual,* National Ski Patrol, 1998
- *Ski and Toboggan Training Manual,* National Ski Patrol, 1994
- *Mountain Travel and Rescue,* National Ski Patrol, 1995
- *NSP Policies and Procedures,* National Ski Patrol, current edition
- PSIA materials:
  - *The American Teaching System: Nordic Skiing*
  - *ATS Nordic Handbook*

Course Objectives

The learner will address the categories that follow to fulfill the course objectives.

Equipment

Toboggans and Their Construction

- Identify the types of toboggans used at the local area.
- Describe how each toboggan component contributes to effective operation.

Rescue Packs

- Demonstrate proper preparation of rescue pack for toboggan storage.

Table 16.1 Nordic and Alpine Skiing and Toboggan-handling Maneuvers		
Nordic	**Alpine**	
Skiing Maneuvers	**Skiing Maneuvers**	
Diagonal stride (traditional)	N/A	
Double pole (with and without kick)	N/A	
Wedge	Wedge	
Wedge turn	Wedge turn	
Stem turn	Stem turn	
Sideslip	Sideslip	
Falling leaf	Falling leaf	
Moving direction changes	Moving direction changes	
Skating	Skating	
V-skate (V1, V2, V2 alternate)	N/A	
Diagonal V-skate	N/A	
Parallel turns	Parallel turns	
Step turns	N/A	
Skate turns	N/A	
Traversing, both sides (climbing and descending)	Traversing, both sides	
Herringbone, sidestep (up-down)	Herringbone, sidestep (up-down)	
Static direction change (kick turn)	Static direction change (kick turn)	
Telemark turn	N/A	
Operating an Unloaded Toboggan	**Operating an Unloaded Toboggan**	
Quick check/setup	Quick check/setup	
Route selection	Route selection	
Traversing	Traversing	
Descending the fall line	Descending the fall line	
Moving belays (wide and narrow trail and sidehill)	N/A	
Static belays (lowering)	N/A	
Moving direction changes	Moving direction changes	
Static direction changes	Static direction changes	
Emergency stop	Emergency stop	
Wheelbarrow	Wheelbarrow	
Rear run (four-handled toboggan)	Rear run (four-handled toboggan)	

Table 16.1 (continued)

Nordic

Toboggan Fabrication

Materials and equipment
Construction techniques

Managing the Incident Site

Approach
Securing the toboggan
Anchoring the skis
Bivouac/subject survival
Loading the patient

Operating a Loaded Toboggan

Route selection
Traversing
Descending the fall line
Moving belays (wide and narrow trail and sidehill)
Static belays (raising and lowering)
Moving direction changes
Turns
  Wedge
  Step
  Parallel
Sideslip
Falling leaf
Static direction changes
Emergency stop

Operating the Tail Rope

Traversing
Descending
Moving direction changes
Sideslip to wedge
Falling leaf to diagonal falling leaf
Static belay

Operating a Four-Handled Toboggan

Route selection
Descending and traversing
Moving direction changes
Static direction changes
Emergency stops

Uphill Transportation

Lift carry
Z-pulley

Alpine

Toboggan Fabrication

N/A
N/A

Managing the Incident Site

Approach
Securing the toboggan
Anchoring the skis
N/A
Loading the patient

Operating a Loaded Toboggan

Route selection
Traversing
Descending the fall line
N/A
N/A
Moving direction changes
Turns
  Wedge
  Step
  Parallel (skidded and carved)
Sideslip
Falling leaf
Static direction changes
Emergency stop

Operating the Tail Rope

Traversing
Descending
Moving direction changes
Sideslip to wedge turn
Falling leaf to diagonal falling leaf
Static belay

Operating a Four-Handled Toboggan

Route selection
Descending and traversing
Moving direction changes
Static direction changes
Emergency stops

Uphill Transportation

Lift carry
N/A

Fabricated Toboggans and Their Construction

- Identify the types of fabricated toboggans used at the local area.
- Describe and demonstrate how each fabricated toboggan component contributes to effective operation.
- Fabricate a toboggan—sufficient for patient transport over a specified distance and type of terrain—from materials available at an incident scene and carried in a standard patrol pack.

Toboggan Storage, Inspection, and Setup Procedures

- Inspect a toboggan stored at the local area by systematically checking its components for safety and function.
- Position the toboggan on the hill/trail by considering the immediate surroundings and using appropriate anchoring and setup procedures.

General Nordic Toboggan Operation

Skiing Maneuvers for Toboggan Operations

- Demonstrate in a stable, controlled manner the following skiing maneuvers, which are essential to safe and effective toboggan operation.
  - Kick turn without poles on a moderately steep, packed slope
  - Kick turn without poles in moguls
  - Uphill sidestep on steep terrain
  - Downhill sidestep on difficult terrain
  - Herringbone ascent on moderate terrain
- Demonstrate the following skiing maneuvers, using a combination of balance and edge-, rotary-, and pressure-control movements to maintain stable position and controlled

speed while handling a toboggan on a variety of terrain and snow conditions at the local area.
- Diagonal stride with and without poles
- Fall-line traverse (climbing and descending) while varying the width between skis and lifting the uphill ski off the snow
- Fall-line sideslip (holding poles at mid-shaft)
- Falling leaf sideslip (holding poles at mid-shaft)
- Wedge
- Wedge transitions (wedge to sideslip and back to wedge)
- Gliding wedge turn
- Stem/step turn from wedge
- Parallel turn
- Sideslip transitions
- Moving direction changes (wedge, sideslip, parallel)
- Skating
- Emergency stops

Operating an Unloaded Toboggan

Quick Check and Initial Setup

- Inspect the toboggan by following quick-check procedures, and prepare it for safe, unloaded transportation from a standby toboggan location.
- Demonstrate how to properly rig both a commercial and fabricated toboggan.

From Position in Control Handles and as Belay Leader

- Demonstrate proper positioning in the handles when operating an unloaded toboggan.
- Demonstrate effective positioning of an additional patroller for efficient transport over varied terrain and trail conditions.

Route Selection

- Describe the factors and/or demonstrate the most appropriate route to follow when approaching an ill or injured skier given a specific location and snow condition.
- Demonstrate how to effectively position yourself and an additional patroller to safely and efficiently transport an unloaded toboggan on wide and narrow trails and on sidehills.

Traversing

- With stability, control, and a combination of turns, transitions, and operating positions, demonstrate a smooth and confident traverse while descending the fall line with an unloaded toboggan in the following local area conditions.
  - Packed or groomed trail/slope
  - Ungroomed terrain, powder, crud, or ice

Descending the Fall Line and Turning

- Demonstrate how to operate the front of an unloaded toboggan while descending the fall line in a variety of terrain and snow conditions.
- Demonstrate how to turn and transition between wedge, sideslip, stem, and parallel ski positions while operating the front of an unloaded toboggan in a variety of terrain and snow conditions.

Static Belays—Raising and Lowering

- Demonstrate how to properly rig a commercial or fabricated toboggan to raise or lower it in a static belay.
- Demonstrate the proper use of natural and constructed anchors.
- Demonstrate a sitting hip belay, using skis as anchors, to lower a patroller and an unloaded toboggan.

- Demonstrate how to use a "figure eight" (or other friction device) and a Muenter hitch to lower an unloaded toboggan and a patroller.

Static Direction Changes

- Perform a balanced and stable kick turn while maintaining contact with the toboggan handles on steep or moguled terrain.

Managing the Incident Site

Approaching the Incident Site and Securing the Toboggan

- Explain and demonstrate how to safely approach an incident site with an unloaded toboggan and secure the toboggan properly in preparation for loading a patient.
- Describe how all available resources (e.g., time, personnel, equipment) can best be used to effectively manage an incident site.

Bivouac/Subject Survival

- Describe the requirements of extended patient care in a wilderness setting.
- Demonstrate an ability to quickly construct an efficient overnight shelter to protect the patient from the elements while awaiting evacuation.
- Demonstrate an ability to provide a heat source to keep the patient warm and to prepare warm fluids.

Positioning the Patient in the Toboggan and Preparing for Transport

- Describe how the patient's position in the toboggan is influenced by the nature and extent of the injury, the patient's mobility, the number of people able to assist, the terrain, snow conditions, and type of toboggan.
- With an empty toboggan, approach a simulated incident on a more

difficult slope, secure the toboggan in an appropriate position for the patient, lift the patient into the toboggan, and secure the patient for transport.
- Prepare the toboggan for departure.

Operating a Loaded Two-Handled or Improvised Toboggan

General Principles

- Describe the general principles of operating the front of a loaded toboggan to ensure a safe, smooth, and controlled descent.

Route Selection

- Identify the appropriate route to follow with a loaded toboggan to provide the safest and smoothest patient ride at various trails and locations throughout the local area.

Traversing and Descending the Fall Line

- Traverse a loaded toboggan in a stable and controlled manner with minimal lateral slippage in the following conditions.
  - Packed or groomed trail/slope on the most challenging terrain at the local area
  - Trail/slope with obstacles
  - Ungroomed terrain, powder, crud, and ice
- Descend the fall line with a loaded toboggan while demonstrating the stability, control, and effective combination of turns, transitions, and braking techniques that will ensure a safe, smooth ride for the patient in the following conditions.
  - Packed or groomed trail/slope on the most challenging terrain at the local area
  - Trail/slope with obstacles
  - Ungroomed terrain, powder, crud, and ice

Moving Belays—Wide and Narrow Trail and Across a Sidehill

- Demonstrate how to properly rig a commercial and a fabricated toboggan for a moving belay.
- Identify the functions of each of the following members of a three- and four-patroller toboggan team.
  - Leader
  - Mule
  - Swing (three-member team)
  - Wings (four-member team)
- Demonstrate how to effectively position yourself and up to four additional patrollers for safe and efficient transport of a loaded toboggan on wide and narrow trails and on sidehills.

Static Belays—Raising and Lowering

- Demonstrate how to properly rig either a commercial or fabricated toboggan to raise or lower it in a static belay.
- Demonstrate the proper use of natural and constructed anchors for raising and lowering a loaded toboggan.
- Demonstrate a sitting hip belay, using skis as anchors, to lower a patroller and a loaded toboggan.
- Demonstrate a "figure eight" (or other friction device) and a Muenter hitch to lower a loaded toboggan and a patroller.
- Demonstrate how to use a z-pulley system to raise a loaded toboggan and a patroller.

Moving Direction Changes, Front Operator Training

- Perform the following maneuvers with a loaded toboggan on a packed slope, a moguled slope, and on powder, crud, and ice.
  - Wedge and sideslip transitions
  - Wedge turn
  - Step/stem turn
  - Parallel turn (skidded and/or carved)
  - Falling leaf sideslip

Static Direction Changes, Front Operator Training

- Perform a balanced and stable kick turn while maintaining contact with the toboggan handles on steep or moguled terrain.

Toboggan Maneuvers In Varying Conditions, Front Operator Training

- Descend the fall line with a loaded toboggan while demonstrating the stability, control, and effective combination of turns, transitions, and braking techniques that will ensure a safe and smooth ride for the patient in the following conditions.
  - Packed or groomed trail/slope on steep terrain
  - Trail/slope with obstacles
  - Ungroomed terrain, powder, crud, and ice
  - Flat terrain

Operating the Tail Rope of a Loaded Two-Handled Toboggan

General Principles

- Describe the general principles of operating the tail rope of a loaded toboggan to ensure a safe, smooth, and controlled descent.

Descending and Traversing the Fall Line

- While operating the tail rope of a loaded toboggan, demonstrate stability and control while maintaining an appropriate position and rope tension to assist the front operator in the following conditions.
  - Packed or groomed trail/slope on moderate to steep terrain
  - Trail/slope with obstacles
  - Powder, crud, and ice

Moving Direction Changes

- While operating the tail rope of a loaded toboggan, perform the following maneuvers with stability and control while descending the fall line.
  - Transitions from sideslip to wedge
  - Transitions from sideslip facing left to sideslip facing right
  - Wedge turns, right and left
  - Step turns, right and left
  - Falling leaf sideslip
  - Diagonal fall-line descent

Mechanical Transport of Toboggans

Transporting Empty Toboggans

- Demonstrate how to transport an empty toboggan uphill on surface lifts using the established method(s) for the local area.

Using Over-the-Snow Vehicles for Transport

The National Ski Patrol does not create training standards or advise patrollers concerning the use of motorized over-the-snow vehicles (grooming machines, snowmobiles, all-terrain vehicles, etc.). The substantial variations in equipment, regulatory requirements, and expected use by area management make it impracticable to develop a training component in this area. While such equipment may be useful in the operation of a ski area, any training and use of such machinery is, and must be, the responsibility of area management and its agents. All personnel operating such vehicles should follow the manufacturer's recommendations and area management's training and operating procedures.

Helicopter Rescue

The National Ski Patrol does not create training standards or advise patrollers concerning the coordination of evacuation and medical care with helicopter services. Area management should determine whether helicopter rescue is necessary and appropriate, and establish protocols for determining when such assistance will be requested. If the patrol needs to evacuate patients by helicopter, the patrol should require each member to participate in a helicopter orientation program (and subsequent refreshers) conducted by the helicopter service in coordination with area management. All patrollers working with helicopter rescue services should follow the protocols and procedures established by area management and the helicopter service.

Evacuation of Toboggans from Aerial Tramways

By agreement with the National Ski Areas Association, patrollers participate in lift evacuation and lift evacuation training (including the evacuation of toboggans from aerial tramways) only as ski area management shall direct. The establishment of necessary policies and procedures for lift evacuation, lift evacuation training, and the selection of equipment to be used in conjunction with such evacuation or training is the sole responsibility of ski area management.

Area management's lift evacuation plan should incorporate the appropriate procedures for the evacuation of loaded toboggans from the lift. Patrollers conduct lift evacuation training (and actual evacuations) as agents of area management. The equipment and skills used to evacuate toboggans from aerial tramways are beyond the scope of a toboggan training program and are more appropriately covered as part of lift evacuation training.

On-the-Hill/Trail Refresher

Training and skill requirements are specifically applicable, and often unique, to the local ski area as directed by area management's policies and procedures. The ski patrol director is generally responsible for organizing or delegating the responsibility for conducting the on-the-hill/trail refreshers.

Refresher Training Considerations

When organizing and conducting an on-the-hill/trail refresher, the ski patrol director (or delegated patrol member) might incorporate but is not limited to the following review of skills and knowledge into the appropriate section of the refresher.

Skiing Proficiency Refresher

- Perform classic and telemark (as appropriate) skating, and nordic downhill maneuvers with stability, control, and effective use of edging, turning, and pressure-control skills on moderate to difficult terrain, trails, or groomed, set track.
- Ski a moderate tour (in terms of distance or duration) in varied terrain and conditions with full patrol packs to allow evaluation of conditioning and technique.
- Ski a controlled course while demonstrating climbing, braking, transitions, and survival skiing (pole drag) techniques.

Toboggan Handling Refresher

- Transport an empty toboggan to a simulated accident site.
- Approach an incident site using proper procedures, and appropriately position the unloaded toboggan at the incident site.
- Using teams of up to four patrollers (including a leader), transport a loaded toboggan while demonstrating effective positioning, teamwork, control, smoothness, and appropriate route selection on the area's moderate to difficult terrain/trails.
- From all operating positions for a loaded toboggan (front, back, and lateral), demonstrate specific skiing skills, including sideslip (forward, backward, and fall line), sidestep, wedge, transition maneuvers, braking techniques, and straight running on both wide and narrow trails.

Local Patrol Policies Refresher

- Describe the location of facilities, equipment, and major landmarks as well as the names, location, degree of difficulty, length, and travel time for all trails at the area patrolled.
- Recite procedures for restocking and returning empty toboggans to their stations.
- Demonstrate the ability to operate the communications system.
- Review area management policies and procedures regarding operation and use of over-the-snow vehicles for transporting patients and toboggans.
- Review ski patrol and ski area management operations procedures, including sign on, assignments, rotations, relief, sweep, search and rescue, and radio procedures.

Skiing Enhancement Seminar (Nordic)

The nordic version of the Skiing Enhancement Seminar is a ski lesson specifically designed to improve the skiing skills of NSP members. Open to all NSP nordic skiers regardless of skiing ability, the seminar features lessons taught by qualified Certified Level III PSIA instructors throughout the season.

Seminar participants can improve their skiing skills by focusing on better techniques that will allow them to ski more efficiently. The seminar also helps patrollers identify their strengths and weaknesses and provides informative exercises for improving their skiing after the seminar.

Scott Markewitz

Credential

- NSP Certificate of Achievement (distributed by instructor)

Continuing Education/ Refresher

- None

Instructor of Record

- PSIA division clinic leaders
- Qualified PSIA Certified Level III instructors

Required Text

- None

Course Objectives

The learner will address the categories that follow to fulfill the course objectives.

- Identify personal skiing strengths and weaknesses.
- Identify good balance and alignment in self and peers.
- Ski with improved efficiency (through better turn shape and speed control).
- Develop (with the PSIA seminar instructor) activities and exercises for continued improvement.
- Identify opportunities for further learning.

Ski Trainer's Workshop (Nordic)

This workshop is designed to improve the skiing-related assessment and training skills of NSP ski and toboggan trainers and evaluators. The program emphasizes a partnership and cooperative effort between PSIA ski instructors and NSP ski and toboggan trainers.

The purpose of the workshop is to give NSP trainers a way to develop a "photographic eye" by using observational clues to improve ski and

Moreover, by helping to increase the skiing proficiency of patrollers, the Skiing Enhancement Seminar presents an opportunity to improve patroller image to the ski industry and the general public.

Prerequisites

- Current NSP membership

Time Commitment

- One day

Fees

- National—none
- Normal PSIA division clinic charges (for course and instructor)
- NSP division—varies
- Trail passes/lift tickets

toboggan evaluation skills. The workshop also allows participants to recognize their abilities and limitations as ski trainers.

Prerequisites

- NSP member
- Instructor Development: Phase I
- PSIA level 2 skier

Recommended Prerequisite

- Skiing Enhancement Seminar, PSIA-level instructor, or other approved option (to be determined by the national program director and division director and nordic supervisor)

Time Commitment

- Objective-based program that can take one to two days

Fees

- National—none
- Normal PSIA division clinic charges (for the course and instructor)
- NSP division—varies
- Trail passes/lift tickets

Credential

- NSP Certificate of Achievement (distributed by instructor)

Continuing Education/ Refresher

- None

Instructor of Record

- PSIA division clinic leaders/examiners selected by PSIA division coordinator

Required Text

- None

Scott Markewitz

Course Objectives

The learner will address the categories that follow to fulfill the course objectives.

- Identify skiing skills necessary for flat track (diagonal stride and skating) as well as backcountry skills.
- Use the NSP evaluation criteria to accurately assess and provide feedback to patrollers regarding skiing skills.
- Explain and demonstrate specific exercises and drills to improve skiing skills necessary for effective toboggan handling and free skiing.
- Recognize NSP training limitations and identify PSIA and other training opportunities to expand or enhance patroller knowledge and skills.

17

Outdoor Emergency Care Program

The National Ski Patrol has always been in a unique position compared to other providers of prehospital care. In addition to caring for illnesses and injuries such as deep frostbite and acute mountain sickness, NSP members often serve in locations far from hospitals and frequently must provide care for an hour or more before patients can be turned over to the EMS system. Nordic ski patrollers may be many hours or even days from a doctor or hospital.

To help instructors educate NSP members about emergency care in the outdoor environment, the National Medical Committee and the National Outdoor Emergency Care Committee have developed specific training objectives to help patrollers maintain these basic patrolling skills and perform their duties in a competent, efficient manner.

Even though the Outdoor Emergency Care (OEC) Program has been designed to fit the specific needs of patrollers, it can serve the needs of any outdoor recreationist or rescue group member who desires a course in non-urban emergency care. The basic lifesaving skills taught in the program are universal and apply to any type of emergency situation.

The Outdoor Emergency Care Course is a standard of training, *not* an operational standard of care. In other words, ski area managers are responsible for the standard of care at their areas, which they establish by putting into place OEC-trained patrollers, patrollers with other medical training, specific equipment, physicians and "doctor patrols," base clinics, advanced life support, and other medical resources.

The OEC program, while not meant to parallel a *complete* Emergency Medical Technician (EMT) Course, is based in part upon the medical criteria contained in the national EMT curriculum established by the U.S. Department of Transportation (DOT). Outdoor Emergency

Care is a sequenced, competency-based educational program with specific knowledge and skill objectives. Where possible, program administrators recognize differences between OEC and EMT curriculum with respect to techniques, equipment, and local medical protocols.

The course is designed to teach patrollers how to manage the various illnesses and injuries they may encounter on any given duty day. A secondary aim of OEC is to prepare students to analyze and devise rational solutions to any unusual problems in emergency care not specifically covered in their training. To this end, OEC administrators emphasize the value of developing a solid foundation in anatomy, physiology, and in-depth patient assessment, and being able to improvise techniques and equipment to fit unusual circumstances. With numerous opportunities to study and take part in emergency care scenarios, students are able to build a strong base of knowledge and a diverse range of techniques from which to choose when called upon to form decisions about appropriate care of patients.

OEC providers who become members of local patrols must follow local policies and protocols developed and/or approved by ski area management. Ski patrols must obtain the review and approval of area management when developing operational protocols. The NSP recognizes that ski area management ultimately supervises, controls, and is responsible for the patrolling activities of individual NSP members and patrols at the area. This is in accordance with Section 1 of

the Joint Statement of Understanding between the National Ski Areas Association and the National Ski Patrol.

Outdoor Emergency Care Course

The OEC course content is taught at the same level as the EMT course content. OEC is designed to prepare candidate patrollers without previous first aid or EMT training to handle the emergency care problems seen at alpine and nordic ski areas. The knowledge and skills to be learned are oriented toward the wilderness setting, with special emphasis on ski injuries, high altitude and cold weather illness, wilderness extrications, and the special equipment patrollers need for emergency care and transportation in the outdoor environment. An individual who completes the course will be prepared to manage a wide range of medical emergencies, regardless of the setting or environment.

Patrols may modify—but not eliminate or reduce—the course content to fit local needs, as long as modifications do not conflict with traditional, well-established principles of first aid.

Prerequisite

- Course—none
- Challenge—current certification or license in medicine or EMS, or First Responder certification at the discretion of the instructor of record

Time Commitment

- Course—no hour requirements. To master the objectives, a candidate needs to devote 80 to 100 hours of class and study time to the course.
- Challenge—Total class hours vary with the candidate's emergency care background, specialty, and experience.

Fees

- National—$15
- Division—$10
- Course—varies
- Cost of materials

Credential

- OEC card (valid for three years)
- NSP Certificate of Achievement (distributed by instructor)

Continuing Education/ Refresher

- Annual OEC refresher consisting of one-third of the total curriculum (skill competency is verified by instructor of record)

Instructor of Record

- OEC instructors

Required Texts

- *Outdoor Emergency Care,* National Ski Patrol, current edition
- *OEC Study Book,* National Ski Patrol, current edition

Recommended Video References

- *History and Physical Examination*
- *Lower Extremity Injuries*
- *Upper Extremity Injuries*
- *Spinal Injury Management*

Course Objectives

The learner will address the categories that follow to fulfill the course objectives.

Adapting to the Outdoor Environment

- Describe the survival requirements of the human body.
- Explain how the outdoor environment affects the major systems of the human body.
- Describe methods of adapting to the outdoor environment.
- Explain the importance of nutrition and physical conditioning in the human body's adaptation to the outdoor environment.
- Demonstrate layering principles using typical ski clothing.

Overview of Human Anatomy and Physiology

- Demonstrate thorough knowledge of anatomical descriptive terms.
- Recite the nine major systems of the human body and explain how they interact in the healthy human body.
- Explain how the human body works, and describe the central concepts behind managing the body's major systems to provide emergency care of an injury or illness.
- Demonstrate comprehension of anatomical positions.

Surface Anatomy and Physiology

- Describe and locate important landmarks of the body.
- Describe and locate vital signs and other important signs.
- Demonstrate the techniques for taking and recording vital signs.
- Explain the importance of exercising universal precautions when using equipment and techniques that may involve contact with a patient's body fluids.
- Demonstrate the proper use and disposal of personal protective equipment.

Basic Assessment

- Explain basic assessment techniques, including first impression and primary and secondary surveys.
- Demonstrate basic assessment techniques as they pertain to a responsive patient.
- Demonstrate basic assessment techniques as they pertain to an unresponsive patient.

Oxygen and Other Types of Respiratory-System Support

- Explain the human body's need

for oxygen.

- Explain how to use oxygen systems and other mechanical aids to resuscitation.
- Explain the importance of exercising universal precautions when using equipment and techniques that may involve contact with a patient's body fluids.
- Demonstrate the basic techniques used for administering oxygen.
- Demonstrate the use of such resuscitation aids as pocket masks, mouth shields, oral airways, and suction devices.

Bleeding and Shock

- Describe the types and causes of bleeding.
- Describe the types of shock.
- Demonstrate appropriate emergency care techniques for controlling external bleeding.
- Demonstrate appropriate emergency care techniques for managing internal bleeding.
- Demonstrate the appropriate care for shock.

Skin and Soft-Tissue Injuries, Burns, and Bandaging

- List and describe closed soft-tissue injuries.
- List and describe open soft-tissue injuries.
- Describe the three degrees and three classifications of thermal burns and their significance in emergency care.
- Describe the characteristics of chemical and electrical burns.
- Define the terms *dressing* and *bandage.*
- Demonstrate basic emergency care techniques for open soft-tissue injuries.
- Demonstrate basic emergency care techniques for closed soft-tissue injuries.
- Demonstrate basic emergency care techniques for burns.

- Demonstrate basic techniques for applying dressings and bandages.
- Demonstrate basic techniques for applying special equipment types and improvised dressings and bandages.

Emergency Care of Bone and Joint Injuries: General Principles

- Describe the general characteristics of sprains, dislocations, and fractures.
- Explain the general principles of emergency care for musculoskeletal injuries.
- Name the types of splints and explain the general principles of their application.
- Demonstrate techniques for long spine-board immobilization
- Demonstrate techniques for traction-splint immobilization.

Mechanisms and Patterns of Injury

- Describe how trauma is influenced by laws of physics.
- Distinguish between various types of trauma and their implications.
- Inspect a simulated incident scene and reconstruct the probable sequence of events.

Specific Injuries to the Upper Extremity

- Describe the features of sprains, dislocations, and fractures of the upper extremities.
- Describe the principles of emergency care for upper-extremity injuries.
- Demonstrate the appropriate assessment and emergency care for sprains, dislocations, and fractures of upper extremities.

Specific Injuries to the Lower Extremity and Pelvis

- Describe the features of sprains,

dislocations, and fractures of the lower extremities.
- Describe the principles of emergency care for lower-extremity injuries.
- Demonstrate the appropriate assessment and emergency care for sprains, dislocations, and fractures of the lower extremities.

Injuries to the Head, Eye, Face, and Throat

- List possible causes of unresponsiveness and appropriate emergency care for an unresponsive patient.
- Describe appropriate emergency care for a responsive patient with head, eye, face, and throat injuries.
- Demonstrate appropriate assessment techniques for a patient with a head injury.
- Demonstrate basic techniques of emergency care for an unresponsive patient.
- Demonstrate basic techniques of emergency care for head, eye, face, and throat injuries.

Injuries to the Neck and Back

- Describe characteristics of spine and spinal cord injuries.
- Demonstrate the appropriate emergency care of a patient with suspected spine or spinal cord injuries.
- Demonstrate the appropriate procedure for logrolling.
- Demonstrate the appropriate procedure for helmet removal.
- Demonstrate the appropriate procedure for immobilizing a patient on a standing spine board.
- Demonstrate the appropriate procedure for a multi-person direct ground lift.

Injuries to the Chest

- List the causes and mechanisms of common types of chest injuries.

- Describe signs and symptoms of common types of chest injuries.
- Demonstrate basic techniques of emergency care for a patient with chest injuries.

Injuries to the Abdomen, Pelvis, and Genitalia

- List the types and causes of injuries to the abdomen, pelvis, and genitalia.
- Describe signs and symptoms of injuries to the abdomen, pelvis, and genitalia.
- Demonstrate basic techniques of emergency care for a patient with specific injuries to abdominal and pelvic areas.
- Demonstrate basic techniques of emergency care for a patient with injuries to the genitalia.

Common Medical Complaints

- Describe characteristics of common medical complaints.
- Describe the general principles of emergency care for patients with common medical complaints.
- Demonstrate appropriate assessment and management of common medical complaints.

Medical Emergencies

- Describe the characteristics of common medical emergencies.
- Describe the general principles of emergency care for patients with common medical emergencies.
- Demonstrate appropriate assessment and management of common medical emergencies.

Environmental Emergencies

- Describe injuries and illnesses caused by exposure to certain environmental conditions.
- Describe the emergency care measures required for cases of environmental emergencies.

- Demonstrate assessment and management of environmental emergencies.

Advanced Assessment

- Further develop assessment techniques as initially learned in the Basic Assessment segment.
- Fully assess a situation, name and describe probable injuries or illnesses, and report treatment.
- Obtain a relevant medical history from a responsive patient.
- Properly prioritize treatment of multiple injuries and/or multiple-patient situations.

Extrication and Transportation

- Describe techniques for obtaining access to, extricating, transferring, packaging, and transporting patients who may be found in remote areas, unstable positions, and/or awkward positions.
- Align an injured person into a supine neutral position.
- Perform emergency and non-emergency patient moves, lifts, and carries.
- Demonstrate an ability to appropriately extricate or move an injured person from a difficult or confining location.

Ski Injuries

- Describe basic types of ski accidents and common injuries resulting from each type.
- Describe the safety aspects of modern alpine (ski/snowboard) and nordic ski equipment.
- Describe ways of increasing ski capability and preventing accidents.
- Describe the correct way to approach an incident scene with a rescue toboggan.
- Demonstrate the appropriate way to load and secure an injured patient in a toboggan.

Triage

- Explain the purpose and use of the triage process.
- Apply the four color-coded categories to a multiple-casualty incident.
- Apply the proper sequence of emergency care for a single patient with multiple injuries.

Other Situations Requiring Emergency Care

- Describe the causes of and the general emergency care for illness and injuries from poisoning through ingestion, inhalation, injection, or absorption.
- Describe the causes of and general emergency care for illness and injuries from contact with hazardous plants and animals.
- Describe the dangers of and typical injuries associated with water-sport recreation activities and the proper emergency care for submersion injuries.
- Describe the proper handling and care of a newborn and mother before, during, and after a normal out-of-hospital childbirth.
- Explain and demonstrate the local procedures for handling illness and injuries that are not typical of the winter environment.

Evaluation Component

For the final practical evaluation, which counts for 60 percent of the final evaluation, each OEC trainee must assume the leadership role in two application-level, realistic patrol environment scenarios performed on the snow if possible. Skill performance guidelines, published in the *OEC Study Book*, serve as checklists for evaluation purposes. Scenarios are designed to help the instructor of record evaluate the skills of two or three students working together after an initial assessment by one individual. The following skills *must* be incorporated into the scenarios.

- Patient assessment (primary and secondary) and vital signs
- Airway management with oxygen equipment
- Management of bleeding and bandaging
- Management of upper- and lower-extremity fractures
- Spinal immobilization
- Lifting and transport techniques, including moving a patient into a toboggan
- Medical and environmental emergencies

The final written exam consists of 100 questions that check student comprehension. The final exam counts for no more than 40 percent of the total evaluation score required to pass the OEC course.

OEC Refresher

The annual Outdoor Emergency Care refresher reviews one-third of the material covered in the complete course; over a three-year period, the entire course is reviewed. The annual refresher topics are featured in the *Refresher Study Guide*, which is distributed to all NSP members in the summer issue of *Ski Patrol Magazine*. The *Refresher Study Guide* also provides material to help patrollers prepare for fall refresher training. It includes new information that relates to the OEC course, new emergency care techniques, sample skill sheets, and an open-book pre-test. Additional planning materials are published in the *OEC Instructor's Bulletin,* which is mailed to OEC instructors each summer.

Each year's OEC refresher is designed to

- provide NSP members with OEC continuing education, the opportunity to review OEC content, and access to updated EMS and medical information and techniques;

- require patrollers to demonstrate competency in selected OEC skills; and
- provide patrollers emergency medical training in a winter, patrol-like setting.

Refreshers provide a means for patrollers to meet these objectives by allowing them to

- annually review a different third of the OEC curriculum;
- annually refresh a set of OEC *core* topics;
- demonstrate competency or receive remedial training in one-third of the OEC skill performance guidelines; and
- meet local needs for reviewing techniques, subjects, protocols, and equipment use.

While there are no stated time requirements for completing an OEC refresher, generally any successful program that meets the above objectives will take most of a day to accomplish. Patrollers who merely demonstrate several skills in an assembly-line checkout are missing out on at least two of the refresher's principle objectives.

CPR Refresher

NSP members are required to recertify their professional-rescuer CPR credentials each year by following guidelines set forth in the American Heart Association's *Basic Life Support for the Professional Rescuer*, the American Red Cross's *Basic Life Support for Health Care Providers,* or the National Safety Council's *Cardiopulmonary Resuscitation and First Aid for Choking*. Even if recertification is not necessary for the credentialing agency, NSP still requires that all members refresh their professional-rescuer CPR skills annually.

OEC Continuing Education

The purpose of continuing education within the NSP is to help members maintain the quality of their patrol knowledge and skills. In turn, competent patrollers benefit the ski industry and outdoor recreation community at large. At a patrol level, it is extremely important to implement systematic on-hill reviews and gauge the medical effectiveness of patroller contact with patients. To accomplish this portion of continuing education on a regular basis each patrol must follow these six steps.

1. Evaluate the treatment provided by reviewing accident reports and soliciting feedback from hospitals, physicians, and patients. Within this scope of this evaluation the patrol should do the following.
   - Determine if the response and operations process was acceptable.
   - Identify any problems or system failures (e.g., with patients, patrollers, the process, or equipment).
   - Identify issues that can be resolved with additional training (i.e., continuing education).
2. Re-educate the patrollers with regard to the performance expected of them. To this end, the patrol can do the following.
   - Conduct consistent debriefing of accidents by a person assigned that responsibility at the patrol level (e.g., OEC instructor, medical advisor, or risk manager).
   - Monitor continuing education.
3. Strive to improve the patrol's emergency care system.
4. Re-evaluate the process following re-education and improvements.
5. Review refresher program content.
6. Recommend to the OEC Program Administrative Committee (OECPAC) any program needs,

content changes, and additional education tools required (based on actual use of OEC at an area).

Outdoor First Care

Outdoor First Care is a emergency care training program designed for ski area personnel and anyone else who works or plays in the outdoor environment who may encounter medical emergencies before the ski patrol or other response team arrives. Based on Outdoor Emergency Care concepts, this course introduces basic assessment skills to help a first-care-trained individual determine appropriate support for patients with life-threatening illness or injury. Personal protection and infection control procedures are emphasized in accordance with universal precautions.

In addition to providing an extra safety measure for recreationists, another benefit of Outdoor First Care is that it promotes strong working relationships between ski area management (or the all-season recreational area) and its employees. Moreover, ski areas and other agencies that train personnel in Outdoor First Care send a signal to the general public that the safety and welfare of guests is a priority at that area. The course is designed to be flexible enough to fit into any ski/recreation area's training schedule.

People who benefit most from completing an Outdoor First Care course are ski area personnel, e.g., ski school instructors, food service personnel, skier service providers (other than ski patrollers), children's day-care employees, maintenance workers, lift operators, snowmaking crews, and security personnel. The course is also appropriate for ski and little league coaches, summer area employees, mountain bike park hosts and ambassadors, outdoor enthusiasts, camp counselors, and outdoor day-trip leaders.

Prerequisites

- None

Time Commitment

- Six to eight hours (The course is skill-oriented and performance-driven. It does not depend on exact time requirements.)

Fees

- National—$5
- Local—varies
- Cost of materials

Credential

- OFC Card (valid for three years)

Continuing Education/ Refresher

- None

Instructor of Record

- NSP OEC instructor
- Emergency care/first aid instructors credentialed by a recognized agency

Required Text

- *Outdoor First Care,* National Ski Patrol, 1994
- For OFC instructors: *Outdoor First Care Instructor's Guide,* National Ski Patrol, 1994

Course Objectives

The participants must demonstrate the following knowledge and abilities as they pertain to Outdoor First Care.
- Describe universal precautions and demonstrate personal protection procedures to minimize exposure to blood-borne pathogens while providing first care.
- Control an incident scene, call for the appropriate help (trained emergency care responder or team), and be able to assist any emergency care responders who arrive on the scene.
- Recognize the mechanisms of injury.
- Perform a brief patient assessment (primary and cursory secondary survey).
- Perform basic life support, rescue breathing, and cardiopulmonary resuscitation (CPR), as necessary.
- Demonstrate taking the radial pulse and carotid pulse; list vital signs and diagnostic signs; and document changes in these signs.
- Control external bleeding.
- Recognize and provide first care for shock.
- Explain the principles of bandaging and splinting.
- Recognize and provide first care for common medical problems.
- Recognize and provide first care for environmental problems.

During the final evaluation section of the course, students must demonstrate each objective in a hands-on summary exercise.

CPR Certification

Cardiopulmonary resuscitation training—one-person adult, obstructed airway, responsive and unresponsive—and certification is recommended but optional with the Outdoor First Care course. If taught, the program must use American Red Cross, American Heart Association, National Safety Council, or other nationally-recognized CPR guidelines.

NSP's Senior Program is tailor-made for members who aspire to perform at the upper levels of skiing/snowboarding, emergency care proficiency, and other skills used while patrolling. The Senior Program is designed to provide a forum in which patrollers can enhance personal skiing/snowboarding and toboggan-handling proficiency, improve their ability to manage OEC-related problems, and expand their overall patrolling knowledge and skills. In addition, the program prepares patrollers for leadership roles within the NSP.

The Senior Program consists of core and elective requirements that must be completed within three years. It is designed for alpine, nordic, and auxiliary patrollers with appropriate variations in requirements for each.

Training is an essential part of the program. Senior candidates are expected to spend a significant amount of time reviewing senior criteria and using the required knowledge and skills to practice scenarios on challenging, senior-level terrain under various conditions in the patrolling environment. Senior candidates can also take advantage of clinics in which they receive constructive and corrective feedback on their performance.

Training varies throughout the system, depending on the resources of time, personnel, locations, equipment, etc., but its purpose is the same in all divisions: to provide suggestions for improvement, an understanding of the required level of performance, and increased awareness of advanced patroller skills. It is unrealistic and inadvisable to participate in any evaluation clinic and expect to pass without training.

Appendices E—H include study and training exercises for alpine, nordic, OEC, and auxiliary components of the Senior Program as well as application forms. Performance on key maneuvers and scenarios are scored by senior examiners, and these evaluations may either be conducted during a clinic held immediately after a training session for a particular skiing/snowboarding technique, toboggan maneuver, or OEC scenario, *or* at the end of the evaluation clinic process. Some divisions hold formal evaluation clinics to determine whether a senior candidate is able to fulfill the senior requirements.

Senior candidates are responsible for keeping their own records of completing core and elective requirements. Authorized instructors or region/division supervisors then verify the completion of core and elective modules and send course records to the national office. It is the patrol director's responsibility to submit to the national office a change of classification form when a member has completed all the senior requirements. Personnel at the national office then verify the request for a classification change against instructor course records.

Senior *auxiliary patrollers* may achieve senior *patroller* status by successfully completing the ski/snowboard and toboggan components of the Senior Program and all elective requirements. In other words, basic ski/snowboard patrollers are not eligible to achieve the senior patroller classification by way of the Senior Auxiliary Program.

Senior patrollers who wish to reregister as auxiliary patrollers will forfeit their senior ski/snowboard patroller classification. To become a senior auxiliary patroller, these individuals must complete the senior auxiliary core requirements and all elective requirements. Achievement of the senior auxiliary classification qualifies a person for a Leadership Commendation Appointment but does not qualify a person for a National Appointment.

Changes instituted in the Senior Program in 1992 have necessitated a few grandfather provisions. Alpine seniors who completed all the existing division senior requirements by June 30, 1992, are grandfathered into the new Senior Program. To maintain their senior status, all grandfathered seniors must participate in a skiing/snowboarding and toboggan-handling skill review in a division-authorized continuing education clinic (i.e., a skiing/snowboarding and toboggan-handling refresher on a senior-rated hill) by May 1, 1997.

Nordic and auxiliary seniors who completed the existing division senior requirements by June 30, 1993, are grandfathered into the Senior Programs for those disciplines. All nordic and auxiliary seniors must participate in a senior continuing education review meeting criteria for those disciplines (i.e., refresher) by May 1, 1998.

Senior Certification

Prerequisites

- NSP membership status—patroller (alpine and nordic)
- Patrol director's recommendation
- Senior Candidate Application (See form in appendix J.)

Time Commitment

- Each core component includes local and division training clinics
- Evaluation clinics—time commitment varies by division

Fees

National—none
Division—varies
Cost of materials

Credential

- NSP Certificate of Achievement (distributed by the instructor for each component)

Continuing Education/ Refresher

- Varies with component. (A patroller who does not complete the continuing education requirements for alpine ski and toboggan must retake those core components to regain senior status. The Senior OEC component need only be completed one time, but as part of membership requirements OEC is refreshed on an annual basis.)
- Completion of an on-the-hill/trail refresher at the senior-performance level on a senior-rated hill once every three years. Senior alpine and nordic skiing/snowboarding and toboggan-handling skills recertification (administered within the division).

Instructor of Record

- NSP division-trained senior instructors
- Division-trained senior evaluators

Required Text

- *The Ski Patroller's Manual,* National Ski Patrol, 14th edition

Senior Program Requirements

The following tables (18.1—18.3) list the core and elective requirements to become a senior alpine patroller, senior nordic patroller, and senior auxiliary patroller, respectively. Also listed are the requirements for maintaining senior status.

A senior candidate need only complete the senior OEC component one time. In other words, a candidate who completes the OEC component

Table 18.1 Senior Alpine (Ski/Snowboard) Patrollers

Core and Elective Requirements	Recertification
Alpine skiing/snowboarding	Continuing education review once every three years
Toboggan handling	Continuing education review once every three years
Senior OEC	Satisfied by completing annual OEC refreshers
Three electives from the senior elective list	Not required to maintain senior status

Table 18.2 Senior Nordic Patrollers

Core and Elective Requirements	Recertification
Nordic skiing	Continuing education review once every three years
Toboggan transport and belay	Continuing education review once every three years
Extended nordic ski tour	Continuing education review once every three years
Senior OEC	Satisfied by completing annual OEC refreshers
Advanced Mountaineering Course	Not required to maintain senior status
Two additional electives from the senior elective list	Not required to maintain senior status

Table 18.3 Senior Auxiliary Patrollers

Core and Elective Requirements	Recertification
Patroller Enrichment Seminar	Continuing education review once every three years (satisfied by fulfilling one of the following requirements): • Hold a leadership position. • Complete an additional senior elective. • Complete a special project (approved and documented by division leadership supervisor). • Retake PES.
One education course or one leadership course from the senior elective list	Not required to maintain senior status
Senior OEC	Satisfied by completing annual OEC refreshers
Three additional electives from the senior elective list	Not required to maintain senior status

but does not complete the skiing/ snowboarding or toboggan-handling component need not repeat the OEC component in the next effort to achieve senior certification.

In contrast, a candidate who completes the skiing component, for example, but does not complete the toboggan-handling and OEC components must retake all three in his or her next effort to achieve senior certification. Furthermore, a senior auxiliary patroller need not complete the senior OEC component when attempting to earn senior patroller certification.

Senior Electives

Each division has the option to require one of the following electives of its members. These electives represent the approved education* and leadership** credentials.

- Instructor Development: Phase I*
- Phase II Instructor Development courses* (all modules required for a specific discipline)
- Basic Mountaineering*
- Advanced Mountaineering*
- Basic Avalanche*
- Advanced Avalanche*
- National Avalanche School (classroom and field sessions)
- Powderfall* (with documented attendance)
- Patroller Enrichment Seminar**
- Professional Ski Instructors of America (PSIA) full certification (Level III)**
- NSP Instructor Certification (any discipline)**
- NSP Instructor Trainer Appointment (any discipline)**
- American Heart Association Basic Life Support CPR instructor or instructor trainer** (documentation required)
- American Red Cross BLS CPR instructor or instructor trainer** (documentation required)
- Equivalent education programs or division-option elective (submitted in advance through an NSP

board-approved application process with review by the National Education Committee)

Disciplines include Alpine Toboggan, Avalanche, Instructor Development, Mountaineering, Nordic, Outdoor Emergency Care, and Patroller Enrichment Seminar.

Senior Core Component: Alpine Skiing/ Snowboarding

The senior alpine skiing/snowboarding component is a national education program that allows patrollers to participate in skiing/snowboarding exercises that require edging, weight transfer, and upper and lower body movements.

The emphasis in the skiing/snowboarding component is to help the senior candidate identify and practice skiing/snowboarding fundamentals related to patrolling in a variety of conditions and on a variety of terrain. Moreover, this component enables the evaluation of the senior candidate's ability to perform specific skiing/ snowboarding maneuvers while incorporating good skiing/snowboarding fundamentals under specified conditions and on specified terrain.

Prerequisites

- Training clinics (local, region, division)
- Warm-up exercises before the evaluation clinic

Recommended References

- Alpine Exercises (appendix E)
- PSIA American Teaching System materials:
    PSIA Alpine Manual
    PSIA Alpine Handbook
    PSIA Alpine References video
    The American Teaching System: Snowboard Skiing
    Snowboarding Images video

General Terrain Requirements

To host senior alpine training and evaluation activities, an area should have a slope that averages 40 percent grade (22 degrees) for at least 800 feet. Senior training and evaluation clinics may be on a shorter slope if it is steeper and if the hill is configured in such a way that many repetitions are reasonably possible. Terrain should be both smooth and moguled. (Moguls may be unexpectedly unavailable because of last-minute grooming, snowfall, etc., but every effort must be made to select ski areas that meet terrain requirements under normal operating conditions.)

In the demonstration and evaluation criteria, terrain is described as "easy," "difficult," and "more difficult" to correspond with the terminology used at most ski areas.

Course Objectives

The skiing/snowboarding portion of the Senior Program consists of training clinics and evaluation on the following turn variations on varied terrain. In the following descriptions, specifications for the size of long-, medium-, and short-radius turns are *approximations*. Rather than focus on these specifications, the candidate should concentrate on the rounded or elliptical shape and comparative size of each turn. Variations in these descriptions will be necessary for the snowboarder to accomplish the course objectives.

Long-Radius Turns

Long-radius turns have an arc of more than 40 feet long and a cord length (the length straight down the fall line) of more than 30 feet. Long-radius turns emphasize lateral movements and balance over the whole foot. Fine adjustments in the feet and ankles and gross adjustments in the

Scott Markewitz

- An appearance of ease and control
- Turns that are long, connected arcs, rather than short arcs connected by traverses
- A quiet upper body

Medium-Radius Turns

The arc of a medium-radius turn is approximately 40 feet long and the cord is about 30 feet long. When initiating the turn, the skier's upper body faces the center of the arc of the turn. He or she then projects the body downhill toward the center of the turn by extending (rising up on and straightening) the outside leg, pushing the knees and hips toward the center of the turn, and using rotary movements to guide the ski tips across the fall line. To complete the turn, the skier flexes to pressure the inside edge of the outside ski with the weight centered on that ski. The completion should lead smoothly to the next turn without a traverse in between. Maintaining consistent, rounded, carved turns while absorbing moguls requires excellent edging, pressuring, and balancing skills.

For the following segments of the clinics and evaluations, medium-radius turns should be performed on the terrain indicated.

- Demonstration and practice: smooth terrain on easier slopes; smooth and moguled terrain on more difficult slopes
- Evaluation: smooth and moguled terrain on more difficult slopes

Performance Objectives for Medium-Radius Turns

When performing medium-radius turns, the candidate must demonstrate the following.

- Turns with consistent size and rounded shape
- Parallel turns
- Consistent, controlled speed
- Weight transfer to the outside ski or snowboard heel or toe

knees and legs improve gliding. Positive edge engagement is achieved during the turn to maximize the benefits from the design of the ski. Weight transfer begins with edge release, and weight increases over the outside ski, or snowboard heel or toe, with edge engagement.

For the following segments of the clinics and evaluations, long-radius turns should be performed on the terrain indicated.

- Demonstration and practice: smooth terrain on easy to more difficult slopes
- Evaluation: smooth terrain on more difficult slopes

Performance Objectives for Long-Radius Turns

When performing long-radius turns, the candidate must demonstrate the following.

- Turns with consistent size and rounded shape
- Parallel turns
- Consistent, controlled speed
- An ability to carve turns (with weight centered over inside edge of the outside ski/snowboard)
- An ability to skid turns
- Balance
- Stability
- Fluid vertical motion

- Turn completion, in both carved and skidded turns
- Balance
- Stability
- Fluid vertical motion
- Turns that are connected arcs without traverses
- Smooth absorption of moguls (between turns)
- Adaptability to terrain changes

Short-Radius Turns

The arc of short-radius turns is approximately 15 to 30 feet long, and the cord is about 15 feet long. Turns should be made consistently down the fall line except when the skier/snowboarder encounters terrain irregularities or changes in pitch.

The proper short-radius turn is mostly carved with little skidding. At the initiation of the turn, the skier transfers 90 percent or more of his or her weight to the outside ski, steers both skis into the turn, and changes edges. He or she then increases the edge angle as the weighted outside ski controls the arc of the turn. The skier actively steers the inside ski as well. The upper body faces the predominant direction of travel (e.g., downhill if making fall-line turns) while the skis turn back and forth. The snowboarder needs to adjust the weight on the heel and toe edge to accomplish the same maneuver.

The turning action of the legs is separate from the upper body, and the turning rhythm is faster than in long- or medium-radius turns. When performing short-radius turns, the skier/snowboarder emphasizes consistent speed, control over change of direction, and rounded turns.

Speed control is achieved by completing the turn. The skier/snowboarder concentrates on carving through the arc of the turn rather than setting edges at the end of the turn. Rounded turn shape is achieved by the proper blending of edging, pressure control, and rotary

Scott Markewitz

movements throughout the arc of the turn. The skier/snowboarder experiments with each of these movements to vary the shape of the turn. The upper body in the short-radius turn should face down the fall line.

For the following segments of the clinics and evaluations, short-radius turns should be performed on the terrain indicated.

- Demonstration and practice: smooth terrain on more difficult slopes; smooth and moguled terrain on most difficult slopes
- Evaluation: smooth terrain on more to most difficult slopes; moguled terrain on most difficult slopes

Performance Objectives for Short-Radius Turns

When performing long-radius turns, the candidate must demonstrate the following.

- Turns with consistent size and rounded shape
- Parallel turns
- Consistent, controlled speed
- Carved turns with little skidding
- An upper body that faces downhill in fall-line turns
- Balance
- Stability
- A lower body in almost continuous motion while the upper body

remains relatively quiet
- Weight transfer to the outside ski or snowboard heel or toe
- Use of edges and pressure to complete turns
- Control over direction changes
- Adaptability to terrain changes

Unpacked Snow and Icy Conditions

Senior candidates will be expected to ski/snowboard any slope in almost any type of snow condition.

If crud, powder, or icy conditions exist only in isolated places along the slope, the instructor may place bamboo poles to create a corridor through these areas and ask the senior candidates to ski/snowboard within it. Senior candidates should be able to stop within a short distance at any time.

Turns may be short, medium, or long radius. Candidates should avoid long traverses between turns, turning continuously as they progress down the hill.

For the following segments of the clinics and evaluations, proficiency in unpacked snow or icy conditions should be demonstrated on the terrain indicated.
- Demonstration and practice: more difficult
- Evaluation: more difficult

Performance Objectives for Unpacked Snow and Icy Conditions

When skiing/snowboarding in unpacked snow and icy conditions, the candidate must demonstrate the following.
- Balance
- Stability
- Control
- Rounded, linked parallel turns
- Moderate, constant, safe speed for his or her ability level
- An appearance of ease and confidence

Equipment Carry

Patrollers are often asked to carry equipment on the ski hill. Due to logistics and liability, inclusion of this maneuver during the senior clinic should be limited to asking the senior candidates to transport items routinely carried during patrol duty, such as toboggan packs, skis, and poles. The senior candidates may select the position to carry the equipment.

Alternatively, instructors should consider asking the senior candidates to carry their ski poles over their shoulders or in front of them.

Instructors should not ask senior candidates to carry extremely heavy or cumbersome loads. On steep, moguled terrain, the equipment carry may involve some sideslipping or stem turns.

For the following segments of the clinics and evaluations, equipment carries should be performed on the terrain indicated.
- Demonstration and practice: more to most difficult slopes
- Evaluation: more to most difficult slopes

Performance Objectives for Equipment Carry

When performing equipment carries, the candidate must demonstrate the following.
- Balance
- Stability
- Control
- Rounded, parallel, linked turns*
- Consistent, moderate speed
- Some sideslipping on steep or moguled terrain
- Equipment securely held

*These turns may be less polished than in the free-skiing/snowboarding portion of the clinic, but the senior candidates should continue to exhibit sound skiing/snowboarding fundamentals.

Evaluation

The senior candidate must pass each of the five evaluated performance objectives (short-, medium-, and long-radius turns, unpacked snow and icy conditions, and equipment carry) to successfully complete the skiing/snowboarding component of the Senior Program. The following is a general definition for evaluating alpine skiing/snowboarding in each category on the score sheet.

Above Senior Level (+)
The senior candidate demonstrates outstanding skill, ability, and technique in skiing/snowboarding (as measured by the program's performance objectives, using the applicable criteria). The senior candidate consistently demonstrates exceptional stability and control in difficult terrain and snow conditions. He or she makes efficient and effective use of equipment and skiing/snowboarding technique to produce a fast, safe, smooth, and consistent run. The senior candidate displays confidence in adapting his or her skiing/snowboarding skills to varying terrain and conditions.

At Senior Level (=)
The senior candidate demonstrates the ability to ski/snowboard in a safe and efficient manner using an effective combination of skill, ability, and technique (as measured by the program's performance objectives, using the applicable criteria). The senior candidate demonstrates better-than-average stability and control in all terrain and snow conditions, producing a safe, smooth, and consistent run.

Below Senior Level (-)
The senior candidate is inconsistent in meeting the minimal skiing/snowboarding requirements (as measured by the program's performance objectives, using the applicable criteria). The candidate

makes critical or frequent errors in speed, control, stability, route selection, communication, or equipment usage. The senior candidate performs skills at a level below that expected of a senior patroller.

Continuing Education

The skiing/snowboarding portion of the senior continuing education program consists of both clinic training and evaluation in the following five maneuvers on varied terrain:

1. Long-radius turns
2. Medium-radius turns
3. Short-radius turns
4. Skiing/snowboarding in unpacked snow and icy conditions
5. Equipment carry

To qualify for senior continuing education, the skiing/snowboarding review must be conducted by a qualified instructor and contain instructional components followed by evaluation and direct feedback that correspond to senior skiing/snowboarding guidelines. It is preferable but not mandatory to run the continuing education session on a senior-rated hill. The continuing education session may be sponsored by one or more patrols, or by a section, region, or division of the NSP. Continuing education may be conducted for groups or on an individual basis.

Senior Core Component: Alpine Toboggan Handling

Good toboggan handling is closely tied to good skiing/snowboarding technique. The senior alpine toboggan-handling component covers the mechanics and components of various rescue toboggans. It also addresses the fundamental principles for operating loaded and unloaded toboggans from the front and rear positions in a variety of conditions and on slopes with different degrees of difficulty.

Toboggan-handling criteria vary with the wide range of equipment used across the country and the differences between alpine and nordic techniques. However, the focus is on improving the patroller's ability to safely, smoothly, and efficiently bring an ill or injured skier down the hill in a controlled toboggan run. Instructors should incorporate into their training sessions strategies for approaching and managing incident sites.

Prerequisites

- Training sessions (local, region, division)
- Warm-up exercises before evaluation clinic

Recommended References

- Alpine Exercises (appendix E)
- *Ski and Toboggan Training Manual*, National Ski Patrol, 1994

General Terrain Requirements

To host senior alpine toboggan-handling training and evaluation activities, an area should have a slope that averages 40 percent grade (22 degrees) for at least 800 feet. Senior training and evaluation clinics may be held on a shorter slope if it is steeper and if the hill is configured in such a way that many repetitions are reasonably possible. Terrain should provide both smooth and moguled terrain as specified in the skiing/snowboarding and toboggan-handling clinic sections. (Moguls may be unexpectedly unavailable because of last-minute grooming, snowfall, etc., but every effort must be made to select ski areas that meet terrain requirements under normal operating conditions.)

In the demonstration and evaluation criteria, terrain is described as "easy," "difficult," and "more difficult" to correspond with the terminology used at most ski areas.

Course Objectives

The toboggan-handling portion of the Senior Program consists of training and evaluation clinics (held on varied terrain) on three main skills: operating the front of an unloaded toboggan, operating the front of a loaded toboggan, and operating the rear of a loaded toboggan. Strategies for

approaching and managing an incident site are also part of the program.

If a senior candidate wants to use a particular type of toboggan for the clinic/evaluation, it is the candidate's responsibility to have that toboggan on the hill and available for his or her use. The candidate should coordinate this effort with the person responsible for running the clinic and evaluation. If no such effort is made, candidates will be expected to use whatever toboggan is available at the time of the clinic and evaluation.

Unloaded Toboggan—Front Operator Skills

Clinics and evaluation on unloaded toboggan operations should cover skiing to a simulated incident site (using appropriate route selection) while senior candidates perform the following skills.

- Straight running
- Short-, medium-, and long-radius turns
- Direction changes (transitions) while keeping the toboggan in the fall line
- Sideslips (fall line and falling leaf)
- Traversing left and right on more difficult terrain
- Linked, rhythmic parallel turns, smoothly executed
- Emergency stops
- Recovery techniques (at least one)

For the following segments of the clinics and evaluations, toboggan-handling maneuvers should be performed on the terrain indicated.

- Demonstration and practice: more to most difficult—smooth and moguled
- Evaluation: more to most difficult— smooth and moguled

Performance Objectives for Front Operator of an Unloaded Toboggan

When operating the front of an unloaded toboggan, the candidate must do the following.

- Select an appropriate route.
  - Pick the safest, fastest, and smoothest route possible.
  - Generally stay to the side of the run and in the fall line as the terrain dictates.
- Operate at an efficient, safe, controlled speed appropriate to the terrain and skier/snowboarder traffic, yet quickly reach the incident site.
- Perform smooth, parallel turns as needed.
- Maintain proper body position.
  - Exhibit solid skiing/snowboarding stance with balance and stability.
  - Hold the toboggan handles waist high with the hands in front of the body.
  - Do not hit the toboggan with the tails of the skis.
- Perform appropriate transitions.
  - Change the direction of the skis while keeping the toboggan in the fall line.
- Perform sideslips.
  - Maintain a consistent speed.
  - Keep the toboggan in or close to the fall line.
  - Overcome the buildup of snow, if any.
- Perform traverses (left and right).
- Ensure minimal bouncing or slipping of the toboggan.
  - Be at ease and in control over the speed and direction of the toboggan under all conditions.
- Perform emergency stops.
  - Stop the toboggan in a short distance on command while keeping the toboggan in the fall line.
- Demonstrate at least one recovery technique.

Approaching and Managing an Incident Site

Incident site approach and management is not part of the final evaluation, but candidates should nevertheless be given the opportunity to demonstrate, discuss, and practice (as time permits) incident site approach and management on varied terrain and snow conditions. Practice should include toboggan approaches and positioning (front and back), various methods of securing and anchoring toboggans, putting on handles, placing the tail rope, checking rescue package details, etc. Techniques for marking incident sites should also be included in practice time.

Loaded Toboggan—Front Operator Skills

The local ski area management or public lands administration sets the policy for operating a loaded two-handled toboggan, with or without a tail rope, although some strategies are generally left to the discretion of the patroller. Under most circumstances, two-handled toboggans are designed to be run by a single operator, with assistance at the tail rope position only when requested by the front operator.

Since the ability of a senior candidate to operate the front of a loaded toboggan in the terrain and conditions required at the senior level is an unknown until final evaluation, certain safety considerations are warranted during training and evaluation. Thus, a capable patroller should assist with the tail rope or rear handles during loaded-toboggan maneuvers.

The rear operator acts as a safety reserve with a slack rope and will only assist the front operator if the front operator requests assistance or if safety considerations make assistance necessary (or during traversing maneuvers). If the person at the rear is not competent, he or she should be replaced with someone who is, so that the front operator has a fair chance to be evaluated on his or her own skills.

The rear operator actively assists

senior candidates who choose to use a four-handled toboggan. Four-handled toboggans should be operated under standard procedures over the same terrain as two-handled toboggans. If candidates usually have access to both two- and four-handled toboggans, they may be required to be trained and evaluated on both types as the rear operator.

While descending the fall line, senior candidates should require little assistance from the tail rope operator on terrain categorized as "most difficult—smooth" and "more difficult—moguled." The toboggan generally should stay in or close to the fall line unless terrain or skier traffic dictates otherwise.

Maneuvers that require two-handled toboggans and a tail rope are referred to as "single operator with safety tail." Senior candidates may rely on the tail rope as needed for braking, stability, or traversing terrain categorized as "most difficult—moguled." The front operator must be aware of the rear operator at all times, and the two should work as a team to communicate and coordinate speed, route selection, and change of direction.

Training clinics and evaluation on operating the front of a loaded toboggan should cover the following topics.

- Route selection that is appropriate to terrain, skier traffic, and patient injury
- Fall-line maneuvers
  - Wedges
  - Transitions
  - Straight running
- Traversing left and right on more difficult and most difficult terrain
  - Candidate trains with and without active assistance from tail rope or rear operator.
  - Candidate chooses whether to use active assistance of tail rope or rear operator during evaluation.
- Braking techniques
  - Front operator
  - Chain brake and other control

surfaces of toboggan
  - Rear operator
- Maneuvering toboggan through moguls
- Crossing flat terrain
- Techniques in soft or deep snow (if available)
- Static and moving direction changes
- Communication with patient and rear operator
- Emergency stops
- Smooth starts
- Ride-smoothing techniques
  - Lifting front of toboggan
  - Lifting toboggan over terrain (This maneuver is for four-handled toboggans only.)

For the following segments of the clinics and evaluations, these toboggan-handling maneuvers should be performed on the terrain indicated.
- Demonstration, practice, and evaluation for single operator with safety tail: smooth terrain on most difficult slopes, moguled terrain on more difficult slopes
- Demonstration, practice, and evaluation for front operator with tail operator: moguled terrain on most difficult slopes

Performance Objectives for Front Operator of a Loaded Toboggan

When operating the front of a loaded toboggan, the candidate must do the following.
- Select appropriate route.
- Control speed while skiing/snowboarding safely and expediently.
- Provide a smooth, safe, and comfortable ride for the patient.
- Ski/snowboard in a balanced and stable position.
- Control descent with a wedge or sideslip.
- Control direction with turns and falling-leaf maneuver.
- Brake toboggan as needed.
- Communicate as necessary with the patient and tail rope operator.

- Perform effective wedge, sideslip, and transition maneuvers with stability and control as appropriate.
- Avoid slipping during traverses.

Loaded Toboggan—Rear Operator or Tail Rope Skills

The rear operator should be able to assist with braking and traversing the toboggan as requested by the front operator, use one or more safe belay techniques, and communicate with the patient and the front operator. In addition, the rear operator should use sound rope management and skiing/snowboarding skills, help move the toboggan across flat terrain, and be able to stop the toboggan in an emergency.

There are at least three basic methods of tail roping:
1. Holding the tail rope in the hands in front of the body
2. Using a belay across the front of the body and over the uphill thigh
3. Using a climbing belay around the waist

Each of these techniques has its advantages and disadvantages, and there are times when one is more appropriate than another. A senior-level patroller should operate the front of the loaded toboggan during the rear-operator training and evaluation portions of the Senior Program.

Training clinics and evaluation on operating the rear of a loaded toboggan should cover the following topics.
- Traversing left and right on more difficult and most difficult terrain with minimal sideways slipping of the toboggan
- Running the toboggan in the fall line while using a safe technique for the terrain
  - Active braking assistance and passive reserve
  - Wedge
  - Sideslips (fall line and falling leaf)
  - Transitions

- Moving direction changes (turning)
- Positioning
  - The rear operator's skis generally face the same direction as front operator's skis.
  - The tail rope should run down the fall line from the rear operator to the toboggan or forward over the front of the rear operator's skis/snowboard to the toboggan (not backward over the rear operator's heels or the back of his or her skis/snowboard to the toboggan).
  - The tail rope need not always be in the fall line.
- Belay techniques
  - Moving belay
    - Hands only
    - Uphill thigh
    - Climber's waist belay
  - Static belay
- Rope management
  - Using knots in rope
  - Different length of rope on different types of terrain and during moving direction changes
  - Tension versus slack as appropriate
  - Movement up and down the length of the rope
  - Handling extra rope
- Coordination with front operator
  - Communication
  - Speed
  - Obstacles
  - Direction changes
  - Active versus passive role of tail rope
- Communicating with and monitoring patient
- Techniques for crossing flat terrain
- Considerations for special snow conditions
  - Powder
  - Ice
  - Windcrust or crud
  - Heavy slush
- Emergency stops (Front operator should always remain in position with hands on toboggan handles ready to stop the toboggan if this becomes necessary.)

- Four-handled toboggan use
  - Special skill techniques for rear operator

The terrain for demonstration, practice, and evaluation should be more to most difficult—smooth and moguled.

Performance Objectives for Rear Operator of a Loaded Toboggan

When operating the rear of a loaded toboggan, the candidate must do the following.
- Traverse left and right with minimal slipping of the toboggan.
- Assist with braking as needed.
- Brake the toboggan with edge and pressure movements.
- Control speed using wedge, sideslip, and transitions.
- Make smooth and controlled turns and transitions.
- Coordinate changes of direction with the front operator.
- Generally sideslip in the same direction as the front operator.
- Maintain the rear of the toboggan in a stable position.
- Control the rope with the hand or belay position.
- Ski with stability and control.
- Adapt to terrain and condition changes.
- Monitor the condition of the patient.
- Maintain a safe distance from the toboggan.

Evaluation

The senior candidate must pass each of these three evaluated areas (operating the front of an unloaded toboggan, operating the front of a loaded toboggan, and operating the rear of a loaded toboggan) to successfully complete the toboggan component of the Senior Program. If a division has had ample opportunity to conduct pretraining in rear operation of both types of two- and four-handled

toboggans, the division can require evaluation of each. The following is a general definition for evaluating toboggan handling in each of the categories on the score sheet.

Above Senior Level (+)

The senior candidate demonstrates outstanding skill, ability, and technique in operating a toboggan (as measured by the program's performance objectives, using the applicable criteria). The candidate consistently demonstrates exceptional stability and control in difficult terrain and snow conditions. He or she makes efficient and effective use of equipment and skiing/snowboarding technique to produce a safe, smooth, expedient, and consistent run. The candidate displays confidence in adapting his or her skiing/snowboarding or toboggan-handling skills to varying terrain and conditions.

At Senior Level (=)

The senior candidate demonstrates the ability to operate a toboggan in a safe and efficient manner using an effective combination of skill, ability, and technique (as measured by the program's performance objectives, using the applicable criteria). The candidate demonstrates above-average stability and control in all terrain and snow conditions, producing a safe, smooth, and consistent run.

Below Senior Level (-)

The senior candidate is inconsistent in meeting the minimal toboggan-handling requirements (as measured by the program's performance objectives, using the applicable criteria). The candidate makes critical or frequent errors in speed, control, stability, route selection, communication, or equipment usage. The candidate fails to meet one or more critical standards for toboggan handling or performs skills at a level below that expected of a senior patroller.

Continuing Education

All seniors must complete this review once every three years to maintain senior status. It is preferable but not mandatory to run the continuing education session on a senior-rated hill. Here are the four components for continuing education reviews (refreshers) of toboggan handling.

1. Operating the front of an unloaded toboggan
2. Approaching and managing an incident site
3. Operating the front of a loaded toboggan
4. Operating the rear of a loaded toboggan

Senior Core Component: Nordic Skiing

Prerequisites

- Training clinics (local, region, division)
- Warm-up exercises before evaluation clinic
- Daypack containing equipment and materials normally used in the patrol environment

Recommended References

- Nordic Exercises (appendix F)
- *Nordic Training Manual,* National Ski Patrol, 1998
- PSIA American Teaching System materials:
    *The American Teaching System: Nordic Skiing
    ATS Nordic Handbook*

The skiing portion of the Nordic Senior Program consists of using good nordic skiing fundamentals to demonstrate effective skiing maneuvers in all varieties of terrain and conditions. Nordic skiing clinics emphasize maneuvers used in traditional, skating, and nordic downhill skiing; specifically, the diagonal stride, the double-pole with and without kick,

skate turns, uphill traverses, kick turns, the herringbone, cross-country downhill turns, step turns, the pole drag, and nordic skiing in unpacked snow and icy conditions.

During evaluation, elegant, stylistic technique is not necessary; however, the candidate is expected to demonstrate proficiency equivalent to that of a PSIA Certified Level II instructor (advanced intermediate).

Diagonal Stride and Double Pole

A clear understanding of the technical components of diagonal stride and double pole methods are necessary for a successful evaluation. The weight shift, timing, and balance required for proper rhythm and flow are essential.

For the following segments of the

clinics and evaluations, diagonal stride and double pole maneuvers should be performed on the terrain indicated.

- Demonstration, practice, and evaluation: mildly rolling, track or prepared smooth surfaces

Performance Objectives for Track or Prepared-Surface Techniques

When performing diagonal stride and double pole techniques, the candidate must demonstrate the following.

- An emphasis on correct body position
- Balancing movements
  - An ability to move from ski to ski with rhythm and flow
  - An ability to balance on gliding skis during upper-body propulsion movements
- Rotary movements
  - Active guidance of the unweighted ski to complement steering the weighted ski during the diagonal stride
  - Complementary arm/leg movements
  - Active guidance of both skis during the double pole
- Edging movements
  - An ability to maintain a flat, sliding ski
  - Use of knee/ankle control for edge angle control
- Pressure-control movements
  - Smooth, effective weight shift from ski to ski (kick)
  - Effective compression guided by abdominal muscles
  - Refined pole use and timing
  - Movement of weight to the heels during double-pole push, then toward the balls of the feet as the arms swing forward after pole push

Double Pole With Kick

The nordic senior candidate is expected to combine foot propulsion with proper double-pole technique.

For the following segments of the clinics and evaluations, double poling with a kick should be performed on the terrain indicated.

- Demonstration and practice: easier, set track, flat, or slight downhill; more difficult, rolling set track
- Evaluation: more difficult, rolling set track

Performance Objectives for Double Pole With Kick

When performing a double-pole-with-kick technique, the candidate must demonstrate the following.

- Balancing movements
  - Coordinated movement of one foot with both arms
  - Timing combined with dynamic balance
- Rotary movements
  - Active guidance of the unweighted ski to complement steering of weighted ski
- Edging movements
  - An ability to maintain flat, gliding skis
  - Use of knee/ankle control for edge angle control
- Pressure-control movements of the skis and poles
  - Smooth, effective weight shift from ski to ski (kick)
  - Effective poling due to compression guided by abdominal muscles

Skating

For the following segments of the clinics and evaluations, skating maneuvers (V-1 Skate, V-2, and V-2 Alternate) should be performed on the terrain indicated.

- Demonstration and practice: flat terrain to mild rolling trails
- Evaluation: mild rolling to more difficult trails

Performance Objectives for V-1 Skate

When performing V-1 skate techniques, the candidate must demonstrate the following.

- Balancing movements
  - Effective ski-to-ski movement that maintains glide and contributes to propulsion
- Rotary movements
  - Active foot/leg steering of the unweighted ski
  - Maintaining a "v" relation with the skis
  - Aligning the body to face the gliding ski
  - Maintaining the skis' divergent relationship; the size of the "v" depends on the skier's speed and steepness of terrain
- Edging movements
  - Edged ski to push; flat ski to glide
  - Refinement of edge angle on push ski and appropriate adjustment on glide ski
- Pressure-control movements
  - Complete weight transfer from push ski to glide ski
  - Skate push begins with the foot under the hips
  - Upper body and hips align with push ski before a smooth weight transfer, then move toward glide
  - Timing of pole plant, pull, and push becomes more refined

Performance Objectives for V-2, V-2 Alternate

When performing V-2 and V-2 Alternate skate techniques, the candidate must demonstrate the following.

- Balance movements
  - Makes effective ski-to-ski movements that maintain glide and contribute to propulsion.
  - Shows ability to maintain extended glide, balanced on one ski.
- Rotary movements
  - Aligns body to face the gliding

ski after weight transfer.
- Maintains the skis' divergent relationship, yet the size of the "v" is smaller due to gliding nature and higher speed of the maneuver.
- Edging movements
  - Maintains a flat ski during poling and recovery phases.
  - Uses fine edge-angle control to enhance the gliding nature of the maneuver.
- Pressure-control movement
  - Maintains propulsion by poling, effective pole push, and upper body compression.
  - Begins poling before skating.
  - Prepares body for compression with forward lean of body before pole plant.

Skate Turns

For the following segments of the clinics and evaluations, skate turns should be performed on set nordic track on the terrain indicated.
- Demonstration and practice: easier, flat or gentle downhill, groomed trail; moderate, gentle downhill groomed trail
- Evaluation: moderate, gentle downhill groomed trail

Performance Objectives for Skate Turns

When performing skate turns, the candidate must demonstrate the following.
- Powerful extension of the leg from a firm platform
- An edged ski for the push; a flat ski for the glide
- Simultaneous use of both poles with each skating motion
- Timing—weight is transferred to the divergent ski as the extension of the pushing leg is complete
- Rhythm achieved by smooth, sequential motion
- Marked acceleration out of turn

Uphill Traverse

The uphill traverse is an important maneuver for travel on and off track. This maneuver should be practiced and evaluated during the extended ski tour. For the following segments of the clinics and evaluations, the uphill traverse should be performed on slopes with the terrain indicated.
- Demonstration and practice: more difficult, open moderate slopes (30 to 45 percent grade); most difficult, moderate slopes with obstacles
- Evaluation: most difficult, moderate slopes with obstacles

Performance Objectives for Uphill Traverse

When performing uphill traverses, the candidate must demonstrate the following.
- Definite weight transfer at push-off to front ski
- Shortened stride and arm swing as pitch increases
- Forward body lean, eyes looking forward
- Proper rhythm, position, and recovery of poles
- Effective use of terrain

Kick Turns

A kick turn is a stationary turn of 180 degrees for the purpose of changing direction when other techniques are undesirable or ineffective. It is often executed in confined areas such as woods. Practice and evaluation should take place during the extended ski tour while performing an uphill climbing traverse and a downhill traverse. For the following segments of the clinics and evaluations, kick turns should be performed on slopes with the terrain indicated.
- Demonstration and practice: easier, open gentle slopes (less than 30 percent grade); more difficult, moderate slopes with obstacles

- Evaluation: more difficult, moderate slopes with obstacles

Performance Objectives for Kick Turns

When performing kick turns, the candidate must demonstrate the following.
- Balance with effective use of poles
- The tail of the ski clearing the snow
- The tail of the ski planted well forward
- The poles clear of the skis
- Complete change of direction while remaining in the same spot

Herringbone

Demonstration of this maneuver should occur on a section of flat groomed track with a gentle uphill grade (5 percent). Practice and evaluation should occur on a slope with a more moderate to steep section of flat groomed terrain (8 to 10 percent) to clearly demonstrate strong edge set. For the following segments of the clinics and evaluations, herringbone maneuvers should be performed on groomed, nordic tracks with the terrain indicated.
- Demonstration and practice: easier, gentle uphill set track; more difficult, moderate uphill set track
- Evaluation: more difficult, moderate uphill set track

Performance Objectives for Herringbone

When performing the herringbone, the candidate must demonstrate the following.
- "V" stance sufficient to maintain forward motion
- Weight on inside edge of holding ski with knees and ankle flexed
- Diagonal poling technique with poles planted well behind and out to the side

- A quick ankle, knee, and hip extension to help maintain uphill momentum
- Head up, body committed forward

Cross-Country Downhill Turns

The purpose of performing advanced cross-country downhill techniques is to refine turning skills, rhythmically link turns on open slopes, and employ a variety of techniques that are dictated by snow conditions and terrain. Skiing control and stability are necessary to ski safely and rapidly to an incident scene.

Accepted cross-country downhill maneuvers include wedge turns (snowplow), stem turns, parallel turns (three to four linked) and telemark turns (three to four linked). For the following segments of the clinics and evaluations, cross-country downhill maneuvers should be performed on slopes with the terrain indicated.

- Demonstration and practice: easier, open, packed slope (less than 30 percent grade) more difficult, open, groomed and ungroomed slopes (30 to 45 percent grade)
- Evaluation: more difficult, open, groomed and ungroomed slopes (30 to 45 percent grade)

Performance Objectives for Cross-Country Downhill Turns

When performing cross-country downhill turns, the candidate must demonstrate the following.
- Balancing movements
  - An ability to maintain a stable, relaxed stance through a broad range of speed, terrain, and snow conditions
- Rotary movements
  - Earlier matching and active guidance of the inside leg
  - An ability to accurately steer the legs sequentially and simultaneously
  - Round turn shape with improved accuracy and control
- Edging movements
  - Smooth increase or decrease of edge angles (progressive edging)
  - Minimized braking, which encourages gliding through the turn
  - Developed timing of edge change movements
- Pressure-control movements of skis and poles
  - Smooth weight shift
  - Movement of the center of mass in the direction of the turn

Step Turns

Step turns are a moderate- to high-speed maneuver. The nordic senior candidate needs to demonstrate the ability to change direction on gradual downhill grades and in varying snow conditions.

For the following segments of the clinics and evaluations, steps turns should be performed on set track with the terrain indicated.
- Demonstration and practice: easier, set track; more difficult, rolling set track
- Evaluation: more difficult, rolling set track

Performance Objectives for Step Turns

When performing step turns, the candidate must demonstrate the following.
- Balancing movements—moving from foot to foot
- Rotary movements—development of foot/leg steering as sequential movements
- Edging movements—stepping sequentially from ski to diverging ski using enough edging on push ski to prevent sideslipping
- Pressure-control movements of skis and poles
  - Moving from foot to foot, while standing on whole foot

- Using poles for balance and propulsion

Pole Drag

The pole drag is a survival skiing technique used when terrain, obstacles, or snow conditions make other cross-country downhill skiing techniques impractical. Nordic senior candidates should be able to demonstrate control, stopping within a short distance at any time.

For the following segments of the clinics and evaluations, the pole drag should be performed on the terrain indicated.
- Demonstration, practice, and evaluation: more difficult, steep narrow trails

Performance Objectives for Pole Drag

When performing pole-drag maneuvers, the candidate must do the following.
- Remove straps to prevent injury in case the baskets catch on an obstruction; baskets drag in snow with pressure applied to poles.
- Maintain good body position (low and stable).
- Adequately control the speed of descent.

Overall Skiing—Unpacked Snow or Icy Conditions

During training clinics and evaluation, nordic senior candidates will be expected to ski any trails or slopes under most any type of snow conditions in the following terrain:
- Demonstration, practice, and evaluation: more difficult

Performance Objectives for Unpacked Snow and Icy Conditions

When skiing in unpacked snow and icy conditions, the candidate must demonstrate the following.

- Balance
- Stability
- Control
- Linked, downhill turns
- Moderate, constant, safe speed for his or her ability level
- An appearance of ease and confidence

Evaluation

The nordic senior skiing evaluation will concentrate on the skier's control, style, and ability to handle the terrain, rather than on testing basic skiing maneuvers. The group tour will allow the senior candidate to be evaluated on some of the required skills during the continuous evaluation on the tour. The following is the general definition for evaluating nordic skiing in each of the categories on the score sheet.

Above Senior Level (+)

The nordic senior candidate demonstrates outstanding skill, ability, and technique in nordic skiing (as measured by the program's performance objectives, using the applicable criteria). The senior candidate consistently demonstrates exceptional stability and control in difficult terrain and snow conditions. He or she makes efficient and effective use of equipment and skiing technique to produce a fast, safe, smooth, and consistent run. The senior candidate displays confidence in adapting nordic skiing skills to varying terrain and conditions.

At Senior Level (=)

The nordic senior candidate demonstrates the ability to ski in a safe and efficient manner using an efficient combination of skill, ability, and technique (as measured by the program's performance objectives, using the applicable criteria). The senior candidate demonstrates better-than-average stability and control in all terrain and snow conditions, to produce a

safe, smooth, and consistent run.

Below Senior Level (-)

The nordic senior candidate is inconsistent in meeting the minimal skiing requirements (as measured by the program's performance objectives, using the applicable criteria). The candidate makes occasional or frequent errors in speed, control, stability, route selection, communication, or equipment usage. The candidate fails to meet one or more critical standards for nordic skiing or performs skills at a level below that expected of a nordic senior patroller.

Senior Core Component: Extended Nordic Ski Tour

The extended nordic ski tour is the basis for evaluating senior candidates' overall nordic and mountaineering knowledge, skills, and abilities as they demonstrate their physical conditioning and orienteering, route selection, toboggan fabrication, bivouac, and subject-survival skills. Aspects of nordic skiing, toboggan transport, and belay evaluation are frequently evaluated during this tour. The extended ski tour should last four or more hours.

Prerequisites

- Training sessions (local, region, division)
- Daypack containing equipment and materials normally used in the patrol environment

General Terrain Requirements

- 1,000 feet of vertical elevation gain or 25 kilometer of trails
- Variety of trails and slopes, rated from easiest to most difficult

Course Objectives

The learner will address the cate-

gories that follow to fulfill the course objectives.

Orienteering

- Follow a compass heading over such a distance and with enough heading changes to demonstrate reasonable orienteering proficiency.
- Plot current location on a map by taking sighting on known landmarks and converting them to a location on a map.

Toboggan Fabrication

- Only use materials from a daypack and natural materials in the field to fabricate a toboggan.
- Load a person into the toboggan and transport the person 50 yards in a traverse, then 50 yards downhill. The instructor of record will evaluate the toboggan for stability, construction, and sturdiness to determine if it is adequate for long-distance evacuation.

Bivouac and Patient-Survival Skills

- Select an appropriate bivouac site for a severe winter condition as described by the instructor of record.
- Build a bivouac shelter large enough for one patroller and one "patient."
- Either build a fire or use a stove to prepare a hot drink or meal.

Performance Objectives for the Extended Nordic Ski Tour

When participating in the extended nordic ski tour, the candidate must demonstrate competency in the following.
- Skiing technique and proficiency
- Stamina
- Strength
- Rate of travel

- Proper route selection
- Map and compass proficiency
- Recognition of avalanche or other potential travel hazard
- Toboggan fabrication (sturdy after three 50-yard tests)
- Construction of emergency shelter in terms of site, size, and protection offered
- Ability to heat and provide a hot drink or meal

Evaluation

The following is a general definition for evaluating the extended ski tour in each of the categories on the score sheet.

Above Senior Level (+)

The nordic senior candidate demonstrates outstanding leadership, mountaineering skills, stamina, and adaptability throughout the extended ski tour. The candidate consistently demonstrates exceptional endurance and overall ski skills in difficult terrain and snow conditions. The candidate makes consistent reasoned decisions based on knowledge of mountaineering skills. The candidate makes efficient and effective use of equipment available in his or her patrol pack for all situations encountered. He or she demonstrates skill at securing the incident scene, managing the incident, and preparing an effective bivouac. The nordic senior candidate displays confidence in adapting to the variety of circumstances presented in the tour.

At Senior Level (=)

The nordic senior candidate demonstrates effective leadership, mountaineering skills, ability, and technique. The candidate demonstrates better-than-average endurance and overall skiing ability in most terrain and snow conditions. The candidate demonstrates knowledge of

mountaineering skills. He or she makes reasonable use of equipment available from his or her patrol pack for most situations encountered. The candidate provides a serviceable bivouac within a reasonable timeframe. The nordic senior candidate demonstrates reasonable adaptability to the circumstances presented in the extended ski tour.

Below Senior Level (-)

The nordic senior candidate is inconsistent in meeting the objectives of the extended ski tour. The candidate regularly defers leadership and decision making to others or makes occasional or frequent errors in leadership judgment, equipment use, or takes excessive time to grasp and perform skills. The nordic senior candidate fails to meet the critical standards for the extended ski tour or performs skills at a level equivalent to a basic patroller.

Senior Core Component: Nordic Toboggan Transport and Belay

The nordic senior candidate must demonstrate leadership ability when setting up and moving a nordic toboggan. Also, the candidate must demonstrate an ability to use specific equipment effectively and apply his or her knowledge of knots, routes, patient packaging techniques, and patroller safety considerations. In addition, the successful candidate must demonstrate the technical skills required to successfully evacuate a patient under any existing weather and terrain condition. He or she must also have the ability to coordinate a team to conduct a toboggan transport in a smooth, efficient, and safe manner.

The nordic senior candidate should be able to work as a team

member and provide leadership when constructing a sturdy toboggan from available materials (which may include an injured person's skis). The candidate should be able to transport the patient a considerable distance under various conditions, using appropriate moving and static belays. Items to be considered when constructing a toboggan include skis, carabiners, webbing, ropes, knots, and any other available building materials. The nordic senior candidate must demonstrate the ability to improvise in an emergency situation.

Moreover, the nordic senior candidate must consider the time and nature of the illness or injury to properly package and care for a patient. The candidate does not have to demonstrate OEC skills for specific injuries during this component. Instructors should identify the nature of the injury so the candidate can use that information to determine appropriate patient management and proper route selection.

While on the extended ski tour the nordic senior candidates may be evaluated on their ability to fabricate a toboggan (from available materials), transport a subject a significant distance, and demonstrate good belaying and patient-handling techniques.

Prerequisites

- Training clinics (local, region, division)
- Warm-up exercises before evaluation clinic
- Daypack containing equipment and materials normally used in the patrol environment

Recommended References

- Nordic Exercises (appendix F)
- *Nordic Training Manual*, National Ski Patrol, 1998
- *Mountain Travel and Rescue*, National Ski Patrol, 1995

Course Objectives

The learner will address the categories that follow to fulfill the course objectives.

Organization and Leadership of a Toboggan Transport/Belay

The candidates will work as a team to rig toboggan belay and haul ropes in such a way that when transported over varied terrain, the toboggan will not have to be re-rigged in the transitions from uphill to downhill, across a hill, or when going from wide to narrow trails, etc.

Performance Objectives for Organization and Leadership of a Toboggan Transport/Belay

When participating in the toboggan transport/belay exercise, the candidate must demonstrate the following.

- Proper selection of knots
- Proper selection of anchor(s)
- Suitable belay position
- Confidence in belay
- Ability to establish belay time through effective communication
- Successful construction of toboggan (if appropriate)
- Leadership in conducting a rescue operation
- Communication with proper authorities
- Team versus an individual approach to the exercise

Up-slope Transport and Belay of a Loaded Toboggan

Training and evaluation content will include route selection, negotiating obstacles, determining the availability of terrain anchors, and a discussion of patient injury. Other important topics to be incorporated into training and evaluation of belay setup and operation include communications, belay commands, teamwork, and effective use of assistance. Demonstration, practice, and evaluation will take place on most difficult terrain consisting of steep slopes between parallel roads or trails with obstacles.

Performance Objectives for Up-slope Transport and Belay of a Loaded Toboggan

When participating in the up-slope transport and belay exercise, the candidate must demonstrate the following.

- Appropriate route selection
- Communication with subject and team members
- Proper belay setup
- Effective operation of belay
- A smooth, safe, and comfortable ride for the patient
- Confident leadership

Down-slope Transport and Belay of a Loaded Toboggan

A portion of the down-slope transport and belay exercise should include a static-belay lowering of a loaded toboggan with the same anchor and hauling system used for the up-slope exercise. The remainder of the exercise should involve moving and moving-static belay techniques.

The terrain for demonstration, practice, and evaluation of the static belay should be on the most difficult, steep slope between parallel roads or trails with obstacles. Terrain for demonstration, practice, and evaluation of moving and moving-static belays should be on more difficult groomed and ungroomed slopes.

Performance Objectives for Downslope Transport and Belay of a Loaded Toboggan

When participating in the down-slope transport and belay exercise, the candidate must demonstrate the following.

- Appropriate route selection
- Communication with subject and team members
- Proper belay setup
- Effective operation of belay
- Speed control using wedge, sideslip, and transitions
- Traverse the slope with minimal slipping
- Coordinated movements with other team members
- Stable position of the rear of toboggan (maintained throughout the exercise)
- Control of rope with hand or belay position
- Skiing with stability and control
- Adaptability to terrain and condition changes
- A smooth, safe, and comfortable ride for the patient
- Confident leadership

On-Trail, Flatland Transport of a Loaded Toboggan

This exercise covers the leader's positioning versus that of the other operator(s), along with the leader's transition and communication with the other operator(s). Another evaluation component is the leader's and operators' attention to the patient and the patient's ride.

For the following segments of the clinics and evaluations, these toboggan-transport maneuvers should be performed on the terrain indicated.

- Demonstration and practice: easier, set track (narrow and wide trails); more difficult, rolling set track (narrow and wide trails)
- Evaluation: more difficult, rolling set track (narrow and wide trails)

Performance Objectives for On-Trail, Flatland Transport of a Loaded Toboggan

When participating in on-trail, flatland toboggan transport, the candidate must demonstrate the following.

- Appropriate positioning of the leader and other team members
- Communication with subject and team members
- A smooth, safe, and comfortable ride for the patient
- Confident leadership

Evaluation

The following are general guidelines for evaluating the nordic senior candidate's ability to construct and handle the toboggan in each of the categories on the scoring sheet.

Above Senior Level (+)

The nordic senior candidate demonstrates outstanding leadership, skill, ability, and technique in operating a nordic toboggan (as measured by the program's performance objectives, using the applicable criteria). The candidate con-sistently demonstrates exceptional stability and control in difficult terrain and snow conditions. The candidate makes efficient and effective use of equipment, belay techniques, and skiing movements to produce a safe, smooth, expedient, and consistent run. The nordic senior candidate displays confidence in adapting nordic toboggan transport, belay, and skiing skills to varying terrain and conditions.

At Senior Level (=)

The nordic senior candidate demonstrates the ability to operate a nordic toboggan in a safe and efficient manner using an efficient combination of leadership, skill, abilities, and technique (as measured by the program's performance objectives, using the applicable criteria). The candidate demonstrates better-than-average stability and control in all terrain and snow conditions, producing a safe, smooth, and consistent run.

Below Senior Level (-)

The nordic senior candidate is inconsistent in meeting the minimal nordic toboggan handling requirements (as measured by the program's performance objectives, using the applicable criteria). The candidate makes occasional or frequent errors in leadership judgment, control, stability, route selection, communication, equipment use, or takes excessive time to grasp and perform skills. The candidate fails to meet one or more critical objectives for nordic toboggan handling or performs skills at a level equivalent to a basic patroller.

Senior Core Component: Senior OEC

The senior OEC component is a national education opportunity that allows members to participate in ski patrol-relevant exercises. These exer-

cises are designed to develop and enhance the skills of decision making, problem management, and leadership as applied to the management of emergency care situations in a typical ski patrol environment. Their purpose is to build on but not duplicate the Outdoor Emergency Care Program.

Senior OEC training provides an opportunity for senior candidates to gain new and different perspectives on their own style of leadership in emergency medical situations. Division senior staffs provide scenarios for written and on-snow practice exercises. These scenarios emphasize leadership, triage, and managing multiple-injury problems.

Local training for the senior OEC program may be accomplished at the patrol, section, or region level, depending on geography, instructor availability, and other considerations. Training of senior OEC candidates should be done under conditions and on terrain similar to that which will be used for the clinic evaluations. It is recommended that training be done on snow for the benefit of the candidate.

During the clinic evaluations, the senior OEC candidates will be assigned an advocate whose primary responsibility is to observe the candidates throughout the clinic, be a mentor for the candidates, and be another set of eyes for the examiners in support of the candidates' actions.

Prerequisites

- Review basic skills (OEC and Basic Life Support CPR).

- Submit written answers to two open-ended practice scenario problems (select from appendix G).
- Create one new senior-level training scenario.
- Participate as a leader in a minimum of four practice scenarios.
- Participate in training clinics.

Recommended References

- *Outdoor Emergency Care,* National Ski Patrol, current edition
- *OEC Study Book,* National Ski Patrol, current edition

Terrain Requirements

On-hill scenarios (typical patrol emergency care situations) must be scheduled during the ski season, on the snow, and comply with requirements described in the scenario. There must be sufficient snow to accomplish all evaluation criteria. Other scenario types, i.e., non-ski run emergencies, such as those that occur in the patrol room, cafeteria, or base-area facility, must also be in their realistic settings. The evaluation clinic must be held at a ski area although the ski area does not need to be open at the time of the evaluation.

Under exceptional circumstances, an alternative location (not a ski area) may be used, but only if the division OEC supervisor has approved the location in advance. The location must meet all the requirements for a senior OEC clinic/evaluation, including terrain, skiing capabilities, scenarios, emergency care equipment, patrol toboggans, etc. If there is no snow at the time of the evaluation, the clinic/evaluation must be canceled or rescheduled.

National senior-rated scenarios will be used in all warm-up and evaluation rounds. No props, other than moulage, may be used to simulate conditions specified in a scenario. For example, a bamboo pole may not be substituted for a tree. Alpine and nordic candidates may be evaluated as a leader in no more than one non-ski run problem (e.g., incident in a patrol room, cafeteria, or base-area facility). If the scenario specifies a snow environment, the candidate being evaluated as the leader must be able to ski up to the "incident." Reasonable accommodations must be made for non-skiing senior auxiliary candidates to access all scenarios, e.g., snowmobile transport. Any equipment or helpers that are part of the scenario should be waiting out of sight of the scenario and the helpers should be able to ski up when responding to the leader's request for assistance.

Senior auxiliary candidates must be evaluated as a leader in one non-ski run problem.

Performance Objectives for Senior OEC

At each scenario, candidates are evaluated on their ability to meet the standardized performance objectives for decision making, problem management, and leadership. Each objective carries equal weight. What follows is an explanation of how the terms "decision making, problem management, and leadership" relate to expected performance.

Decision Making
- Problem assessment: The candidate approaches the incident appropriately, evaluates the situation, and determines all essential issues and safety needs.
- Patient assessment: The candidate conducts a primary survey and secondary survey, and during a "patient" interview considers the trauma and likely medical outcome.
- Appropriate prioritizing: The candidate addresses a single patient and determines whether the patient is a priority case. The candidate also assigns priority status to multiple patients and conducts triage.
- Overall safety: The candidate takes all appropriate actions to identify, protect, mark, and move patients.

Problem Management
- People resources: The candidate requests, uses, and directs available resources appropriately; keeping people involved without allowing independent actions.
- Equipment resources: The candidate requests and uses equipment appropriately and ensures that other patrollers also use equipment appropriately.
- Plan of action: The candidate manages the problem, avoids repeating actions, directs logical follow-through given the patient's condition, and allots the appropriate

amount of time for action points.
- Anticipation: The candidate plans for what may happen next, avoids common problems and duplication of services, and unnecessary movement of the patient.
- OEC skills: The candidate directs or applies appropriate OEC skills according to patient need and in accordance with OEC skill performance guidelines.
- Transportation: The candidate uses planned, supportive, and appropriate means to arrange transportation for priority cases and for others, securing an adequate number of helpers.

Leadership
- Communication with the patient, helpers, bystanders: The candidate informs the patient of what is happening, gives appropriate instructions to helpers, and directs bystanders without introducing confusion.
- Attitude: The candidate is positive, reassuring, and outgoing.
- Ability to direct: The candidate is assertive, makes independent decisions, and demonstrates an ability to use resources and provide clear direction to helpers.
- Confidence: The candidate demonstrates that he or she knows what to do and how to do it.
- Delegating: The candidate builds and uses a controlled team approach and doesn't try to do everything alone.

Course Objectives—Final Evaluation

The senior OEC candidate will demonstrate the following knowledge and abilities as they pertain to various elements of Outdoor Emergency Care.

At the end of every scenario, each evaluator will independently complete an evaluation sheet. The advocate for the senior and the two station evaluators must reach a consensus evaluation regarding the senior candidate's performance on that scenario. The point of striving for consensus is to have a well-reasoned decision to share with the candidate. Station evaluators should defer non-critical performance issues to the advocate. Since advocates have observed candidate performance throughout the entire day of warm-ups and evaluations, they must be allowed to overrule decisions concerning the candidate's *minor* errors if they believe the error was misunderstood by the examiners.

If the basic skill review and practice scenarios have been administered correctly during senior OEC training, the candidate should be able to meet all of the program objectives. If the senior candidate feels comfortable with his or her ability to deliver high-quality emergency care, the candidate's decision-making efforts will reflect that confidence.

There are several options, approved by the NSP Board, for running a final senior OEC evaluation. Each region may decide, in collaboration with the division OEC supervisor, which option will be used (see current options in the following sections or check most current edition of *NSP Policies and Procedures*).

Option A—Warm-Up Round

Senior OEC candidates will participate in group exercises at three stations of about 20 minutes each. These exercises are designed to help the senior candidates—who have been randomly assigned to the various stations—team advocates, and station instructors begin the process of building a team.

The instructor of record should allot time for positive learning opportunities, critique, feedback, and rotation to the next station. Constructive feedback should include discussion of expectations, suggestions for improvement, procedural issues, and alternative strategies for the incident. The warm-up/socialization rotations are designed to help senior candidates decrease jitters and to give each person at least one opportunity to be the primary caregiver at an incident before the evaluation rotations begin. Under no circumstances are these warm-ups to be used for evaluation purposes. Warm-ups must be done the day of the evaluation.

Option A—Evaluation Rounds

Candidates are evaluated on their ability to perform as the leader in a senior-level OEC scenario. One evaluation consists of being the leader in a multiple-injury scenario. The second evaluation as the leader in a multiple-patient (triage) scenario.

Option B—Evaluation Rounds

If this option is chosen, the evaluation is accomplished as part of the training sessions. During a series of clinics, candidates will have to successfully complete six scenarios as leader. These six scenarios must include two multiple-injury problems, two multiple-patient problems, and two bystander problems. Candidates may be evaluated by a senior OEC trainer/evaluator from their home area on only two scenarios (one each from two out of the three different categories). The other four scenarios must be evaluated by senior trainer/evaluators from other areas.

Option C—Warm-up Round

The warm-up round is identical to Option A.

Option C—Evaluation Round

Candidates are evaluated once as the leader in a multiple-patient (triage) scenario. The candidate may pass, fail, or be reevaluated, based on the decision of the senior trainer/evaluators. Reevaluations will only be given under extreme circumstances when the candidate's performance was jeopardized by a scenario-based situation, e.g., patient giving wrong vitals.

Evaluation

The following is a general definition for evaluating OEC scenarios in each of the categories on the score sheet.

Above Senior Level (+)
The senior candidate demonstrates outstanding decision-making, problem management, and leadership abilities (as measured by the program's performance objectives, using the applicable criteria). The senior candidate consistently demonstrates exceptional problem assessment, resource management, communication, and team interaction in every scenario. The patroller does an exceptional job of identifying and coordinating all actions necessary to manage the helper(s), bystander(s), and the scene to satisfy OEC skill performance objectives while ensuring the safety of the patient(s).

At Senior Level (=)
The senior candidate demonstrates above-average decision-making, problem management, and leadership abilities (as measured by the program's performance objectives, using the applicable criteria). The senior candidate demonstrates above-average problem assessment, resource management, communication, and team interaction in every scenario. The patroller identifies and coordinates all actions necessary to manage the helper(s), bystander(s), and the scene to satisfy OEC skill performance objectives while ensuring the safety of the patient(s).

Below Senior Level (-)

The senior candidate is inconsistent in meeting the minimal decision-making, problem management, and leadership abilities (as measured by the program's performance objectives, using the applicable criteria). The candidate makes critical or frequent errors in problem assessment, resource management, OEC skill performance, communication, and team interaction. The senior candidate identifies and coordinates actions necessary to manage the helper(s), bystander(s), the scene, and the patient(s) at a level below that expected of a senior patroller.

Continuing Education

To maintain senior OEC skills, patrollers must complete established annual OEC refreshers and local OEC continuing education programs. The Senior OEC Program does not require any additional training or evaluation beyond attending annual refreshers and continuing education sessions.

Senior Auxiliary Core Component: Patroller Enrichment Seminar

The Patroller Enrichment Seminar (PES) is an approved senior core component for senior auxiliary and a senior elective for alpine and nordic patrollers. It is a national education course that allows patrollers to participate in practical, relevant exercises that help enhance their patrolling experience.

PES encourages patrollers to increase their knowledge of education and leadership opportunities within the patrolling environment, to provide more effective services for area management, and to seek personal achievements as members of a national education association. This national education course—which consists of four two-hour modules—offers a goal-oriented, objective-based, interactive clinic that may be modified to address local patrolling responsibilities.

For details on the specific modules, see chapter 14 and appendix H.

PART

III

Appendices

Whenever patrollers represent themselves as members of the National Ski Patrol or wear the NSP uniform or other insignia, they are expected to display appropriate behavior that projects a positive image of themselves, their patrol, and the national organization. Conduct that adversely impacts the relationship of the NSP to area management or the ability of the NSP to fulfill its mission is an appropriate basis for evaluation of the membership status of the person who acted improperly, regardless of the time or place of the conduct. NSP may discipline its members on the basis of such conduct to the extent the association determines such conduct adversely affects the organization.

The NSP has a code of conduct that outlines the behavior generally expected of the association's members. (The code of conduct also is provided in the *NSP Policies and Procedures* manual, which contains the most recent information about the association's programs, rules, and regulations.)

The code does *not* regulate the relationship of NSP members to area management or the public lands administration. When performing patrol services on behalf of area management or the public lands administration, NSP members are agents of area management or the public lands administration and are subject to the control, direction, and discipline of area management and/or the public lands administration. In this regard, the patrol director acts as the representative of area management and/or the public lands administration. Area management and/or the agency administering public lands are free to limit, condition, revoke, or otherwise govern a member's privilege of providing services at a ski area. This authority may be exercised by an authorized representative of the area, including the patrol director.

NSP encourages local patrols to adopt standards of conduct that meet

APPENDIX

A

Code of Conduct

local patrol needs. These standards should be reviewed and approved by area management. The NSP Code of Conduct does not apply to local patrols when disciplining their members at the local level for conduct relating to the delivery of patrol services.

The code does not grant any individual any legally enforceable rights but merely sets forth general performance standards and procedural guidelines for dealing with violations of those standards.

Standards of Conduct

The standards of conduct in the code establish the behavior generally expected of NSP members. These standards are phrased in general terms. Examples of violations are listed to alert NSP members to the more commonplace kinds of disciplinary issues. However, human conduct is far from predictable. There likely will arise instances of unacceptable conduct not listed in this chapter that may be an appropriate basis for discipline. The standards, and the accompanying examples, are therefore merely indicative of the kind of conduct expected of NSP members, the violation of which is deemed detrimental to the NSP.

General Decorum

Members will display a positive attitude, good judgment, respect for the law, diplomacy, honesty, integrity, and courtesy when dealing with fellow members, patrol candidates, area employees, public lands administrators, members of other organizations, and the public. Members will main-

tain a neat, professional appearance as appropriate during NSP activities and when representing or acting on behalf of the association. Examples of violations include

- conduct unbecoming a member of the NSP that tends to bring the NSP into disrepute or discredit;
- willful submission of false or misleading information in connection with any aspect of NSP membership, training, or performance;
- cheating on NSP tests and examinations;
- interfering with or obstructing area management or the public lands administration, other than to enforce authorized and documented NSP national training standards;
- theft or destruction of property;
- an unprovoked physical attack or altercation of any kind;
- unsubstantiated criticism of the NSP, area management, public lands administration, or their respective directors, officers, staff, or members; and
- misappropriation, misuse, defalcation, or neglect of money or property owned by the NSP, an NSP subdivision, area management, or public lands administrator.

NSP Rules and Regulations

Members will follow the NSP rules and regulations as provided in the NSP bylaws, *NSP Policies and Procedures*, division policies, and the authorized directives of NSP officers and advisors. Examples of violations include

- failure to attend required meetings or training sessions without the prior knowledge and approval of the supervising officer, advisor, or instructor;
- failure to maintain NSP membership requirements;
- willful, reckless, or repeated violation of NSP rules, policies, or procedures;
- insubordination—failure to carry

out an authorized, reasonable directive or assignment issued by a supervising officer, advisor, or instructor;

- willful, reckless, or repeated violation of established safety rules, policies, and procedures;
- refusal or inability to improve performance to meet the reasonable demands of NSP membership status or classification, or any instructional, advisory, or leadership position, after notification of the need to improve and a reasonable period to make such improvement;
- unauthorized release of confidential information or records of the NSP or its subdivisions, including information generated by proceedings under the code; and
- refusal to accept or comply with sanctions imposed pursuant to the code.

Equal Opportunity

The NSP is committed to the equal opportunity of all members and prospective members. In recruitment, selection, training, utilization, advancement, awards, discipline, revocation of membership, or other actions, no member will discriminate on the basis of race, creed, color, religious belief, sex, marital status, pregnancy, age (provided the person meets the minimum age requirements of the NSP), national origin, ancestry, physical or mental handicap, veteran status, or any basis prohibited by applicable federal or state law.

This provision does not prohibit the NSP from requiring a person to meet the reasonable performance standards of NSP membership, membership status, membership classification, training programs, or any instructional, advisory, or leadership position the person occupies or seeks.

Sexual Harassment

Sexual harassment may interfere with

performance; create an intimidating, hostile, or offensive environment; or influence or tend to affect the participation, contributions, or advancement of members. Accordingly, NSP will not tolerate any form of sexual harassment within the organization.

Sexual harassment, as the term is used in the code, includes unwelcome sexual advances, verbal or physical conduct of a sexual nature, visual forms of a sexual nature (e.g., signs, posters, and the like), or requests for sexual favors, when (1) submission to such conduct is made either explicitly or implicitly a term or condition of a person's membership in NSP, (2) submission to or rejection of such conduct by a person is used as the basis for decisions affecting such a person's membership or participation or advancement in NSP, or (3) such conduct has the purpose or effect of unreasonably interfering with a person's performance as a member of NSP or creating an intimidating, hostile, or offensive membership environment.

In determining whether alleged conduct constitutes sexual harassment, the NSP will look at the record as a whole and at the totality of the circumstances, such as the nature of the sexual advances and the context in which the alleged incidents occurred.

Substance Abuse

A member must not use or be impaired by any mind-altering substances (including alcohol or illegal drugs) while participating in NSP activities, while acting on behalf of or representing the NSP, or while wearing any authorized official NSP patrol uniform. A member may use legally obtained medications while participating in NSP activities only if the medications do not impair the member's performance.

Special Arrangements for Acquisition of Equipment

From time to time, NSP members

may be invited to participate in special arrangements for the acquisition of ski or snowboard equipment or other merchandise or services. These arrangements typically require that the equipment or services be used only by NSP members, and the equipment or services may not be resold to persons other than NSP members for a certain time. The arrangements may have other restrictions.

Failure to follow the rules of any such arrangement may have serious consequences for all members and the NSP. Members will observe and follow all stipulations and conditions of any such arrangements.

Misrepresentation or Abuse of NSP Positions of Authority

NSP members and others respect and accord deference to those who occupy leadership or instructional positions within the organization. Members will not misrepresent their position or authority within the NSP. Members will not use their positions of authority within the NSP to obtain special privileges not ordinarily accorded all NSP members, unless the privilege is inherent in the position or necessary to fulfill the obligations of the position.

Misfeasance or Incompetence in NSP Positions of Authority

NSP officers, advisors, instructors, and other members in positions of authority will fulfill the qualifications, duties, and responsibilities of their respective positions as set forth in *NSP Policies and Procedures* and other NSP publications. Examples of violations include

- failure to meet or maintain qualifications or requirements for an NSP office, or for a staff, advisor, or instructor position; and
- incompetence, inefficiency, or negligence in the performance of duties as an officer, advisor, or instructor.

False Accusations of Code Violations

NSP members will not accuse another member of violating the code with knowledge that the accusation is false or with reckless disregard for the truth of the accusation. Any accusation must be based on reasonably reliable information known or made known to the person who makes the accusation.

NSP Disciplinary Procedures

The NSP Board of Directors has adopted guidelines for members to follow when addressing disciplinary issues regulating NSP membership. These procedures do not apply to local patrols when disciplining their members at the local level for conduct relating to the delivery of patrol services.

Sanctions for Violations of the Code

A member who violates the NSP Code of Conduct is subject to discipline. If, after following the procedures outlined below, the violation is confirmed, the disciplinary sanctions may include one or more of the following:
- no sanction;
- verbal reprimand of the member;
- written reprimand sent to the member and retained in the records of national and division registration records for the division in which the accused member is registered;
- direction that the member take some action reasonably calculated to cure or otherwise address the violation of the code;
- restrictions on the participation of the member in NSP programs;
- suspension from any office, advisory, instructor status, or other position with NSP for a defined period;
- removal from any office, advisory, instructor status, or other position

with NSP;
- suspension of NSP membership for a defined period, not to exceed one year;
- revocation of NSP membership.

No other sanctions are permitted.

Reporting of Code Violations

Members or others who observe conduct that violates the code should report the matter to the line officer immediately superior to the accused member.

If the accused member is an NSP instructor, and the conduct involves an NSP education or training program in which the accused member was participating as an instructor, the conduct should also be reported to the instructor trainer who supervises the accused member.

Investigation of Accusations

The line officer or instructor trainer to whom the conduct is reported should perform an expeditious investigation of the allegations. The officer or instructor trainer informs the member of the accusation and provides an opportunity for the accused member to make a response or to appear at a meeting called for the purpose of hearing the accusation and response.

Where the contemplated sanctions include suspension or revocation of NSP membership or the suspension or revocation from a position as an officer, advisor, or instructor, the officer or instructor trainer gives written notice to the affected member of the accusation at least 10 days before any sanction is imposed and before any meeting called for the purpose of hearing the accusation and response.

The notice includes a statement of the accusation, copies of any supporting documents or materials, the range of possible sanctions contemplated by the officer or trainer, and an invitation to respond in writing and to

attend the meeting for the purpose of hearing the accusation and response, setting forth the date, time, and place of the meeting. The accused member provides any written response or other documents to the officer or trainer before the meeting.

After an accusation has been made, the line officer(s) or instructor trainer handling the matter conducts the investigation in a confidential manner. The officer(s) or instructor trainer notifies only those who are authorized by the code or whose notifications are reasonably required to conduct a proper investigation. This requirement of confidentiality applies to all members of the National Ski Patrol who receive notification of the accusation during the investigation.

Once the investigation is concluded, the findings and any sanctions are communicated to the accused, and to the officers, advisors, area management representatives, and public lands administrators who need to know in order to enforce any such sanction. The same confidentiality requirement applies to any appeal of the initial decision.

Report to Area Management or Public Lands Administration

If the conduct of the accused member involves the provision of services on behalf of the ski area management or public lands administration, the line officer reports the matter to the local patrol director. The local patrol then reviews the matter pursuant to the policies of the local patrol, area management, and/or the public lands administration.

The procedures and sanctions under the code regulating NSP membership are separate from whatever procedures and sanctions may exist regulating local patrol membership.

Temporary Suspension of Membership for Serious and Continuing Violations

If the conduct appears to be a serious or continuing violation of the code, the line officer may, after consulting his or her directly superior line officer, temporarily suspend the membership of the accused member; and the instructor trainer, after consulting his or her supervisor, may temporarily suspend the instructor certification of the accused member, pending resolution of the accusation.

Unless earlier terminated, the temporary suspension expires 10 days after its imposition. A temporary suspension may be extended for a reasonable period if personally approved by the division director or national chairman. In all other cases, no sanctions are imposed before the member has an opportunity to respond to the accusation.

Finding of No Violation or Minor Violation

If the line officer or instructor trainer finds no violation of the NSP Code of Conduct, or a minor or *de minimis* violation without substantial consequence, he or she so informs the accused member and those who made the accusation. Any member (including the original complainant) aggrieved by any such decision may appeal as provided in the grievance procedures set forth in NSP Bylaws, Article Xa.

Finding of a Violation by Line Officer

If the officer finds the member in violation of the NSP Code of Conduct, the officer is authorized to impose any of the following sanctions:
- no sanction;
- verbal reprimand of the member;
- written reprimand sent to the member and retained in the

records of national and division registration records for the division in which the accused member is registered;
- direction that the member take some action reasonably calculated to cure or otherwise address the violation of the code;
- restrictions on the participation of the member in NSP programs.

The imposition of any sanction is accompanied by information concerning the member's right to appeal the officer's decision.

In addition, the line officer may recommend to the division director that the membership status of the member be revoked or suspended or that the member be removed from an office or advisory within the NSP. In any such recommendation the line officer makes a written report of his or her findings and recommendations, and forwards them, along with supporting and responding documents, to the division director.

The division director, or a committee established by the division, conducts any additional investigation deemed necessary by the division director or committee. If a committee is established, the committee makes its findings and recommendations in writing to the division director.

If the division director finds the member in violation of the NSP Code of Conduct, the division director is authorized to impose any of the sanctions except those relating to instructor certification or participation. The division director sets forth in writing his or her findings, conclusions, and the sanction, if any is imposed.

Members aggrieved by a decision of the line officer, division director, or national chairman may appeal as provided in the NSP Bylaws, Article Xa, provided the appeal is presented within 60 days of the notification to the aggrieved member. Grievance procedures and appeal deadlines are set forth in NSP Bylaws, Article Xa.

Nothing in the procedures requires a superior line officer to follow these procedures in order to discharge from office a member who serves at the prerogative of the superior line officer. A line officer is always free to discharge the officer or advisor with or without cause and without following these procedures.

Finding of a Violation by an Instructor Trainer

If the instructor trainer finds the member in violation of the rules and procedures applicable to the NSP program in which the accused member instructs, the instructor trainer is authorized to impose any of the following sanctions:
- no sanction;
- verbal reprimand of the member;
- written reprimand sent to the member and retained in the records of NSP;
- direction that the member take some action reasonably calculated to cure or otherwise address the violation of the code;
- restrictions on the participation of the instructor in teaching classes or refreshers in the program.

The imposition of any sanction is accompanied by information concerning the member's right to appeal the instructor trainer's decision. Grievance procedures and appeal deadlines are set forth in NSP Bylaws Article Xa.

In addition to any sanction listed above, the instructor trainer may recommend to his or her supervisor or division advisor that the instructor status of the member be revoked or suspended. In making such a recommendation, the instructor trainer prepares a written report of his or her findings and recommendations to the supervisor of the instructor trainer.

The supervisor is authorized to impose any of the following sanctions:
- no sanction;

- written reprimand sent to the member and retained in the records of NSP;
- direction that the member take some action reasonably calculated to cure or otherwise address the violation of the code;
- restrictions on the participation of the instructor in teaching classes or refreshers in the program;
- suspension of the member's certification as an instructor for a defined period of time;
- revocation of the member's certification as an NSP instructor.

The imposition of any sanction is accompanied by information concerning the member's right to appeal the officer's decision.

Members aggrieved by the decision of the instructor trainer may appeal to the supervisor or division advisor for the program. Members aggrieved by the decision of the supervisor or division advisor may appeal as provided in the NSP Bylaws Article Xa, provided that such appeal must be presented within 60 days of the notification to the aggrieved member.

Grievance Procedures

Any member aggrieved by a final decision made pursuant to the Code of Conduct may appeal the decision as provided in the grievance procedures set forth in NSP Bylaws Article Xa. An appeal from a decision must be in writing and must be made within 60 days after the rendition of the final decision. A member desiring to appeal a final decision must follow the procedures outlined in the NSP Bylaws.

A patroller's uniform presents a unified, positive, and professional image to the skiing and snowboarding public and is easily recognized in case of emergency. It is ski area management's prerogative to determine what uniforms its volunteer and/or paid patrollers will wear while on duty at the ski area.

If area management has a uniform code that directs area patrollers to wear the National Ski Patrol's standardized uniform, then the NSP requirements for this uniform must be met. These requirements are established by the NSP Board of Directors and are enforceable through the division, region, section, and patrol. The details for each classification (alpine, nordic, and auxiliary) are found in *NSP Policies and Procedures,* chapter 7.

All NSP members should present a neat, professional appearance to the public and area management while on duty. Members may wear their NSP patrolling uniform when traveling to and from duty at a ski area or when attending recognized ski patrol functions. Members may not wear the NSP uniform where alcoholic beverages are served unless responding to an accident.

Candidates; members registered as inactive; medical associates; alumni members; and associate or affiliate registrants may not wear the NSP standardized uniform. Candidates may not wear any type of NSP insignia, primarily because they are in training and have not yet demonstrated the knowledge and skills required of patrollers. When candidates successfully complete the required training and examinations, they may then wear the NSP standardized uniform.

The NSP Standardized Uniform

The NSP official parkas meet the association's standards for uniformity

B

Uniforms and Insignia

of color and design, and offer numerous features to help ensure the wearer's comfort. These parkas, along with other specially priced patrolling apparel and equipment, are available through the *Winter Catalog.* Specific requirements for the official uniform are provided annually in the *NSP Policies and Procedures* manual.

Parkas and Jackets

The NSP provides two types of parkas: a red parka with the NSP-approved white back cross, and a rust and blue parka with the NSP-approved gold back cross. These garments identify NSP members as qualified, registered patrollers capable of providing emergency care and rescue of ill or injured skiers and snowboarders. Parka styles offered through the *NSP Winter Catalog* periodically change based on manufacturer's current designs and availability.

At its January 1997 meeting, the NSP Board of Directors voted to abolish rust and blue as official parka colors for the National Ski Patrol as of the 2000-2001 ski season. Patrols and NSP members may continue to use rust and blue uniforms at the local level after 2000 if deemed the appropriate colors for uniforms by local area management.

Aid Belts and Packs

The NSP aid belts/packs currently available through the *NSP Winter Catalog* are the recommended aid belt/packs for NSP members. The styles vary according to the type of assigned duty.

Pants

Pants worn while patrolling should be designed for skiing or snowboarding. The recommended color for pants is navy or black. When wearing the NSP parka and while on duty, patrollers should not wear jeans or other pants that are not designed for skiing or snowboarding.

Head Gear

Any type of hat may be worn providing it is neat, practical, and projects a professional appearance.

Equipment

Skis, snowboards, boots, poles, and bindings should meet current DIN standards, be well maintained, and in good condition.

Insignia, Patches, and Other Identification

The NSP back cross, chest badge, a ski area patch, and an I.D. bar are the only items authorized to be worn on NSP parkas. (The back cross, chest badge, and I.D. bar are illustrated and available through the *NSP Winter Catalog.*) The back cross identifies patrol certification and should not be covered up by identifications from other agencies. Patrollers who have been recognized for ski patrol achievement, appointed to ski patrol office, or who have received meritorious recognition may elect to includes these insignia on their I.D. bar.

General guidelines for NSP badges and insignia on parkas are as follows: the circular badge should be on the upper left chest; the I.D. bar should be on the upper left chest, centered below the badge; the area badge, if any, should be on the upper right chest; the back cross should be centered on the back; and there should be no badges on the shoulders or arms.

The *NSP Winter Catalog* carries numerous other apparel (sweaters, wind shirts, vests, etc.) with the proper NSP insignia affixed. Any NSP member may wear these items. Pins and identifications are available for individuals who have achieved certain skill, instructional, or award status (Certified, National Appointment, Instructor, etc.).

The NSP Board of Directors recognizes the need for a united effort among the association's membership to help increase ski and snowboard safety awareness among the general public. The NSP supports safety education programs developed for outdoor recreation. All divisions should encourage their members to promote ski and other outdoor recreation safety education programs, materials, and symbols where possible.

To this end, the snow sports industry has adopted a "code" of behavior to guide skier and snowboarder conduct. This code, entitled Your Responsibility Code, is endorsed by the National Ski Areas Association (NSAA), the Professional Ski Instructors of America (PSIA), and the National Ski Patrol.

Your Responsibility Code

1. Always stay in control, and be able to stop or avoid other people or objects.
2. People ahead of you have the right of way. It is your responsibility to avoid them.
3. You must not stop where you obstruct a trail or are not visible from above.
4. Whenever starting downhill or merging into a trail, look uphill and yield to others.
5. Always use devices to help prevent runaway equipment.
6. Observe all posted signs and warnings. Keep off closed trails and out of closed areas.
7. Prior to using any lift, you must have the knowledge and ability to load, ride, and unload safely.

Know the Code. It is your responsibility. This is a partial list. Be safety conscious.

If you have trouble remembering the entire code, the following mnemonic, or memory aid, can help you recall its

components. It is easy to remember that skiing can cause cramps (spelled "CRAMPPS," in this case). Applied to Your Responsibility Code, the CRAMPPS mnemonic looks like this:

1. **Control.** Always stay in **control,** and be able to stop or avoid other people or objects.
2. **Right of Way.** People ahead of you have the **right of way.** It is your responsibility to avoid them.
3. **Above.** You must not stop where you obstruct a trail, or are not visible from **above.**
4. **Merging.** Whenever starting downhill or **merging** into a trail, look uphill and yield to others.
5. **Prevent.** Always use devices to help **prevent** runaway equipment.
6. **Posted.** Observe all **posted** signs and warnings. Keep off closed trails and out of closed areas.
7. **Safely.** Prior to using any lift, you must have the knowledge and ability to load, ride, and unload **safely.**

NSAA Education Programs

The National Ski Areas Association makes a concentrated effort each year to develop new materials and videos that concentrate on skier education. Their materials are available through the *NSAA Catalog of Videos and Publications.* NSP member areas may purchase these products at NSAA member prices by contacting the National Ski Areas Association, 133 South Van Gordon Street, Suite 300, Lakewood, CO 80228; phone (303) 987-1111; or fax (303) 986-2345.

Ski Area Ecology

A chairlift ride brings an unsurpassed opportunity to observe and enjoy splendid views and heighten awareness of the mountain ecosystem. Patrollers should take the time to become familiar with mountain features, birds and other wildlife indigenous to the region, and other items of local interest. Patrollers can help broaden the ski area guests' appreciation of the natural environment by sharing this information during lift rides with guests.

The Professional Ski Instructors of America supports NSAA programs on environmental awareness and encourages instructors to disseminate this knowledge to students. Patrols should work closely with their area's ski instructors to gather and share ski area ecology information that can be relayed to ski area visitors at appropriate opportunities.

Creating a Safety Education Program

Areas that emphasize the importance of skiing and snowboarding responsibly send a message to the public and the entire industry that safety is a priority at the area. This emphasis—generally most apparent in signage and in one-on-one interaction between employees and guests—helps remind people to ski and snowboard safely, which can contribute to a reduction in accident rates at the area and an increase in the comfort levels of the general clientele. Ski areas that effectively and consistently impart the safety message usually have safety education programs that relate to every area employee and department. Development of a such a program takes commitment and support from management and dedicated staff (paid and volunteer) who are willing to devote thought, time, and energy into organizing and overseeing the program.

Three key elements ensure the

success of such a program: the selection, training, and organization of personnel. Because the personnel involved in skier and snowboarder education maintain a high profile, selecting the right people is very important. Generally the best personality type for such a position is someone who has excellent communication skills and a positive, upbeat attitude, who believes strongly in the concept of safe skiing, and who has the maturity and attitude to handle this authority.

Training should involve discussion, films, demonstrations, and interactive and role-playing sessions. Emphasis should be on the development and encouragement of listening and communication skills. Training might also require Outdoor First Care so those people involved in the skier education program will know what to do until a ski patroller arrives if they come upon a guest who has become seriously ill or injured. Ongoing continuing education, mentoring, and evaluation should be done by the training group.

In terms of organization, the effectiveness of scheduling and work assignments is essential to a well-run safety education program. Personnel in this department must maintain close interaction and communication with other area departments—particularly ski patrol, lifts, parking, and transportation, security, base lodge maintenance, and food service. This rapport will help ensure that all area employees have the most recent information about the area's safety procedures, and in turn, will ensure that the safety education personnel receive information from other departments that may have bearing on the program.

Here are some common components of safety education programs.
- Give talks to bus groups, that is, provide safety discussions to people on shuttle buses and destination buses.

- Set up a safety table in the base lodge and distribute literature, stickers, etc. about skier and snowboarder safety.
- Review certain safety tips for guests in the lift line.
- Coordinate a theater where safety education programs can be viewed by guests, individuals who have been reported as fast and reckless on the slopes, and others.
- Publish weekly safety articles, written by patrollers, in local newspapers and mountain publications.
- Post safety display exhibits and signage in area buses, the base lodge, on lift towers, and on lift shacks.
- Work with local closed television companies that do snow sports series.
- Give safety talks to the community (e.g., schools, clubs, fund raisers).
- Send thank-you letters to guests who have offered constructive comments or expressed concerns.
- Provide puppet shows with safety themes to the children's ski school.
- Give off-mountain talks to schools, kids in day care, and young kids in ski school classes.

Any skier education program requires a great deal of research, planning, preparation, and support from ski area management and its appropriate departments. Essential content should include the following.
- Identify the area's philosophy and attitude toward a skier education program.
- Obtain statistics that support the value of a skier education program.
- Explore the mountain's additional education needs and how they can be met.
- Collect handouts, brochures, videos, etc. to start and enhance a skier education program.

Membership associations represent an important segment in today's economy. Associations represent individuals and organizations and present a forum to advance the cause of the collective group. The continually changing nature of associations affects the way the National Ski Patrol works with its membership.

One part of the NSP's mission is to establish and maintain proactive relationships with government, the snow sports industry, and related organizations. The success of the NSP in several areas is directly influenced by rules and programs that other organizations develop and publish.

The NSP generally supports and, in many cases, uses education programs that have been developed by other organizations within the snow sport industry and the outdoor recreation community at-large.

Additionally, the NSP participates as a partner in the development of other association's programs. The NSP is a recognized leader in Outdoor Emergency Care and winter rescue. NSP's expertise is sought by numerous organizations and its participation is basic to several of its partnerships.

The NSP actively participates in national standard-setting processes that impact the ski industry as well as its own education programs. These activities include participating on committees that set federal and state statutes and regulations, and developing educational curriculums and standards that impact ski area and ski patrol operations or the NSP's own education programs.

The NSP Board of Directors recognizes the need for a united effort by its members to help increase ski safety awareness and promote the integrity and use of NSP education programs among the membership and other outdoor recreation organizations and enthusiasts.

Snow Sports Industry Associations and Partnerships

It is essential that the National Ski Patrol work in close partnership with other associations in the snow sports industry. How these associations operate and interact with the NSP greatly impacts the benefits NSP members receive from the association.

National Ski Areas Association (NSAA)

The NSAA serves as the trade association for ski area owners and operators. Its mission is to stimulate and promote on-snow sports and safety, and to meet the needs of the snow sports industry.

Joint Statement of Understanding Between the National Ski Patrol and the National Ski Areas Association (Revised July 1993)

This Joint Statement of Understanding is intended to define the relative positions of general ski area management, through the auspices of the National Ski Areas Association (hereafter NSAA), and the National Ski Patrol (hereafter NSP) and its member volunteer patrols and patrollers. It is recognized that matters which may not be covered in this Joint Statement may develop from time to time in the future, and that such matters may, by mutual agreement, be the subject of a further expansion of this Joint

Statement of Understanding, if necessary and agreed upon.

It is recognized between the parties to this Joint Statement or Agreement that individual groups of volunteer patrollers may form and/or belong to a patrol organization that is itself a member of the NSP. However, any NSP member or group of patrollers performing ski patrol services at a ski area in the United States is subject to the following:

1. A patrol, once established at a given ski area, is under the supervision of the ski area management and must abide by the policies and procedures established by that management.

2. The patrol director of any NSP volunteer patrol shall, if required by area management, certify that all patrollers at that area have completed the training and educational requirements set forth by the NSP Board of Directors and have met all Outdoor Emergency Care (OEC) requirements. The NSAA encourages its member areas to require patrollers at each area to meet the current NSP training and educational criteria or their equivalent.

3. Management shall, at all times, have the right to approve the selection of the volunteer patrol director. Management shall likewise have the right to dismiss the patrol director or any patroller at any time. If requested by area management, the NSP division director shall confirm management's decision in this regard.

4. NSP and NSAA recognize the importance of educating lift evacuation participants as to appropriate lift evacuation techniques and the specific implementation details in the ski area lift evacuation plan. The establishment of necessary policies and procedures for lift evacuation, lift evacuation training, and the selection of equipment to be used in conjunction with such evacuation or

training is the sole responsibility of ski area management. Patrollers will participate in lift evacuation and lift evacuation training only as ski area management shall direct.

5. Both the NSP and ski area management agree that incident investigation and documentation is an important element of patrol activity. To that end, ski area management shall establish a procedure for accurate compilation, safe retention, authorized disclosure of, and controlled access to information and documentation relating to any incident. As such, no patroller shall make any statement regarding any incident to anyone, other than to proper authorities having rightful jurisdiction. Any such inquiry shall, in any event, and in the first instance, be referred to area management or its appointed representative.

6. It is recognized that ski area management ultimately supervises and controls many of the patrolling activities of individual NSP members and patrols at each ski area. As such, it may be asserted that the ski area bears legal responsibility for such acts of its patrollers. It is also understood and agreed that there are services provided by individual NSP members based upon their training received from NSP. To the extent that claims are made against individual ski areas relating to activities over which ski area management has ultimate supervision or control, it is agreed that the ski area should make no claim or demand or suit against NSP or its directors, officers, and employees. Likewise, to the extent that the basis for any such claim relates to areas of specialty training of individual patrollers by NSP, NSP should not make any claim against individual ski areas, regardless of any claim made against them.

7. It is specifically understood

between the parties to this Agreement that nothing herein, and nothing contained in any individual agreement between the NSP and individual ski areas based on the Joint Statement of Understanding, shall in any way vary the clear, non-employee status of individual volunteer patrollers. In fact, it is expressly understood between the NSP and the NSAA, as well as the membership of both organizations, that the volunteer patrollers are not and have not been employees, but agents when acting within the scope of their assigned duties, in view of the voluntary nature of their patrolling services.

Professional Ski Instructors of America (PSIA)

The NSP and PSIA have consolidated administrative services under the management of the same executive director. Consolidation of national office services has provided both organizations with long-term benefits through cost-savings in the delivery of membership services, expanded opportunities through improved marketing, and improved relations with area management.

Through the administrative consolidation, NSP and PSIA have strengthened their position with other organizations and have improved their ability to respond to the ever-changing demands of the mountain recreation industry.

Each organization continues to operate independently, and each board of directors reviews and approves its own budget. Likewise, the programs of both organizations continue to operate independently.

Statement of Understanding Between the National Ski Patrol and the Professional Ski Instructors of America (January 1990)

This Joint Statement of Understanding is intended to provide to the National Ski Patrol (NSP) and the Professional Ski Instructors of America (PSIA) a clear statement and understanding of the consolidation of office services agreed to by each organization and its respective board of directors. It is anticipated that, for the most part, problems will be handled and resolved among the PSIA president, the NSP national chairman, and the PSIA/NSP executive director, working through each executive committee, when appropriate. In all cases, it will be the aim and intention of each group, through its mutual interest, to provide a practical and dignified means of friendly adjustment of differences in settling any disputes between the parties.

Each party shall be free to bring matters to the attention of the other at any time without prejudicing the harmonious relationship or office operations, and the parties shall be available at all times for the proper and effective adjustment of any differences either by mail, telephone, or meeting under professional and courteous circumstances.

Agreement

Each respective board of directors has agreed that certain areas of operations will be consolidated as outlined in the proposal presented and approved by the PSIA Board of Directors in October 1989 and the NSP Board of Directors in January 1990; and, in addition

- that each organization has accepted the organizational chart with respect to the line of authority;
- that the executive director has the responsibility and authority as outlined in the attached executive

director job description;
- that each organization has accepted the budgeting flow-chart process; and
- that each organization has appointed three individuals—the national treasurer, president/national chairman, and one other member of their respective executive committees—to the Joint NSP/PSIA Review Committee to review finances. It is also agreed that the Joint Review Committee will be the body entrusted with the responsibility to resolve any impasse that might arise between the NSP national chairman, the PSIA president, and the PSIA/NSP executive director.

Dissolution

Each organization will have the right to, without cause, unilaterally terminate this agreement of national office services consolidation by providing the other organization with written notice from its respective board of directors *120 days prior* to the end of the other organization's financial year end (June 30). The date of dissolution will then be the fiscal year end. In such case, the settlement of financial involvement between the two groups will be handled by the PSIA/NSP Joint Review Committee through the respective executive committees, and their decision will be binding on each respective group. If the review committee fails to reach agreement, formal arbitration as set forth in this agreement will take place.

Arbitration

Except as otherwise provided for in this statement, a failure to reach an agreement or adjustment with regard to any differences, or to settle any dispute or claim that may arise, shall thereupon make the same a matter for arbitration, upon the written request of either party to the other. Such arbi-

tration shall be in accordance with either the commercial arbitration rules then in effect or with the American Arbitration Association.

Additions

Any additional elements which the parties may from time to time consider desirable, and which are not in conflict with the terms and conditions of this statement, or which may be amended to the terms and conditions of this statement, shall be embodied in a document entitled "Schedule C," labeled and attached as "additional items," signed by the responsible parties, and, thus, made a part of this "Statement of Understanding."

Cross Country Ski Areas Association (CCSAA)

The CCSAA is an organization that represents the business interests of the cross-country touring centers in the United States. This association promotes the advancement and development of new touring centers and the sport of cross-country skiing.

Fedération Internationale des Patrouilles de Ski (FIPS)

FIPS is an international association of ski patrol organizations. A delegation of international patrollers meets periodically to demonstrate various methods of handling common emergency care and rescue situations and to exchange information on the patrolling activities of the various patrol associations.

National Avalanche Foundation (NAF)

The National Avalanche Foundation is an education foundation dedicated to providing introductory avalanche education to ski industry and government agencies whose employees are involved with avalanches in their day-to-day work. The National Avalanche

Foundation's bylaws identify its members who serve on various committees. The NSP appoints representatives to the National Avalanche Foundation Board of Directors and its committees.

The National Avalanche School is administered by the NSP for the National Avalanche Foundation. The school is held every two years (odd-numbered years) in a location approved by the National Avalanche Foundation Board. The school is a two-part program: in the first phase, students learn about the fundamentals and concepts of avalanche control and snow physics; in the second phase, students have an opportunity for field-relevant practice and observation.

United States Skiing (U.S. Skiing)

U.S. Skiing is the national governing body for the sport of skiing in the United States. U.S. Skiing, together with the United States Ski Association (USSA) and the U.S. Ski Team Foundation (USSTF), manages all aspects of competitive skiing from junior development programs through the national and Olympic team, including programs for masters skiers and disabled skiers. These organizations also manage various recreational skiing programs.

SnowSports Industries of America (SIA)

SIA is the association representing the snow sports industry's hard-goods manufacturers. This organization coordinates an annual trade show in which the manufacturers display their products for the coming ski season. The NSP marketing and purchasing staff attend this event to determine what products are appropriate for the *NSP Winter Catalog*, negotiate purchases with the manufacturers, and finalize contractual agreements for the delivery of products to the NSP warehouse.

Canadian Ski Patrol System (CSPS)

The CSPS is a nonprofit corporation comprising highly trained volunteer and professional ski patrollers. This national organization was formed to promote safe skiing at areas throughout the Canadian provinces and to provide assistance to injured skiers. Like NSP members, CSPS members provide uniform, highly skilled patrolling services to the skiing and snowboarding public.

National Ski Retailers Association (NSRA)

The National Ski Retailers Association represents the snow sport retailers throughout the United States. The NSP and NSRA have worked diligently to develop a structured program that promotes the opportunity for members to purchase professional snow sport equipment as well as provide the desired administrative control for industry manufacturers and retailers.

National, State, and Local Government Agencies

These agencies affect the manner in which the snow sport business, ski areas, and ski patrols manage their businesses and operations.

U.S. Department of Agriculture

Many, if not most, of the ski areas in the western United States are on public land that is administered by the United States Forest Service (USFS). These ski areas operate under a special use permit issued to the area by the USFS. The Bureau of Land Management (BLM) manages other outdoor recreation land resources.

U.S. Information Agency

The NSP's Professional Division has been approved by the U.S. Information Agency to facilitate a limited number of applications for reciprocal patroller exchange visas. The agency offers J-1 visas to individuals in qualified ski patrol programs such as the National Ski Patrol for the foreseeable future. Exchange programs must have the approval of area management and an agreement should be in place with a foreign resort to exchange ski patrol personnel.

Working out all arrangements (other than the J-1 visa), including travel plans, insurance, housing, wages, a work permit for the U.S. citizen to work abroad, and other details, is the responsibility of the two participating areas. For further details on program sponsor guidelines and insurance requirements, please contact the administrative department at the NSP national office.

U.S. Department of Transportation

The National Highway Traffic Safety Administration (NHTSA) has assumed the responsibility of providing national standards within the national Emergency Medical Services (EMS) community. The overall objective is to provide a standard of training for emergency medical technicians (EMTs) who render care to victims of accidents and illnesses. NSP's Outdoor Emergency Care Program contains the same standard of training requirements derived from the U.S. Department of Transportation national EMS course curriculum.

U.S. Department of Labor

The Occupational Safety and Health Administration (OSHA) is given broad powers through the Occupational Safety and Health Act of 1970 to regulate safety practices in the workplace.

In general, the act does not directly regulate volunteers, and it does not appear that OSHA asserts jurisdiction over volunteers.

Individual state statutes and regulations, and the interpretations of them, may vary. Every employer is responsible for providing each of his or her employees a place of employment that is free from recognized hazards that are causing or are likely to cause death or serious physical harm to the employees.

Voluntary compliance with the content of OSHA regulations is the most prudent standard for NSP volunteer members. It is not the NSP's place to tell area management how to deal with OSHA federal or state regulations with respect to its patrollers, so long as no immutable national policy is implicated. It is up to area management to determine the law and make whatever provision for its patrollers is required.

Organizations That Establish Standards

The specific organizations described below establish standards that impact ski area operations.

American National Standards Institute, Inc. (ANSI)

The B77 Committee of ANSI reviews standards for aerial passenger tramways as the accredited standards committee for the American National Standards Institute, Inc. (ANSI). Ski industry lift training, operations, and evacuation must comply with ANSI standards. State tramway regulatory authorities may also impact ski area operations and patrolling.

American Society for Testing and Materials (ASTM)

The ASTM F30 Committee is an accredited standards committee that reviews standards for emergency medical services. The F32 Committee reviews standards for search and rescue.

Associated and Partnership Organizations

Following our mission to support and participate in the ski and outdoor recreation community, the National Ski Patrol participates on various committees and interacts with the organizations described below on a frequent basis.

National Mountain Bike Patrol

U.S. Cycling has an association within its organization called the National Off-Road Bicycle Association (NORBA). The National Mountain Bike Patrol is a joint program between NORBA and the International Mountain Bicycle Association (IMBA) to promote the positive image of mountain biking in the United States and to promote safe, enjoyable off-road cycling opportunities. NSP and BLM participate on a committee with NORBA and IMBA that has been established to develop consistent training guidelines for mountain bike patrols.

Mountain bike patrollers must satisfy all training requirements established by their local area, demonstrate adequate skills in mountain bike patrolling, and follow all local policies and procedures. NSP's involvement with this program is to make accessible its Outdoor Emergency Care and Outdoor First Care programs to the local bike patrols.

Outdoor Recreation Coalition of America (ORCA)

ORCA is the trade association for the human-powered outdoor recreation industry. Its members represent a wide spectrum of organizations from retailers to manufacturers and provide educational information to the media. NSP participates as a provider of emergency care training information relevant to ORCA's membership.

National Search and Rescue Association (NASAR)

NASAR is a national education association that fulfills its educational charter through training courses, curriculum development, publishing, and various outreach programs involved with search and rescue fundamentals, search management, incident command, basic water rescue, and wilderness medicine.

The NSP Board of Directors adopted a resolution providing for mutual cooperation with and support of the National Association for Search and Rescue. The NSP has a representative on NASAR's Program Advisory Board for wilderness medicine programs.

Wilderness Medical Society (WMS)

The Wilderness Medical Society is the world's largest organization devoted to wilderness medical issues. The society is traditional in its commitment to medical knowledge, education, and research, yet it is unique in its focus on wilderness environments and the challenges they present. Society members include physicians and other professionals who share medical, ecological, and recreational interest in wilderness activities.

American Red Cross, American Heart Association, National Safety Council

These associations provide consistent, reliable education and training in the prevention and control of injury and illness. Their programs are geared to many different groups, including the general public, life-guards, and search and rescue groups, among others.

Affiliate Organizations

NSP may enter into affiliation agreements with outside organizations for the purpose of allowing the outside organization to organize and teach NSP education programs on behalf of members of the outside organization. An outside organization desiring to obtain NSP educational programs for its members must submit an application in the form established by the NSP.

The application is initially considered by the NSP education department in coordination with the national program director for the NSP program(s) that the outside organization desires to access. The factors considered include the nature of the outside organization to deliver quality educational programs; the fees to be charged students for the programs; the revenue to be returned to the NSP; the use of NSP materials; the procedures to be established by the outside organization to conduct instructor recruitment, qualifications, training, orientation, maintenance, and recertification; procedures for quality assurance; the provisions for enforcing NSP training and administration standards; and the procedure for discontinuing the relationship.

Based upon this review, the NSP may enter into negotiations with the outside organization with the objective of reaching a mutually satisfactory agreement for the delivery of the desired NSP education program(s). As part of the agreement, NSP may consent to credential individual members of affiliate organizations to teach NSP education programs.

Any agreement negotiated pursuant to this section must be approved by the NSP Executive Committee before the implementation of the agreement. The Executive Committee may consider and approve or

reject the proposed agreement without holding a formal meeting.

Associate Registration

An associate is an individual who has a need or desire to participate in NSP-organized education programs and be credentialed through NSP training, receive NSP magazines, etc. There is an annual fee of $30 and any appropriate course or subunit fees. An associate may not perform any on-the-hill/trail ski patrolling duties at NSP-affiliated areas.

Initially, the person seeking the associate designation must complete a registration form and send it to the NSP national office along with the annual registration fee. In subsequent years, an associate receives an invoice to register for another year.

Each person registered in this category shall be designated as an associate; there are no patrol skill designations. The individual is not a *member* of the National Ski Patrol. He or she has no voting rights and is not considered in geographical membership counts.

An associate receives *Ski Patrol Magazine* and may purchase all catalog items except those that would identify the person as an active member of the NSP.

An associate is not eligible to receive awards or appointments that are restricted to NSP members. Also, an associate is not authorized to wear the official NSP uniform.

NSP Acronyms and Buzzwords

The following list contains numerous acronyms and buzzwords, along with their meanings, that are commonly used throughout the NSP. This is a partial list.

ADD	Assistant Division Directors
Advisors	Titles have been changed to national program directors, division supervisors, and region administrators
ANC	Assistant National Chairman
ANSI	American National Standards Institute
ARC	American Red Cross
ASTM	American Society for Testing and Materials
B77	A committee of ANSI (Committee on Standards for Aerial Passenger Tramways) dealing with lifts: equipment, evacuation, training standards
Basic M	NSP Basic Mountaineering Course
Basic A	NSP Basic Avalanche Course
BLM	Bureau of Land Management
Board Committees	
	Operations, Administration
BOD	Board of Directors
BR	Board Representative
CCSAA	Cross Country Ski Areas Association
CE	Continuing Education
Circle M	Old name for NSP Basic Mountaineering Course
Circle A	Old name for NSP Basic Avalanche Course
CPR	Cardiopulmonary Resuscitation
CSCUSA	Colorado Ski Country USA
DD	Division Director
DOD	Department of Defense
DOT	U.S. Department of Transportation
EC	Executive Committee
EMT	Emergency Medical Technician
ExCom	Executive Committee
F32	The Committee on Search and Rescue for ASTM
FCC	Federal Communications Commission
FED	Federal Equipment Distribution
FIPS	Fedération Internationale des Patrouilles de Ski
Geographic Divisions	
	Alaska, Central, Eastern, European, Far West, Intermountain, Northern, Pacific Northwest, Rocky Mountain, Southern
HIV	Human immunodeficiency virus
HBV	Hepatitis B virus (disease of the liver)
Joint Statement of Understanding	
	NSAA
	PSIA
NAF	National Avalanche Foundation
NAS	National Avalanche School
NASAR	National Association for Search and Rescue

National	Patroller who has received a National Appointment
	Patrollers who are volunteers on a combined paid and volunteer patrol staff
	National office
NOLS	National Outdoor Leadership School
NSAA	National Ski Areas Association
NSP	National Ski Patrol
OEC	Outdoor Emergency Care
OECPAC	Outdoor Emergency Care Program Administration Committee
OFC	Outdoor First Care
OSHA	Occupational Safety and Health Administration

Patroller Classifications

       Skill Classification

              Alpine (Ski/Snowboard), Auxiliary, Nordic

       Type of Service

              Volunteer, Professional

       Member Level

              Candidate, Patroller (Basic), Senior (Alpine or Nordic), Senior Auxiliary, Certified

PD	Patrol Director
Phase I	Initial instructor development program (Part I)—Completion is a pre-requisite for taking Phase II
Phase II	Initial instructional skills program (Part II)—a global module plus instructor skills training for a specific discipline, i.e., OEC, Alpine Toboggan, Avalanche, Mountaineering, Nordic, PES
Pro Division	Professional Division
PSIA	Professional Ski Instructors of America
QA	Quality Assurance
QM	Quality Management
RD	Region Director
SIA	SnowSports Industries of America
S&T	Ski and Toboggan
SC	Section chief
SOLO	For-profit organization that provides wilderness emergency medical programs
SPM	*Ski Patrol Magazine*

Statement of Understanding

       The agreement that defines the relationship between NSP volunteers and ski area management; also the agreement that defines the relationship between NSP and PSIA, with respect to the administrative consolidation

Tax Exemption

       501 (c)(1)—Status granted to federally chartered non-profit organizations

       501 (c)(3)—Nonprofit status

       501 (c)(6)—Nonprofit educational foundation

USSCA	United States Ski Coaches Association
USFS	United States Forest Service
WEC	Winter Emergency Care (former name for Outdoor Emergency Care)
WFR	NASAR Course—Wilderness First Responder
WSO	Winter Special Olympics

The *Ski and Toboggan Training Manual* outlines the generally accepted training standards and procedures for the NSP alpine toboggan training program. This manual should be used as the reference for further detail on training activities and exercises.

Basic Skiing and Snowboarding Definitions

The following basic skiing and snowboarding terminology may be used in clinics and evaluations.

Stance and balance. A functional relationship of the legs that is not forced or contrived while skiing or snowboarding. A slightly flexed, upright stance allows for muscular/skeletal efficiency and accuracy of movements. The individual balances on the whole foot with the ability to work the entire ski or snowboard.

- For the skier, the body is in a slightly countered relationship with the skis. The upper body must be disciplined and should have a dynamic relationship with the skis.
- For the snowboarder, the body is countered with the snowboard and bindings, based on the setting and angulation of the bindings to the snowboard. The upper body must be disciplined and should have a dynamic relationship with the snowboard.

Rotary movements. Movements that reorient the direction of travel of the skis or snowboard through muscular effort coupled with the forces generated by the interaction of the edged skis/snowboard and the snow. An active guidance of the skis/snowboard exists throughout the turn.

- For the skier, rotary movements of the inside leg enhance the action of the outside leg. Generally there is a stronger application of rotary movements in gliding turns.

- For the snowboarder, rotary movement of the rear foot/leg enhances the action of the forward leg. Generally there is a stronger application of rotary movements in gliding turns.

Edging movements. Adjustments of the angle between the running surface of the skis/snowboard and the slope. Guiding the skis/snowboard onto an edge and using progressive edging throughout the turn creates the desired turn shape. Edging movements start from the center of mass. Fine-tuning adjustments are made with the knees, ankles, and feet.

Pressuring movements. Movements that regulate the pressure on the skis/snowboard to suit the situation.

- For the skier, this concept includes pressure adjustments from ski to ski (also called weight transfer), increasing or decreasing the pressure applied to one or both skis (also called weighting or unweighting), and pressure adjustments made along the length of the skis (also called leverage). The transfer of pressure to the outside ski is smooth and progressive. Flexion and extension movements are used to maintain and control the desired turn shape.
- For the snowboarder, this concept includes much the same format as for the skier, except the weight transfer from edge to edge on the snowboard is a toe-to-heel weight transfer, in addition to the use of pressure adjustments along the length of the snowboard.

Rhythm and flow movements. Movements that link turns with a continuous flow of the center of mass to produce and maintain rhythm. At the turn initiation, the center of mass rises toward the new turn. During turn initiation, active guiding of the inside ski greatly enhances the flow of the turn.

Training progressions can be developed for each movement or for a specific weakness by isolating each of these skills and then varying them independently. For example, an exercise on isolation progression might begin with edging movements and then add rotary movement.

NSP's *Ski Patrol Magazine* and PSIA's *The Professional Skier* magazine contain many articles with exercises that patrollers can use to enhance their skiing/snowboarding and toboggan-handling skills.

Skiing/Snowboarding Exercises

Skiers and snowboarders can improve their skill proficiency by practicing a variety of exercises developed by PSIA. (PSIA instructors can suggest many other exercises in addition to the ones described as follows.) This skill enhancement is beneficial to patrollers, who must maintain a stable position and control speed when maneuvering a toboggan down a slope.

Warm-up Skiing/Snowboarding

The training clinic should start with a few warm-up exercises; those that emphasize rotary, edging, and pressuring movements are most important.

The exercises described in the following sections incorporate basic movement patterns related to skill development. They also emphasize the shape of the turn, balance, stability, and control of speed and direction. Proper application will produce consistent, rounded, linked, and controlled turns, a quiet upper body, and the appearance of ease and control regardless of terrain and conditions.

The skiing/snowboarding component also includes skiing/riding unpacked snow or icy terrain (conditions permitting) and skiing/riding while carrying equipment.

Wedging the Fall Line

Ski in a gliding wedge straight down the fall line while centered over the skis. While making no rotary or pressuring movements, increase then decrease the edging on both skis at the same time. Note the results as the angle increases the ability of the ski to hold, causing a braking action. Next, vary the edge angle on one ski at a time, again noting the results.

Snowboarders may modify this exercise by sideslipping straight down the fall line while applying pressure to the hillside edge of the snowboard. Note the results as the angle increases the board's ability to hold, causing a braking action.

Pressure Changes

Repeat the wedge exercise above, but move the pressuring edge forward on the skis/snowboard and note the results. Next, move the pressure to the tail(s) and note the results. The next step of the progression might involve pressuring the skis independently and then adding rotary motion. In the case of a snowboard, add rotary motion.

Flatland Skate

Skate on flat or very gentle terrain to develop edging and pressuring skills. When done in a straight line (point to point), edging skills can be isolated from rotary movements and also can develop weight transfer awareness through side-to-side and fore-and-aft movements. Skating also helps develop independent leg action and flexing/extending movements. (This exercise does not apply to snowboarding.)

Skate Turns

Execute turns by skating through them rather than by using a more conventional turn approach. Focus on making a complete weight transfer for each skate and skating onto the new ski before entering the fall line. When done on a more difficult slope, this exercise can expand on the basics learned from the flatland skate. Rotary movements are emphasized by stepping or skating in a path to change direction and control speed.

Notice that pressuring movements and steering play a bigger role in this exercise because of the natural edging that occurs on a slope. (This exercise does not apply to snowboarding.)

Crab Walk

The crab walk demonstrates direction change as a result of hard edging. Ski downhill in a wedge, edging one ski without rotary movements while flattening the other ski. This will force you to proceed in an angular direction. Repeat the process by edging the other ski. Proceed down the slope by alternating from ski to ski, producing a zigzag pattern. (This exercise does not apply to snowboarding.)

Sideslips

Perform sideslips down or across the fall line. Experiment with edge angles and weight transfer from side to side, as well as fore and aft, to develop a wide range of results from the skis' or the snowboard's interaction with the slope.

Emergency (Hockey) Stops

This variation of the sideslip requires the addition of rotary skills as well as a keen awareness of pressuring skills.

From a straight run down the fall line, pivot the skis or the snowboard across the fall line. Then increase the edge angle while controlling the direction of the slide down the fall line until forward momentum is stopped.

360-Degree Turns

Make 360-degree turns to practice rotary motion, edge control, and pressure skills. Carry the turn past the point where it is normally completed. When momentum stops, slip backward down the hill. Flatten the edges and pull the ski tips or nose of the snowboard downhill to complete the 360-degree turn. (The turn will not be a complete circle.) The 360-degree turn requires changes in edging and rotary movements.

Long-Radius Turn Exercises

Instructors should select one or two training exercises from the following examples and have the senior candidates follow the stated directions.

Carved and Skidded Turns

Perform both carved and skidded turns to increase the awareness of the difference between the two and the different skills used for each. Hold each turn for four seconds.

To carve the turn, balance on the inside edge of the outside ski or on the toe or heel edge of the snowboard and pressure the middle of the skis/snowboard, maintaining a slightly countered stance (upper body faces slightly downhill, lead with uphill hip and shoulder).

Too much pressure forward on the skis/snowboard during the last half of the turn will cause the tails to skid. Too much pressure backward generally causes increased speed and lack of control. Experiment with putting pressure at different points on the skis/snowboard, and note the sensations and results.

Weighting Middle of Ski

Experiment with weighting the middle of the skis/snowboard, and note the effect on the turn. Generally, the skidded turn involves more rotary force and less edging. Skidded turns also may result from over-edging, lack of flexing, or the center of mass being outside the line of action.

Alternate Weighting

Alternately weight the outside ski, both skis, and the inside ski, and describe the effect. Continuous fluid vertical motion (angular as well as up and down) of the body is required for properly pressured turns. The upper body follows the direction of the skis.

Experiment with static vertical positioning, and compare that feeling with continuous fluid vertical motion. (This exercise does not apply to snowboarding.)

Medium-Radius Turn Exercises

Instructors should select one or two training exercises from the following examples and have the senior candidates follow the stated directions.

Flat Terrain Balance

Stand on flat terrain without skis on, and balance against ski poles. Move the left ski boot in an arc. Rest your body weight on the inside edge of the boot. Try to have the boot slice through the snow, with the heel following the track of the toe, and note the sensation. Repeat the exercise with the right foot. Then repeat with skis on while making carved medium-radius turns (with *both* feet moving in the same arc).

Snowboarders will do this same exercise but change the stance in relation to the snowboard/binding setup.

Flat Terrain Flex

Stand with weight evenly distributed over both feet on flat terrain without skis or snowboard on, using ski poles for balance. Twist your boots to the left and then to the right, and describe the sensation. Try the exercise without flexing, with flexing, with a hop and no flex, and with a hop and flexing. Repeat the exercise with the skis/snowboard on to make skidded turns (little or no edging). Add edging to transform the turns into carved turns. Note that flexing initially assists the rotary or turning movements, then aids in edging.

Leapers

This exercise is designed to help move the body in the direction of the new turn. Flex at the end of one turn. Follow the flex by a leaping extension (unfolding) of the body into the air in the direction of the center of the next turn. Use the uphill or outside leg extension to direct the body toward the center of the new turn. Leap off the snow. Land on the edges of the skis and absorb by flexing the ankles, knees, and hips.

Leap on smooth terrain first, then on small moguls. Leap up on the front side of one mogul, over the trough between moguls, and land on the far side of the second mogul. Decrease the size of the leaps until the skis remain in contact with the snow, all the while making the same type of body movement. (This exercise does not appy to snowboarders.)

Moguls

To ski or snowboard moguls, concentrate on establishing a rhythm, weighting the outside ski or snowboard fully on its inside edge, and maintaining continuous fluid vertical motion. At the initiation of each turn, remember to project the body down the hill in the direction of the new turn. To unweight, try turning on the tops of the moguls. Let the moguls do the unweighting. Approach the mogul, keeping the knees loose and flexing to absorb the mogul.

- For the skier, touch the inside pole to the snow slightly forward and downhill when cresting the mogul, steer the skis around the pole, and press the skis down against the backside of the mogul to complete the turn in the trough.
- For the snowboarder, use a reaching motion with the inside arm slightly forward and downhill when cresting the mogul, steering the snowboard around the point, as if rotating around a pole, and press the snowboard down against the backside of the mogul to complete the turn in the trough.

Vary the edge angle to make carved or skidded turns. Practice absorbing moguls between turns while maintaining a constant speed.

Short-Radius Turn Exercises

Instructors should remember to work with senior candidates on more difficult and most difficult terrain and to include both smooth slopes and moguls since the skiing techniques will vary with the condition.

Crossed Arms

With arms crossed (without poles) and hands lightly touching your shoulders, make short-radius turns down the fall line. Keep the cross formed with your arms facing downhill. Concentrate on complete weight transfer onto the inside edge of the outside ski or snowboard, a strong turning action of the skis or snowboard, and continuous motion from one turn to the next. Start with a slower rhythm and then speed it up. Avoid turning the upper body (rotation), leaning the upper body into the turn (banking), and bending forward at the waist, which will weight the tips too much, causing the tail(s) to skid out.

Tuck Turns

Make short-radius turns from a high tuck position. Aim the hands down the hill to direct the upper body. Start by slightly turning in and out of the fall line, transferring weight from outside ski to outside ski. For snowboarders, this entails transferring weight from the heel to toe edge or visa versa.

Next, complete the turns across the hill, keeping the upper body facing downhill. Try the same exercise from a low tuck position, linking round, short-radius turns. Alternate tuck turns with regular turns. Keep the upper body stable; let the lower body create the turn.

Diagonals

Make short-radius turns while traveling diagonally down the hill. Emphasize turn initiation and completion. For initiation, focus on steering the skis or snowboard into and across the fall line as they are tipped on edge with transfer of weight to the outside ski, or, for a snowboard, to the outside edge. For completion, focus on fully weighting the inside edge of the outside ski or snowboard by flexing the knees, ankles, and hips to transfer weight to that edge.

Moguls

Practice the same exercise for moguls described in the section on medium-radius turns, except establish a smaller turning arc and a faster rhythm. Do not absorb any moguls between turns.

Unpacked Snow or Icy Condition Exercises

Instructors should select training exercises from the following examples and have the senior candidates follow the stated directions.

Powder Exercise

Weight both skis more or less equally (perhaps a little more weight on the outside ski). Too much weight on one ski may cause it to dive deeper while the unweighted ski floats to the surface. Weight the middle of the skis or snowboard—do not sit back.

Turning in powder is a slower process than turning on packed snow. Start with a strong up-unweighting at the beginning of the turn. Actively steer the inside edge of the inside ski or snowboard to help initiate the turn. Extend (unfold) and use a twisting/pushing motion with both feet to guide the ski tip(s) or snowboard toward and across the fall line. Flex to absorb and finish the turn.

Start with long- and medium-radius turns, then progress to short-radius turns. On short-radius turns, when you feel resistance of the snow against the skis/snowboard at the end of one turn, relax and let the snow push your feet, skis/snowboard, and knees upward (unweighting). Then push, twist, and steer the ski tip(s) or snowboard toward and across the fall line and the tail(s) of the skis/snowboard sideways. On steep slopes, push the skis/snowboard down into the snow at the end of the turn to control speed.

Icy Conditions

Maintain sharp edges. Keep the skis/snowboard in constant contact with the snow. Focus on edge control, weight distribution, and fluid, smooth movements.

For edge control, move the skis/snowboard forward along its inside edge instead of skidding sideways. Carve the turns. (Try the boot arc exercise described in the section on medium-radius turns.)

For weight distribution, concentrate on fully weighting the inside edge of the outside skis/snowboard, keeping the weight centered fore and aft on that ski or the snowboard. Icy conditions require maximum edge bite. Too much weight forward or backward will cause a loss of edging. Experiment with shifting the weight fore and aft along the skis/snowboard.

For skiers, try picking up the inside ski of the turn to fully weight the outside ski. To increase angulation, roll the knees and ankles more into the hill. Over-edging will also result in loss of edge control. Experiment with different degrees of edging and notice the difference in control. On steep slopes, lean the upper body over the downhill ski to increase edge bite. Avoid jerky movements, and concentrate on being smooth and fluid.

Crud Snow

Exaggerate the lengthening and shortening movements of the body, otherwise relying on the fundamental turning techniques. Start short by flexing the legs. Extend the body up, out, and across into the center of the turn to unweight and change edges. Commit the upper body across the skis/snowboard toward the fall line to help change edges and pull the skis/snowboard into the turn. Stay balanced over the middle of the skis/snowboard.

Immediately after extending, changing edges, and guiding the tips into the fall line, get short by flexing the knees in the direction of the turn. Sink forcefully and smoothly in the center of the skis/snowboard. Extend off the new downhill ski or snowboard edge to begin the next turn.

Equipment Carry Exercises

Instructors should design training exercises that enable candidates to practice the skills needed to meet the stated objectives.

Progressions

For the skier, the training progression should begin by skiing without the use of poles. The next step is to ski or snowboard while carrying light loads, progressing to heavier and/or bulkier loads.

Toboggan Exercises

When toboggan-handling activities combine skiing and snowboarding, it is extremely important to emphasize communication at all times—verbal and physical. Unexpected direction changes, for example, may create a situation that is detrimental to the individuals involved.

Warm-up Toboggan Exercises

The toboggan training clinic should start with a few warm-up exercises, and these exercises may also be useful as actual training exercises during the toboggan clinic. Instructors may use the following "phantom" toboggan exercises in training the senior candidates.

Phantom Toboggan Exercises

These phantom exercises enable patrollers to simulate toboggan skills without the aid of an actual toboggan.

Bamboo Pole Drills

Two patrollers skis/snowboard while holding two sets of poles to simulate a toboggan. Each set consists of two side-by-side bamboo poles taped together; this makes each simulated "toboggan handle" less likely to break. Rather than act as a rear operator, the person in back uses his or her weight to push the front person to create the effect of a loaded toboggan. The front operator is responsible for direction and speed.

Rope-a-Goat

This drill should help the rear operator develop an understanding of his or her personal limitations in controlling a toboggan. The lead skier/snowboarder goes to the fall line on easier or more difficult terrain in a gliding wedge or sideslip with unset edge(s) imitating a toboggan. The rear operator controls and guides the phantom toboggan down and across the hill, using edge control and skiing/snowboarding techniques appropriate for the terrain and conditions.

Wedge Skills Exercises

Senior candidates should practice wedge skills exercises either with or without a toboggan on easier and more difficult terrain. Experiment with both skidded and carved wedge turns through varying degrees of edge angle and body position. Initiate the turn by shifting or transferring weight and applying a rotary force to the outside ski. Complete the turn by shifting the weight to the opposite ski.

(See the Skiing/Snowboarding Exercise examples at the beginning of this appendix for discussions on exercise options for snowboarding patrollers; these apply to toboggan handling also.)

Skidded and Carved Wedge Turns

Use less edge angle and pressure for skidded turns. Use more edge angle and pressure on the inside edge of the outside ski or snowboard for carved turns. Assure a balanced stance with weight centered fore and aft on the outside ski or snowboard of the turn. Maintain a comfortably high, stable stance with hips centered and knees bent. Turn your feet in the desired direction, and use pressure and rotary motion.

Braking Wedge

With hips centered, brush the tails of the skis out far enough to create significant edge angle between the ski and snow. The more the edge angle of the skis is increased, the more dramatic the braking action. Keep your hands on your hips or comfortably at your sides or on the toboggan handles. The ski tips should stay together, with body weight on the inside edge of feet and skis, centered fore and aft. Keep your body facing down fall line, with knees bent. Stress stability and control. Come to a stop with the ski tips in the fall line on easier terrain and with the ski tips in the fall line or off to one side on more difficult terrain.

In this exercise, a snowboarding patroller uses the sideslip, with edging. An increase in pressure on the hillside edge causes more dramatic braking action. Keep the hands on the hips or comfortable at the sides or on the toboggan handles, with body weight on the heel or toe (side being used for control), centered fore and aft. Keep the body facing down the fall line, with the knees bent. Stress stability and control. Come to a stop with the board off the fall line to one side in all terrain.

Gliding Wedge

Maintain a comfortably high stance with the hips centered and the body supported by the skeletal structure instead of by muscular effort. Keep the ski tips together, pressing them slightly apart. There should be little, if any, edge between the ski and the snow. Keep the knees bent. Apply pressure/balance to the middle of the skis, with weight evenly distributed between the skis. Keep the hands on the hips or comfortably at the sides or on the toboggan handles. The whole body should be facing down the fall line. Travel down the fall line, stressing stability and control. (This exercise does not apply to snow-boarding.)

When done in team format on toboggans, the snowboarding patroller may use the sideslip skill with little or no edging except to control speed.

Straight Run, Glide, Straight Run

Start from a straight-running parallel stance facing down the fall line. Go to a gliding wedge and back to a straight-running position. Repeat three to four times. Concentrate on the key points mentioned in the description of the gliding wedge, especially applying equal pressure on skis and little, if any, on the edge angle. (This exercise does not apply to snowboarding.)

When done in team format on toboggans, the snowboarding patroller may place the snowboard nose into the fall line, then rotate across the fall line, and back, using necessary pressure (edging) to control speed.

Glide and Brake

Alternate back and forth between the gliding wedge and the braking wedge. Notice the difference in the distance between the tails of the skis and the edge angle.

With the instructor, assign a number rating to the size of wedges. (Skis parallel = 0, maximum wedge = 4; gradients of 1, 2, and 3 in between.) When the instructor calls out the numbers, change the shape of the wedge accordingly. Discuss the relationship between edging, speed, wedge size, and terrain.

When done in team format on toboggans, the snowboarding patroller may place the snowboard nose into the fall line, then rotate across the fall line and back, using necessary pressure (edging) to control speed.

Skidded Wedge Turns

Make a series of skidded wedge turns (skiers) or three left and right skidded (snowboard), followed by a series of three left and right carved wedge turns, emphasizing similarities and differences between each type of turn. Describe the differences, and repeat the exercise.

Visualize smashing a wad of sticky gum underneath the outside turning foot for a feeling of rotary motion. Discuss extending into the fall line at turn initiation to help flatten the skis or snowboard and make them easier to steer into the turn. Discuss flexing the knees and ankles in the second half of the turn to increase edge angle and complete the turn. Then alternate with one series of left and right carved wedge turns and one series of left and right skidded (snowboard) or skidded wedge turns (skiers).

Glide and Wedge

Alternate gliding wedge and wedge turns followed by a braking wedge to a stop. On easier terrain, stop with the ski tips in the fall line. On more difficult terrain, stop with ski tips in the fall line or off to one side of the fall line.

For snowboarders, alternate sideslip and skidded turns, followed by a hockey stop.

Sideslip Skills Exercises

Sideslip exercises can be practiced with or without a toboggan. Include sideslipping straight down the fall line as well as sideslipping in a "falling leaf" pattern (forward and backward). Practice the exercises on smooth, packed, more difficult terrain, and moguled terrain, if possible.
- For skiers, use the left and right ski alternately as the downhill ski. Do a kick turn to change direction.
- For snowboarders, use the heel-side and toe-side edges alternately, making quick transition turns to change from each edge.

Downhill (Straight) Sideslips

Begin this section with a simple downhill sideslip. Experiment with varying degrees of edging. The skier's feet should be comfortably apart—at about shoulder width. Avoid a closed stance (feet together), as this provides minimal stability. One foot may be farther forward than the other but should not lead by enough to affect balance or stability. Gently rise, roll the knees and ankles downhill to release the edges, and slip on the bases. Gently sink, roll the knees and ankles uphill to set the edges, and slow or stop. Demonstrate balance, stability, control, constant speed, and edge set and release.

For snowboarders, use the heel-side and toe-side edges alternately, making quick transition turns to change from each edge.

Falling Leaf Lateral Movement

Move the point where the body weight acts on the ski or snowboard forward and backward. (When performed correctly, forward and backward travel are of approximately equal distance.) Change from a forward to a backward sideslip smoothly with no traverse or edge set.

Tracks left in the snow should be rounded and brush like. Sideslip rather than traverse. Discuss and experiment with different methods of adding lateral motion (both forward and backward) to the sideslip.

Weight Shifts

Experiment with extreme weight shifts (leaning the entire body forward and backward) to subtle weight shifts (moving the pressure from the balls of the feet to the heels). Avoid excessive rotary force, i.e., too much twisting of the lower leg, which initiates turns.

Transitions Exercises

Transitions can be defined as the maneuvers a senior candidate uses in front or behind a toboggan to go from a wedge (skier) to a sideslip or from a sideslip facing one way to a sideslip facing the other way. This skill is applied to toboggan handling and should not be confused with drills to improve turn initiation. Transitions allow changing the direction of the skis or snowboard while keeping the toboggan in the fall line. They should be done while maintaining a straight descent without acceleration. Use easier and more difficult, smooth, packed terrain. Transitions may be practiced with or without a toboggan.

Wedge Transitions

From a wedge position pointing straight down the fall line, pivot or turn the skis across the slope 90 degrees without moving more than five feet across the slope. (This exercise does not apply to snowboarding.)

Sideslip Transitions

From a sideslip position facing across the hill, pivot or turn the skis 180 degrees to face across the hill in the opposite direction. Limit boot movement across the slope to no more than a few feet. Use wedge (skier), stem (skier), skidded turns (skiers or snowboarders), or parallel maneuvers (skiers or snowboarders).

To perform the maneuver, rise up on the skis/snowboard to release the edges, flatten the skis/snowboard onto their base(s), turn or pivot the feet and skis/snowboard on their base(s) in the new direction, and sink back down more on the bases than on the edges of the skis/snowboard.

Corridor Skiing

To execute transition maneuvers, keep the skis/snowboard within a pre-established corridor approximately two ski-lengths wide. Another approach is to maneuver while keeping the boots (skiers) between two parallel lines that have been drawn approximately five feet apart. Focus on a point down the slope will help maintain a straight descent.

Unloaded Toboggan—Front Exercises

Refer to *The Ski and Toboggan Training Manual* for guidance in designing unloaded toboggan training exercises. Some examples follow.

Route Selection

Visually inspect the hill. Discuss possible routes and practice to see if the selected route is appropriate. Look for alternatives on the same slope.

Follow the Leader

Use toboggans over varied terrain. Discuss and simulate proper position on a static and moving toboggan in various terrain and conditions.

Chopsticks Drill

Have two patrollers simulate a toboggan by holding two bamboo or wooden poles. The front patroller places a pole under each arm and cups his or her hands over the pole ends. When the team begins to move, the rear operator leans on the poles to create the effect of a loaded toboggan.

Skiing/Snowboarding Skills with Toboggans

Demonstrate sideslips, turns, and transitions.

Recovery Techniques

Practice wheelbarrow, rear run, and 360-degree maneuvers.

Loaded Toboggan—Front Exercises

Refer to *The Ski and Toboggan Training Manual* for guidance in designing unloaded toboggan training exercises. Some examples follow.

Route Selections

Tour the mountain and review route choices using various trails and accident scenarios.

Ride the Walls

There are steep inclines along many cat tracks. Use these to practice traverse stance and toboggan tracking by skiing or snowboarding up on them and working to maintain a stable line with the toboggan.

Long Traverses

Do long traverses on varied terrain. Spend enough time on the edges to gain the feel of the traverse position.

Difficult Terrain Practice

Choose uneven or icy terrain to practice balance and edge control.

Progressive Exercises

Practice making as many turns as possible, progressing from an unloaded to a loaded toboggan. Use bamboo or rope drills in pairs to simulate turns with the toboggan.

Traverses on Varied Terrain

Traverse with and without active assistance from the rear operator on
* easier, more difficult, and most difficult terrain;
* smooth and moguled terrain; and
* packed powder, powder, crud, and icy conditions.

Moguls

Practice techniques to descend smoothly through moguls with a toboggan, including selecting the route; controlling the toboggan's contact with the surface; using the brake chain; positioning in the handles, and lifting and lowering the toboggan handles.

Kick Turns

Practice kick turns in a variety of conditions and terrain, with and without a toboggan and with and without poles.

It is important for skiers and snowboarders to communicate between each other when kick turns are necessary. Snowboarding patrollers may maneuver the mountain with forward and fakie (reverse) motions, not having to make transition changes. However if a skier and snowboarder are operating a toboggan as a team, they must come to a complete stop so the skier has a safe area to perform the maneuver.

Loaded Toboggan—Rear Operator Exercises

Refer to *The Ski and Toboggan Training Manual* for guidance in designing unloaded toboggan training exercises. Some examples follow.

Rope-a-Goat

Practice rear operating techniques by skiing or snowboarding straight down the fall line and controlling turns with the help of another candidate who is simulating the toboggan. Attach a section of rope around the waist of the front person and proceed down the hill.

Traversing

Practice traversing left and right with a loaded toboggan, keeping the toboggan from slipping sideways.

Tail Rope Length

Practice lengthening and shortening the distance along the tail rope according to toboggan speed, snow conditions, and terrain.

Braking

Practice applying increased braking power until effectively braking the entire weight of the loaded toboggan.

Front Commands

Practice responding to the front operator's movement in an effort to lessen the impact of the moguls and dips.

Rear Turning

Practice coordinating left and right turns on smooth slopes and on moguled slopes.

The *Nordic Training Manual* outlines the generally accepted training standards and procedures for the NSP nordic training program. This manual should be used as the reference for further detail on training activities and exercises.

Prepared Track Exercises

Select and design training exercises for the senior candidates that meet stated objectives.

(PSIA instructors can suggest many other warm-up exercises in addition to those described in this appendix.)

Diagonal Stride

Ski in a straight line between two points without poles. Count the number of strides between the points. Try to reduce the number of strides each time. Experiment with push-off, glide length, and body position. This exercise is designed to help develop weight transfer, pushing off, and gliding on one ski.

Poling

Use alternate poling to propel yourself forward in a track. Experiment with shaft angle and arm extension. Vary the pole angle and arm extension to achieve maximum glide and power. Use this exercise to develop arm extension and upper body strength.

Double Pole

On a gentle slope, use both poles to propel yourself downhill. As you stand up, move your hips forward to project the upper body. Use upper body compression, then pole push. This exercise is primarily designed to maintain or increase speed while going downhill.

One-Step Double Pole With Kick

On rolling or bumpy terrain use this maneuver at the crest of a rise. Feel the difference in leg force needed to power the push-off at higher and lower speeds. This exercise is designed to develop sliding, pole push, and push-off.

Step Turn

On a gradual downhill slope, change directions by taking small divergent steps. Lift up on the tips while stepping to keep the tail in the snow and the ski under control. This exercise is designed to develop balance, edging, rotary, and pressure-control movements.

Skate

On flat terrain or a gentle slope, skate in a straight line. Align your toe, knee, and nose over the gliding ski for proper body position. This exercise is designed to develop weight transfer and edging, and it promotes an upright body position.

Skate Turn

On flat terrain ski a figure eight. Vary the size of the figure, and experiment with double and diagonal poling. Start slow, and gradually increase your speed and power. This exercise is designed to develop edging, push-off, pole push, and weight transfer.

Straight Run

Begin with the basic body position: skis comfortably apart and parallel, knees slightly bent, and hands at sides. Use a double-pole push to start the skis sliding. Distribute body weight as evenly as possible over both feet. Transfer weight from foot to foot while in a straight run. Shuffle skis back and forth while in a straight run. This exercise is designed to help develop a balanced stance.

Pole Drag

Remove pole straps and grip poles on the shafts and handles. Drag baskets in the snow to reduce speed. Rest the shafts or your forearm against your knee or thigh to increase leverage and braking power. The pole drag is best used to control speed on steep, narrow, icy trails.

Gliding and Braking Wedge

Let your skis glide downhill in a wedge position while using minimal edging. At a designated point (A), begin a braking wedge, and stop at a designated point (B). Repeat the exercise, gradually decreasing the distance between A and B (and increasing braking power). Note changes in body position and edging. This exercise is designed to develop edging, sliding, and steering.

Crab Walk

Ski downhill in a wedge and edge one ski without rotary (steering) movements, while flattening the other ski. Repeat the process by edging the opposite ski. Proceed down the slope by alternating from ski to ski, producing a zigzag pattern. Crab walking demonstrates direction change as a result of hard edging. This exercise is designed to develop edging and pressure control.

Parallel Turn

Skiers control speed by completing the turn. Concentrate on steering through the arc of the turn rather than pivoting and setting edges at the end of the turn. Experiment with edge control and rotary movements to vary the shape of the turn.

Off-Track Exercise Examples

Conditions in the backcountry vary from prepared track. Consequently, senior candidates must be able to demonstrate skills in varied terrain. The following examples are designed to help candidates prepare to ski off-track conditions.

Herringbone/Half Herringbone

Climb the hill using the herringbone technique, switch to the half herringbone technique on the right, return to the full herringbone, then switch to the half herringbone on the left and back to a full herringbone. Vary the width of the "V" shape and the amount of edging. Keep your weight over your feet. Use this exercise to develop edging, weight transfer, and pole push.

Stem Turn

From a traverse, stem the uphill ski while maintaining the edge of the downhill ski in the traverse. Initiate the turn with a smooth and continuous pressure to the stemmed ski while steering both feet in the direction of the turn. To resume the traverse, steer the uphill ski parallel to the downhill ski. This exercise consists of a steering turn used to change directions and control speed.

Stem Christie

From a traverse, stem the uphill ski with an up and forward motion.

Transfer weight to the outside ski and begin edging. Complete the turn as skidding stops and the skis enter a new traverse. This exercise is useful in toboggan handling and as a downhill turning progression to the parallel and telemark turns.

Wedge Christie

From a traverse, open both skis into a small wedge and steer them into the fall line. The edge change on the inside ski and weight transfer to the outside ski should be as smooth as possible. You may steer the skis parallel before or after the fall line, as needed. This maneuver is useful in nordic toboggan handling and as a downhill turning progression to the parallel and telemark turns.

Traverse (Uphill)

Point your skis at an upward angle to the fall line, and use the uphill diagonal stride. As the hill gets steeper, maintain the upward angle, adjust poling for balance, and edge the skis into the hill to prevent sideslipping.

Traverse (Downhill)

Point your skis at a downward angle to the fall line, and use the downhill diagonal stride. As the hill gets steeper, maintain the downward angle, adjust poling for balance, and edge the skis into the hill to prevent sideslipping.

Traverse with Kick Turn

This exercise involves a stationary turn of 180 degrees to change direction when other techniques are undesirable or ineffective. Place your skis across the fall line, edged if necessary, and face downhill. Plant your poles behind you (uphill) for stability. Your body weight should be on the uphill ski. Kick your downhill ski forward and up, and pivot it around on its trail to the opposite direction, bringing the

feet together, but facing opposite directions. Transfer your weight to the downhill ski, and bring the uphill ski around to point in the same direction. Bring your poles to your sides. On steep terrain, it may be easier to do the kick turn facing uphill.

Sidestep

Position your skis directly across the fall line in an edged position. Then pick up the uphill ski and step laterally uphill. Move the downhill ski alongside the uphill ski (matched). You may also wish to experiment with forward sidestepping, which is a combination of uphill traverse and uphill sidestep. Practice sidestepping downhill, then downhill and forward, downhill and backward, etc. This is a necessary maneuver when belaying or entering steep terrain.

Telemark Position

On rolling terrain, absorb bumps by sinking into the telemark position. After cresting the bump, push down with your legs to maintain snow contact, and sink into the telemark position again at the transition. Experiment with fore-and-aft positions to develop balance. This exercise is designed to develop sliding and balance.

Telemark Turn

As you move from one telemark position to the other, allow your center of mass to create a constant flow of motion. Rise during initiation to release edges, then sink into the telemark position, actively steering both skis. Control speed by completing the turn. Achieve rounded turn shaped by blending edging, pressure control, and rotary motion throughout the arc of the turn. Experiment with varying the shape of the turn and with fore and aft weighting.

The OEC component of the senior program allows patrollers to participate in ski patrol-relevant field exercises. These exercises are designed to develop and enhance the skills of decision making, problem management, and leadership, as applied to the management of emergency care situations in a typical ski patrol environment.

Practice Scenarios

Outdoor Emergency Care supports the OEC standard of training. The Senior OEC clinics provide a setting in which patrollers are evaluated on their ability to meet OEC's standard performance objectives. Patrollers must demonstrate their knowledge and skills in these areas, using decision making, problem management, and leadership abilities. The following scenarios may prove useful in pre-evaluation training clinics. Various factors of the scenario have been rated by a OEC Test Bank Committee to determine the overall degree of difficulty.

OEC Practice Scenario 1

The following table contains an emergency care scenario in which the senior candidate must manage a humerus fracture with resulting nerve paralysis. The degree of difficulty for each scenario component is provided as well as the overall degree of difficulty.

| **Injury** |
| Humerus fracture with complete radial nerve paralysis (3) |
| **Environment** |
| Entangled in a snow gun (or other man-made obstacle) (1) |
| **Personnel** |
| Single patient (0) No trained help (1) |

Degree of Difficulty = 5

General Scenario Description

A snowboarder lost control while jumping a mogul. He became airborne, and when he fell his upper arm struck a snow gun at the edge of the trail. You are the only available patroller for the first 10 to 12 minutes. The patient complains of severe pain in the unstable upper arm, with numbness over the thumb side of the hand and an inability to extend his wrist and fingers.

OEC Practice Scenario 2

The following table contains an emergency care scenario in which the senior candidate must manage an unresponsive patient who has a laceration and a pre-existing medical condition. The degree of difficulty for each component is provided as well as the degree of difficulty.

| **Injury** |
| Unresponsive (4) Laceration with minor bleeding (1) Medical condition (0) |
| **Environment** |
| More difficult slope (narrow area if available) (1) |
| **Personnel** |
| Single patient (0) Trained patrollers (0) |

Degree of Difficulty = 5

General Scenario Description

A skier on a narrow slope became airborne off of a mogul. Upon landing, her head hit a tree and she then fell forward onto a jagged rock. The accident was witnessed by the skier's friend, who has remained on the scene. The patient is unresponsive but stable throughout the entire management of the problem. The bleeding from the thigh laceration is only minor, but the friend reveals that the patient is HIV positive.

OEC Practice Scenario 3

The following table contains an emergency care scenario in which the senior candidate must manage a patient with severe respiratory distress and a facial laceration. The degree of difficulty for each component is provided as well as the overall degree of difficulty.

| **Injury** |
| Severe respiratory distress with flail chest and tension pneumothorax (4) Facial laceration (1) |
| **Environment** |
| Most difficult slope with moguls (0) |
| **Personnel** |
| Single patient (0) Trained patrollers (0) |

Degree of Difficulty = 5

General Scenario Description

A skier hit a mogul unexpectedly and fell forward. When you arrive on the scene, the skier is sitting on the snow. He tells you that the right side of his chest and face are hurting. He is also experiencing some difficulty breathing, especially if he tries to take a deep breath. This symptom worsens as time passes. All breathing is shallow; and any deep breaths or excessive movement cause increased pain.

OEC Practice Scenario 4

The following table contains an emergency care scenario in which the senior candidate must manage two patients: one with first- and second-degree burns and the other with glass in his eye. The degree of difficulty for each component is provided as well as the overall degree of difficulty.

Injury

Burns, first and second degree (2)
Glass in the eye (2)

Environment

Outside of a maintenance shed or kitchen (0)

Personnel

Multiple patients (1)
Trained patrollers (0)

Degree of Difficulty = 5

General Scenario Description

There has been a flash fire, cause unknown, in which an employee sustained burns to the face, neck, and hands. The employee (Patient A) stumbled into a fellow employee (Patient B), breaking his glasses and knocking him down. Patient A has areas of first- and second-degree burns on his palms and the peripheral areas of his face. His eyes and breathing are okay. Patient B has glass in one eye from the broken glasses and is very anxious about the possibility of losing his eye.

OEC Practice Scenario 5

The following table contains an emergency care scenario in which the senior candidate must manage a patient who has fractured his wrist and clavicle. The degree of difficulty for each component is provided as well as the overall degree of difficulty.

Injury

Wrist fracture (2)
Clavicle fracture (2)

Environment

Easiest slope (0)

Personnel

Single patient (0)
Obstructive ski instructor (1)

Degree of Difficulty = 5

General Scenario Description

A first-time skier was on one of the area's easiest slopes with a new ski instructor when he fell forward, his binding released, and he put his hands out to break his fall. When you arrive, the instructor is very upset and is being overly apologetic to the skier, blaming the slope's grooming for causing the accident. The patient is complaining of pain in his wrist and shoulder on the same side. As a first-time skier, he is quite anxious about the situation.

OEC Practice Scenario 6

The following table contains an emergency care scenario in which the senior candidate must manage a patient with an open femur fracture and a humerus fracture. The degree of difficulty for each component is provided as well as the overall degree of difficulty.

Injury

Open femur fracture (3)
Humerus fracture (2)

Environment

Most difficult slope (0)

Personnel

Single patient (0)
Trained patrollers (0)

Degree of Difficulty = 5

General Scenario Description

A skier was jumping and caught some really good air but got out of position for the landing and experienced a hard, twisting, tumbling fall. During one of the tumbles, her ski pole got caught under her body and she felt her upper arm snap. She fell a considerable distance, with various equipment scattered along the way. She has an open mid-shaft fracture on the leg against the slope. She complains of terrible pain in her leg as well as pain in the opposite arm.

OEC Practice Scenario 7

The following table contains an emergency care scenario in which the senior candidate must manage a patient with a pelvic fracture, wrist fracture, and who is wearing a medical-alert tag. The degree of difficulty for each component is provided as well as the overall degree of difficulty.

Injury

Pelvic fracture (3)
Wrist fracture (2)
Medical history (0)

Environment

Lift line (0)
(alternate location—top of the hill at lift exit area)

Personnel

Single patient (0)
One trained patrollers (0)
Bystander help (1)

Degree of Difficulty = 6

General Scenario Description

A 56-year-old female is standing in the lift line (or is standing at the top of the hill near the unloading area) when another skier bumps into her right side, causing her to fall on her left side. When you arrive on the scene, the patient complains of pain and tenderness in the left hip and wrist areas. She is wearing a medical-alert tag for epilepsy.

OEC Practice Scenario 8

The following table contains an emergency care scenario in which the senior candidate must manage a patient with a back injury and lower-leg fracture. The degree of difficulty for each component is provided as well as the overall degree of difficulty.

Injury

Back injury (3)
Lower-leg fracture (2)

Environment

Below chairlift, not accessible by skiing (1)

Personnel

Single patient (0)
Trained patrollers (0)

Degree of Difficulty = 6

General Scenario Description

While riding up the lift, a skier fell about 20 feet out of his chair when the lift made an emergency stop. The area under the lift is not accessible by skiing under the lift, so you take off your skis and walk about 20 feet over to where the patient is lying in the snow. The patient complains of lower back and lower leg pain. You find the patient has deformity in the lower leg, with some specific pain upon palpation. The patient complains of mid-thoracic back pain with numbness and tingling in both legs.

OEC Practice Scenario 9

The following table contains an emergency care scenario in which the senior candidate must manage a patient with severe abdominal pain

and a sprained shoulder. The degree of difficulty for each component is provided as well as the overall degree of difficulty.

Injury

Severe abdominal pain (3)
Third-degree AC joint shoulder sprain (2)

Environment

Most difficult slope (0)

Personnel

Single patient (0)
Trained patrollers (0)

Degree of Difficulty = 6

General Scenario Description

A skier was skiing very fast through the trees when she lost control trying to avoid a collision with a tree. She fell on her own ski pole, which jabbed her in the abdomen (upper left quadrant). She also fell onto her shoulder. When you arrive on the scene, the patient complains of pain in the shoulder, and pain and rigidity in the abdomen. Both of these symptoms worsen.

OEC Practice Scenario 10

The following table contains an emergency care scenario in which the senior candidate must manage a patient with a dislocated shoulder, a fractured patella, and a fractured wrist. The degree of difficulty for each component is provided as well as the overall degree of difficulty.

Injury

Dislocated shoulder (2)
Patella fracture (2)
Wrist fracture (2)

Environment

Bump run (0)

Personnel

Single patient (0)
Trained patrollers (0)

Degree of Difficulty = 6

General Scenario Description

A 16-year-old skier was taking a bump run, caught an edge, and landed on one knee on the hard edge of a bump. He also put out a hand to break the fall, and felt the shoulder go as he hit. You find the knee in a locked position. The patient is complaining of pain in the knee as well as on the right arm and wrist.

OEC Practice Scenario 11

The following table contains an emergency care scenario in which the senior candidate must manage a patient with an acute abdomen. The degree of difficulty for each component is provided as well as the overall degree of difficulty.

Injury

Acute abdomen (4)

Environment

Lodge (0)

Personnel

Single patient (0)
Obstructive parent (1)
No trained help (1)

Degree of Difficulty = 6

General Scenario Description

A 13 year old is sitting in the lodge in obvious abdominal pain. An area employee requests ski patrol assistance. The parent arrives shortly after you do. The patient is complaining of steady, severe pain in the right lower quadrant.

OEC Practice Scenario 12

The following table contains an emergency care scenario in which the senior candidate must manage a patient with a cervical spine injury and head contusion. The degree of difficulty for each component is provided as well as the overall degree of difficulty.

Injury

Cervical spine injury (3)
Head contusion (1)

Environment

Disentanglement (1)
Off slope (1)

Personnel

Single patient (0)
Trained patrollers (0)

Degree of Difficulty = 6

General Scenario Description

A skier went into deep snow in the trees and hit a tree with her forehead. The skier is standing, leaning against the tree with skis on and poles in hand. Her head and neck hurt, and her fingers and toes are tingling, but there is no muscular weakness.

OEC Practice Scenario 13

The following table contains an emergency care scenario in which the senior candidate must manage a patient with a fractured hip and an eye contusion. The degree of difficulty for each component is provided as well as the overall degree of difficulty.

Injury

Hip fracture (3)
Eye contusion (2)

Environment

An icy slope (0)

Personnel

Single patient (0)
Trained patrollers (0)
Difficult spouse (1)

Degree of Difficulty = 6

General Scenario Description

The skier lost control and fell hard onto one hip on the ice, lost both skis, and rolled a couple of times. During one of the rolls, he hit his eye with the ski pole grip, which is still in his hand. When you arrive, the spouse tells you she wants to sue the area because of the "lack of grooming" (ice). The patient complains of pain in his hip. You find swelling and tenderness over one eye.

OEC Practice Scenario 14

The following table contains an emergency care scenario in which the senior candidate must manage a young patient with a severe head injury and a fractured clavicle. The degree of difficulty for each component is provided as well as the overall degree of difficulty.

Injury

Head injury—epidural hematoma (life threatening) (4)
Clavicle fracture (1)

Environment

Off the trail in an area with trees (1)

Personnel

Single patient (0)
Trained patrollers (0)

Degree of Difficulty = 6

General Scenario Description

A 10 year old was skiing with her father in a closed, gladed area. The child lost control and struck a tree with the left side of her face and her left shoulder. You do not arrive until about 15 minutes after the accident. The patient's father tells you that the child was unconscious for a couple of minutes after the impact. The patient is now responsive but is not completely oriented. She is still woozy and unable to stand but has good pupil reaction at the time of your arrival. There is a hematoma in the area of the temple and pain in the shoulder area. Her condition deteriorates as time passes, until finally she is unresponsive with a fixed pupil on the same side as the head injury.

Written Scenario Exercises

To prepare adequately for the evaluation, each candidate must write essay answers to two scenario problems and write one new senior OEC scenario problem. Select from the following scenarios or from the *OEC Test Bank* booklet (degree of difficulty 5 to 6) to write essay answers. Given the general information available below, complete the scenario objectives for decision making, problem management, and leadership. As you do the written scenarios, consider the points that will serve as the evaluation criteria for your leadership attributes.

Decision Making, Problem Management, and Leadership Expectations

One of the goals of the senior OEC component is to motivate, challenge, and facilitate a senior candidate's growth and/or experience level. Everyone involved in ski patrolling has been in a leadership position at one time or another. It may have been at the scene of an accident, while teaching one of NSP's many courses, or while serving as hill leader for the day. When you assume a leadership role, you are expected to fulfill certain responsibilities or duties, either by performing the task personally or by delegating it to another qualified individual.

Some patrollers are very comfortable in a leadership role while others tend to shy away from taking charge. Several factors may help determine whether someone is a better leader or follower, including personality, education, profession, age, and level of ski patrol experience. Each of these factors can affect a person's decision-making abilities in various situations. How do people make sound decisions and apply them to a leadership role? The following steps trace that process.

Decision-making Process

These steps enable a good leader to gain control of the situation.
1. Gather all the information about the problem or situation. Understand the information, and process it rapidly and efficiently.
2. Assess the seriousness of the situation. Set priorities based on the facts.

Communication

3. Instruct and delegate tasks to the people involved at the scene. Be calm, confident, and competent, and give concise orders or commands to anyone who is available to assist you, including other patrollers, area personnel, and bystanders. Everyone involved must clearly understand the course of action and the tasks that are expected of them. (Other patrollers should be able to work under minimal supervision and attend to the details while you address the broader picture.)

Anticipation and Flexibility

4. Anticipate the needs of the injured, the needs of the patrollers tending to the situation, and the problems that may arise. Be ready to initiate a change of plan. (You may decide to change the plan of action suddenly, depending on the time it takes to evacuate the injured, the role the weather may play, what equipment is needed, whether equipment fails or is unavailable, etc.)
5. Evaluate the on-the-scene plan of action. How effectively is the plan working? Remain flexible.

Follow-up

6. Review the events that occurred during the situation (both your actions and the actions of those you directed). In a non-judgmental, positive manner, give constructive feedback to all involved. (You might decide what was done well or what could have been handled better, more efficiently, etc. Alternatively, everyone involved in the situation could discuss these issues.)

Effective Team Characteristics

- Mutually set goals
- Understanding and commitment to goals
- Clearly defined, non-overlapping roles
- Atmosphere that encourages development
- Decisions based on facts, not emotions or personalities
- Efficient, task-oriented meetings that focus on improvement
- Discussions that involve all members
- Members listening and showing respect for each other
- Problem solving versus blaming
- Frequent performance feedback
- Informed members
- Pride and spirit
- Free expression of feelings and ideas
- Cooperation and support of members
- Tolerance for conflict with emphasis on resolution

Sample Exercise

The following section contains a sample essay response to a scenario. This exercise illustrates the knowledge components to be included in any OEC exercise designed by the OEC Test Bank Committee.

General Problem Description

A 60-year-old male (Patient A) is sitting on the snow after climbing uphill to help his wife (Patient B), who fell on a more difficult slope and is complaining of severe lower leg pain. Patient A is short of breath and complaining of chest pain, and he has a history of angina.

Patient Information

Signs and Symptoms
Patient A Complains of severe chest pain, substernal radiating to the left arm. The patient has taken a nitroglycerin tablet but has not felt any relief. The patient also complains of shortness of breath, is anxious, and is concerned for his wife, who is perspiring heavily.

Patient B Complains of severe pain and tenderness at the top of her left boot. The patient's circulation, motor functions, and sensation are within normal limits. (She can wiggle her toes, is not bleeding, and has no open fracture.)

Vital Signs	Patient A	
	Pulse	Respirations
Initial	118	32
5 min.	110	30
10 min.	106	28
15 min.	110	30

Vital Signs   Patient B

	Pulse	Respirations
Initial	110	20
5 min.	112	22
10 min.	100	22
15 min.	104	24

Scenario Objectives

Describe your actions as the leader in this situation.

Equipment: Call for two toboggans equipped with hill packs, as well as blankets, a quick splint, and oxygen.

Decision-making: Ensure the overall safety of the people at the accident site by identifying any immediate hazards, marking the site clearly, and protecting the patients from further possible harm. *Assess* the problem. Determine the *priority* for treatment by performing primary surveys on each patient followed by secondary surveys to determine appropriate medical care for each patient. With the possibility of a heart attack for Patient A, alert the base that this is a hurry case.

Problem management: *Utilize* the available people to assist with the patients and the equipment. Assign people according to their skill and experience. *Direct* bystanders to help secure the site, and assist with splinting and lifting if patrollers are not immediately available. *Request* the appropriate equipment. Have a *plan of action* based on the patients' conditions and the circumstances of the accident and the environment.

The main concern is the need to get Patient A to advanced life support as quickly as possible while still properly handling Patient B.

Patient A should be positioned so that he is comfortable. He should be transported with his head uphill, while having oxygen administered to him. Transport Patient A in a sitting position unless the patient is more comfortable lying down. Patroller assistance also will dictate this transportation decision. Patient B should be transported with the injury uphill.

It is essential that the necessary OEC skills are performed on both patients according to OEC performance guidelines. It is the leader's responsibility to ensure proper skill application by all helpers.

Leadership: *Communication* with both patients and available helpers is crucial. Patient A needs to be reassured about his wife's condition. Patient B needs to be reassured about her husband and treated quickly to avoid further complications with shock.

The leader must direct with *confidence* and a *positive attitude*. Utilize all available helpers aggressively and effectively. Use a *team approach* and control the situation at all times. Give clear, simple directions.

Written OEC Scenario 1

General Scenario

A skier is out of control and goes off the slope at high speed. The skier strikes a tree, bounces off, and collides with a second tree with his lower body. He then lands on a rock. There is a witness to the accident and he has remained on the scene. The patient remains unresponsive throughout the scenario.

Patient Information

Signs and Symptoms

The skier is unresponsive with slight bleeding from the nose. His skull is bruised on the side of the forehead, next to the temple. There is no response to pain. The left leg is at a 45-degree angle.

Vital Signs	Pulse	Respirations
Initial	120	14
5 min.	126	18

10 min.	130	18—secretions begin to affect breathing. Patient is gagging.
15 min.	128	14

Scenario Objectives

Describe your actions as leader. What injuries do you suspect? What are your treatment and transport priorities? What other aspects of the scenario need your attention? Be sure to show how you would handle decision making, problem management, and leadership items.

OEC Written Scenario 2

General Scenario

A skier goes over a jump and crosses her skis when landing. This causes a hard, body-slam fall on a firm packed slope. The fall is on her right side.

Patient Information

Signs and Symptoms

The patient is oriented to person, place, time, and event, but because of deepening shock she is not completely responsive. The patient's right rib case hurts a great deal, with more diffuse pain inside the chest cavity. She is coughing up pink sputum. Her breathing is difficult (rapid and shallow). Her right upper arm is also very painful.

Vital Signs	Pulse	Respirations
Initial	96	26
5 min.	100	28
10 min.	106	30
20 min.	112	32

Scenario Objectives

Describe your actions as leader. What injuries do you suspect? What are your treatment and transport priorities? What other aspects of the scenario need your attention? Be sure to show how you would handle decision making, problem management, and leadership items.

OEC Written Scenario 3

General Scenario

Three kids are goofing around and pushing each other while on the chair lift. One starts to fall, grabs hold of the other two, and all three fall from the chair (about 10 feet).

Patient Information

Signs and Symptoms

Patient A The patient may have broken ribs and is having some trouble breathing. He is sitting up and holding his arm to his chest (in a "V" position with his hand at the opposite shoulder). He is relatively comfortable in this position but feels a little nauseated. He blames the others for the accident.

Patient B The patient has broken his glasses and complains of pain under his eyelid. Glass is in the eye. He blames the others for the accident.

Patient C This patient is shaken and bruised but not injured. He blames the others for almost killing him. He is persistently distracting when not attended to.

Scenario Objectives

Describe your actions as leader. What injuries do you suspect? What are your treatment and transport priorities? What other aspects of the scenario need your attention? Be sure to show how you would handle decision making, problem management, and leadership items.

OEC Written Scenario 4

General Scenario

A 16 year old hits a "pop" fence, which causes a forward fall. When you arrive on the scene, the patient's mental status is fuzzy. He doesn't recall the accident but answers to his name. The patient is wearing a medical-alert tag that says DIABETIC. He can move his jaw, and although it is painful, he is able to swallow with no airway obstruction.

Patient Information

Signs and Symptoms

The patient is conscious of sharp, severe pain one inch anterior to the angle of the jaw. His teeth don't mesh properly. The patient is insulin dependent. He took insulin that morning but skipped lunch.

Vital Signs	Pulse	Respirations
Initial	68	18
5 min.	72	16
10 min.	72	14
15 min.	70	14

Scenario Objectives

Describe your actions as leader. What injuries do you suspect? What are your treatment and transport priorities? What other aspects of the scenario need your attention? Be sure to show how you would handle decision making, problem management, and leadership items.

OEC Written Scenario 5

General Scenario

When you arrive on the scene, the skier tells you he lost control trying to jump a mogul, became airborne, and hit the tree with his right side. He is lying on a significant grade at the tree-lined edge of the slope.

Patient Information

The patient is lying on his right side with the left ski off. The right hip is slightly flexed. He guards the right leg and will not allow the right hip to be extended. The skier complains persistently of groin/hip pain and keeps repeating that he has to go to the bathroom. He has severe pain upon pelvic compression and pain in the lower quadrants. A low pulse rise and increased general abdominal guarding occur. The patient becomes diaphoretic and increasingly insistent about having to void.

Vital Signs	Pulse	Respirations
	100	22 and shallow

Vitals rise gradually throughout the problem.

Scenario Objectives

Describe your actions as leader. What injuries do you suspect? What are your treatment and transport priorities? What other aspects of the scenario need your attention? Be sure to show how you would handle decision making, problem management, and leadership items.

OEC Written Scenario 6

General Scenario

You have just arrived on the scene of an accident involving a guest and an employee who was driving a snowmobile. A bystander states that a member of the snowmaking crew was driving his machinery very recklessly and that he forced the skier off the trail. The skier struck a snowmaking hydrant, then caught her left ski under a snowmaking pipe as she left the trail. The snowmobile operator has driven away.

Patient Information

The skier is lying on her back with her head downhill. She complains of

severe pain in the right upper leg and the left knee. She will not allow the left knee to be straightened.

Vital Signs   Pulse   Respirations
                100   24
Vitals remain stable if patient is treated for shock or become 140 and 35 if not treated for shock.

Scenario Objectives

Describe your actions as leader. What injuries do you suspect? What are your treatment and transport priorities? What other aspects of the scenario need your attention? Be sure to show how you would handle decision making, problem management, and leadership.

OEC Written Scenario 7

General Scenario

A novice skier was skiing out of control down an advanced slope. Another skier collided with the novice as he was finishing a turn. The novice (Patient A) is not moving. The other skier (Patient B) is sitting on the ground.

Patient Information

Patient A is unresponsive and lying face down on the snow. He has blood running from his mouth and is having trouble breathing. The bleeding appears to be where he bit his tongue. Patient B is sitting on the ground complaining of pain in his shoulder. He is very rude and is yelling at the unresponsive skier.

Vital Signs   Patient A
	Pulse	Respirations
	+12	+4
They remain stable at that level.

Vital Signs   Patient B
	Pulse	Respirations
Normal	Normal	when calm
Elevated	Elevated	when not calm

Scenario Objectives

Describe your actions as leader. What injuries do you suspect? What are your treatment and transport priorities? What other aspects of the scenario need your attention? Show how you would handle decision making, problem management, and leadership.

OEC Written Scenario 8

General Scenario

A skier who was jumping off a mogul struck two skiers who crossed his path. All three slid down the hill. One skier slid into the path of a snow-grooming machine. The lift operator tells the you about the accident as you come off the chair, including the fact that the accident happened 10 minutes earlier and that there are no other patrollers available to help. You grab a toboggan and take it to the accident.

Patient Information

Patient A, the skier who jumped off the mogul, has pain in both lower legs; one is bleeding. He is very upset and apologetic. He repeatedly says that he never saw the other skiers until it was too late. He is also the skier who hit the grooming machine.

Patient B is unresponsive when you arrive but comes around as you start to do the assessment. He is unclear about what caused the accident and gets upset when he sees that his friend has been further injured by hitting the grooming machine.

Patient C has a large gash on the side of his neck; there is a pool of blood under him. His pupils are fixed and dilated.

Vital Signs   Patient A and Patient B
	Pulse	Respirations
	+16	+6 above normal
Vitals remain elevated throughout

Vital Signs   Patient C
	Pulse	Respirations
	None	None

Scenario Objectives

Describe your actions as leader. What injuries do you suspect? What are your treatment and transport priorities? What other aspects need your attention? Be sure to show how you would handle decision making, problem management, and leadership.

OEC Written Scenario 9

General Scenario

You and another patroller are standing at the top of a chairlift where you observe two skiers trying to get off the lift. As they rise from the chair, the first skier begins to fall. He grabs for the second skier for support and they both fall. The second skier is hit on the back of the head by the chair as it swings around.

Patient Information

Patient A is nervous and anxious about his friend's reaction to the accident. He complains of pain and tenderness in his right wrist and of pain when trying to move his fingers or wrist.

Patient B has a laceration on the back of his head form the chair, surrounded by some local tenderness, but he reports no generalized head or neck pain or problems with movement. He also complains of a knee that is sore from being twisted during the fall and says he heard it "pop" when falling. At some point during the interview, after the patient realizes he is bleeding, he tells the you that he is HIV-positive. This is a cause for concern as the you had contact with the blood before putting on your gloves.

Vitals are as found. (Use the vitals of the person acting as the patient in this scenario.)

Scenario Objectives

Describe your actions as leader. What injuries do you suspect? What are your treatment and transport priorities? What other aspects of the scenario need your attention? Be sure to show how you would handle decision making, problem management, and leadership.

Patroller Enrichment Seminar Exercises

The Patroller Enrichment Seminar has some preparatory work as a prerequisite to the actual course. The following study activities will assist the learner in fulfilling course objectives.

Study Activity 1

Module: Patrol Facilities Management
Activity: Patrol Facility Duties

Directions

Complete the following items for Study Activity 1.

1. Identify the responsibilities that area management or the public lands administration has given your local patrol. Add other responsibilities to this list as appropriate.

2. Describe in detail, each patrol responsibility.

3. Identify people whose skill level (in the case of a volunteer patroller) or job classification (in the case of an area employee) matches that which is required for a particular responsibility. If the patrol is not directly involved, describe any interaction that occurs with other ski area departments.

4. Prioritize the most important duties for patrollers, for ski area management, and for ski area guests (1 = most important; 10 = least important).

5. Prepare a creative, five-minute presentation of routine patrol facility duties (refer to the chart on the following page) in your patrol. Be prepared to give this presentation during the Patroller Enrichment Seminar (PES) Patrol Facilities Management module.

Patrol Facility Duties

Duties	Local patrol responsibility (yes or no)? If no, who at the ski area is responsible for this duty?	Specific Job Description
Emergency care		
Maintenance of aid room, equipment, and supplies		
Administration and clerical support		
Accident reporting and evaluation		
Education programs a. Candidates b. Other		
Communication a. Operation b. Participation c. Interface with hill patrollers		
Deployment of personnel and supplies		
Liaison with area management		

List any other duties on a separate sheet.

Study Activity 2

Module: Patrol Facilities Management
Activity: Patrol Facility Assessment Tool
(adapted from *Ski Patrol Magazine*, Fall 1991)

Directions

The following checklist is designed to help you conduct an informal assessment of your patrol facility. This assessment tool represents suggestions made by advisors at many ski areas and at training seminars, and is not intended to set forth any formal standards for patrol facility layout, equipment, or services.

To perform the assessment, review each statement realistically and assign it a rating from 0 to 4.

4 = Fully complies.
3 = Substantially complies, but improvement is needed.
2 = Somewhat complies, but improvement is needed.
1 = Minimally complies, and significant improvement is needed.
0 = Does not comply in any way.

After completing the checklist, examine the ratings to determine which areas are satisfactory and which are in need of improvement. Then, total the scores for an overall assessment of the patrol facility. There are 100 points possible.

1. The patrol facility operates under a written policies and procedures guide for patrol operations and for emergency/contingency situations that has been approved by area management.   Score_____
    a. The guide is kept in the main patrol facility for reference purposes. It is easily located and everyone knows where it is.
    b. The guide incorporates plans for exceptional circumstances, such as emergency situations, disasters, and search and rescue. The guide contains the schedule for fire drills and other pertinent drills.

2. The patrol facility is securable.   Score_____

3. The patrol facility is insulated against inclement weather. Adequate temperature is maintained.   Score_____

4. Portable heat sources (if any) are safe for use and are maintained.   Score_____

5. The patrol facility has easy access for toboggans and stretchers.   Score_____

6. The area outside the patrol facility has easy access for an automobile or ambulance.   Score_____
    a. Provisions exist for other evacuation or transportation (e.g., helicopter) and are posted or are detailed in the patrol's policies and procedures guide.

7. There is ample patrol facility for easy transfer of patients to beds and for working effectively at the bedside.   Score_____

8. There is ample bed space to accommodate average peak patient load or there are provisions for efficiently managing patient overflow.   Score_____

9. The patrol facility is well-lighted and has provisions for an emergency or backup light source in the event of a power outage.   Score_____

10. The patrol facility routinely has a neat, orderly, and professional appearance.   Score_____

11. The patrol facility routinely has an adequate stock of emergency care materials in a securable site.   Score_____

12. Materials for transportation assistance (e.g. wheelchair, stretcher, litter) are on hand routinely.   Score_____

13. The patrol facility has a water source and ability to provide warm water.   Score_____

14. The patrol facility has a working fire extinguisher.   Score_____

15. The patrol facility has an oxygen source. Safety measures are established for maintenance and operation.   Score_____

16. The patrol facility has posted "No Smoking" signs, especially if oxygen source is maintained.   Score_____

17. A bed assignment system is used to facilitate room activity flow and care transfer.
    a.   There is easy access to emergency care materials from bed spaces.   Score_____

18. All beds can be seen from the main aid desk.   Score_____

19. At least one bed has a privacy curtain.   Score_____

20. Beds are provided with adequate blankets and pillows.   Score_____
    a.   Blankets, pillow covers, and mattress covers are kept clean, or disposable covers are used.

21. Rest room facilities are easily accessible.   Score_____

22. The locker/equipment/meeting area is sufficiently separated or removed from the patient area to
    minimize excessive noise and activity.   Score_____

23. The patrol facility has appropriate and adequately maintained communication equipment.   Score_____
    a.   The patrol facility has telephone access.
    b.   The patrol facility has radio access.
    c.   An overall communications system has been established with area management, lifts, the
         U.S. Forest Service, law enforcement agencies, etc.

24. Adequate specialized support equipment is provided and maintained.   Score_____
    a. Spine boards   i.   Trauma packs
    b. Portable oxygen   j.   Splints (box, quick, traction)
    c. CPR face mask   k.   Blood pressure cuff
    d. Dish pan   l.   Emesis basin
    e. Disposable gloves   m. Clock with second hand
    f. Protective gown/goggles   n.   Disposable towels
    g. "Red bag" for blood-   o.   Trash receptacles
       stained materials   p.   Accident reports
    h. Scissors   q.   Other

25. The following materials are available and guidelines established for appropriate/required record keeping.   Score_____
    a.   Accident report forms
    b.   Risk management forms
    c.   Patrol administration logs
    d.   Supply and equipment order forms, etc.

Total Score_____

Study Activity 3

Module: Patrol Facilities Management
Activity: Patrol Facility Design and Activity Flow Assessment

Directions

1. Draw a floor plan of your patrol's aid room (as close to scale as possible). Include the location of equipment, supplies, furniture, etc. and any unique aspects within the floor plan.

2. Using the same floor plan, highlight the activity flow (traffic patterns) of the room(s), including patient care and patroller duties.

Study Activity 4

Module: Patrol Facilities Management
Activity: Administrative Implications of Patrol Incident Investigation

Directions

1. Select one practical OEC scenario from the Senior Study Activities.

2. Identify the facts that should be preserved during an incident investigation. Describe how they would be preserved.

Study Activity 5

Module: Administrative Policies Management
Activity: Operational/Administrative Skills

Directions

1. Create a list of administrative procedures used at your ski area or within your patrol. The following are examples of areas in which administrative procedures are created for some ski areas and/or ski patrols.
   - Guest services (e.g., daily trail logs, communication logs)
   - Area equipment (e.g., equipment or toboggan checklists)
   - Communications (e.g., patrol newsletter)
   - Ski area emergencies (e.g., helicopter evacuation, fire, avalanche, lift failure)
   - Patrol management (e.g., duty assignments, proposal process, appeal process)
   - NSP membership (e.g., patrol registration, member registration, change of classification)
   - NSP education programs (e.g., course records, course orders, lesson planning)
   - Instructor/trainer incentives (e.g., awards)

2. Identify the process required to satisfy the operational/administrative procedures (who, how, why, what, when, etc.). Identify any significant issues that need to be addressed to satisfy the procedure.

Study Activity 6

Module: Administrative Policies Management
Activity: Procedures and Policies

Directions

1. Identify some emergencies that could occur at your ski area. Select one emergency to develop into a plan.

2. Prepare an outline of the steps necessary to develop a contingency or emergency plan. (Details of actual procedures are not required.) Use or revise an existing plan at your ski area for this exercise. Consider the following components in your plan:
   a. Plan development
   b. Practice drills
   c. Backup plans
   d. Equipment required
   e. Human resources required

Study Activity 7

Module: Expanded Patroller Services to Ski Areas
Activity: Training for Expanded Responsibilities

Directions

Fill out the Potential Expanded Patroller Services chart on the following page, then use that information to help you complete these steps.

1. Complete a needs assessment for expanded services by your patrol and ski area.

2. List additional job responsibilities you think could be incorporated into your patrol and any additional training that might be required.

3. Outline a plan on how the assessed needs could be implemented.

4. Be prepared to discuss these ideas during the clinic module.

Potential Expanded Patroller Services

	Role	Training	Resources
In the patrol facility			
In the base area			
On the hill			
Out of area			

Outline for Implementation (#3 under Directions)

Study Activity 8

Module: NSP Education and Leadership Opportunities
Activity: Organizational Flow

Directions

1. Prepare any questions you have regarding education certification or credentialing procedures, job descriptions, responsibilities, and their relationship to the NSP.

2. Prepare any questions you have regarding leadership appointments or election procedures, job descriptions, responsibilities, and their relationship to the NSP.

Study Activity 9

Module: NSP Education and Leadership Opportunities
Activity: Selecting an Education or Leadership Path

Directions

1. Select an education or leadership role you would like to have. Research how to obtain this position, and identify the training required and the appointment or election process.

2. Be prepared to share this information at the senior clinic.

APPENDIX

I

Certified Exercises

This appendix contains information on how to prepare for the NSP certified evaluation. The following study activities are designed to help the certified candidate fulfill the course objectives.

Multiple-Casualty Plan Study Questions

The following questions are provided to develop and enhance the skills of decision making, problem management, and leadership, as applied to the management of emergency care situations in a typical ski patrol environment.

1. Define mass casualty.
2. Why is it important for patrollers to be aware of procedures to follow during a mass-casualty incident?
3. What is an incident command center (ICC)?
4. Who operates an ICC? Why?
5. Why is technical support valuable to the ICC?
6. How long is the ICC operated?
7. What is the location of the ICC?
8. What is a forward command center (FCC)?
9. Who operates an FCC? Why?
10. What is the location of the FCC? Why?
11. What types of incidents may require the use of an ICC and FCC?
12. Name several procedures that may be necessary for most incidents.
13. How should an incident be reported?
14. What information is important to obtain? Why?
15. What should happen with radio and telephone communications? Why?
16. What is triage? How should it be used? Who is the triage supervisor?
17. Where is a good place for a staging area?
18. What is a victim's assistance program? Why is it a good idea?

Emergency Care Certified Open-Book Study Guide

Use the following questions to test your knowledge of Outdoor Emergency Care. Because the following is an open-book, take-home study guide, you must provide complete, correct answers. Incomplete study guides will be returned by your division certified examiner for completion. If you have any questions, please see your division certified advisor.

1. Respiration is chemically controlled by the
   a. carbon dioxide in the blood
   b. water vapor in the blood
   c. nitrogen in the blood
   d. oxygen in the blood

2. Put the breathing process into sequence, using the letters a through f.
   ___ Air flows in to equalize the pressure.
   ___ The chest cage enlarges.
   ___ The inside pressure is now lower than the outside pressure.
   ___ The lungs are pushed out by the air.
   ___ The chest cage returns to passive size.
   ___ Air is forced out by chest pressure.

3. In most cases, once respiratory arrest begins, lethal changes in the brain begin in
   a. 10 to 20 minutes
   b. 30 to 60 minutes
   c. 4 to 6 minutes
   d. 3 to 5 seconds

4. List the four components that control the level of blood pressure.
   a. _____
   b. _____
   c. _____
   d. _____

5. An unresponsive, breathing patient who is in shock from blood loss can benefit from oxygen therapy. A good way to deliver oxygen is through a
   a. nasal cannula with 9 liters per minute of oxygen
   b. mask with 2 liters per minute of oxygen
   c. positive pressure valve
   d. mask with 15 liters per minute of oxygen and an oral airway

6. The chest cavity is separated from the abdominal cavity by the
   a. pleura
   b. diaphragm
   c. mediastinum
   d. pericardium

7. Arteries carry oxygenated blood and veins carry unoxygenated blood. What are the two exceptions to this statement?
   _____
   _____

8. Systolic pressure refers to the low reading when taking a blood pressure.
   a. true
   b. false

9. Match the statements with the correct responses.
   a. ___ blood accumulated under the skin,   1. tetanus
        producing a characteristic bluish discoloration   2. laceration
                                                        3. sprain
   b. ___ a muscle that is severely stretched or torn   4. puncture
                                                        5. edema
   c. ___ a disease caused by a soil bacterium   6. strain
        introduced into an open wound   7. abrasion
                                                        8. ecchymosis
   d. ___ the sterile material placed next to an open wound   9. bandage
                                                       10. dressing

10. List six symptoms that may indicate a brain injury.
    _____
    _____
    _____
    _____
    _____
    _____

11. Changes in pupil size, especially in just one pupil, are likely to be seen in
    a. heart attack
    b. drug usage
    c. lack of oxygen
    d. skull fracture

12. Emergency care for a soft-tissue avulsion is to
    a. wrap the avulsion in a sterile dressing, place it in a plastic bag, and pack it in cool water
    b. discard the avulsed tissue, and bandage the wound
    c. reposition the avulsion, cover it with a moist dressing, and bandage it in place
    d. place the avulsion in a container of water and send it with the patient to the hospital

13. When caring for a wet or chemical burn, the most essential emergency care step is to
    a. apply a counteractive chemical
    b. flush the injury immediately with large quantities of water
    c. remove contaminated clothing
    d. transport the patient immediately to the hospital

14. If medical care will be delayed, an infected wound on an arm or leg should be
    a. elevated higher than the heart
    b. kept lower than the heart
    c. flushed and washed before bandaging
    d. covered with cold packs to reduce swelling

15. Loss of more than ___ of blood is life threatening.
    a. 1 pint
    b. 1 quart
    c. 3 pints
    d. 2 quarts

16. Shock accompanying a head injury is
    a. common and to be expected
    b. unusual and should prompt the rescuer to look for additional injuries
    c. usually due to an accompanying injury to the cervical spine
    d. usually due to intercranial bleeding

17. A patient has suffered severe wounds of the lower part of the face and jaw. He is unresponsive. To treat for shock, place the patient on his
    a. back with his legs elevated
    b. stomach
    c. back with his head and shoulders raised
    d. side with his head turned face down

18. List the five regions of the spine from superior to inferior.
    _____
    _____
    _____
    _____
    _____
    _____

19. A comminuted fracture
    a. involves bones that break and commute to different places
    b. is life threatening because of contamination
    c. rarely results in misalignment of a limb
    d. involves a bone broken into more than two fragments

20. The major diagnostic difference between a fractured hip and a dislocated hip is the direction the lower extremity is rotated. The fractured hip rotation is _____ and the dislocated hip rotation is _____.

21. When performing emergency care for a tibia/fibula fracture, and no distal pulse is found, the rescuer should
    a. make no attempt to align the leg/foot
    b. apply a traction splint
    c. splint the injury in the position found and quickly transport
    d. anatomically align the leg/foot, splint, and transport

22. What is the difference between fixation and traction splints?
    _____
    _____
    _____

23. The most important consideration when dealing with a patient with a midshaft femur fracture is that
    a. it is often an open fracture and very painful
    b. the leg may be markedly deformed or rotated
    c. there may be a large amount of blood loss
    d. the bone ends may separate and cause permanent nerve damage

24. A noticeable blue tinge in the tongue, lips, nail beds, and skin is a sign that the brain is getting too little oxygen. This is called
    a. silicosis
    b. halitosis
    c. cyanosis
    d. psoriasis

25. A patient has sustained a pneumothorax from a violent accident. His color is becoming more cyanotic and there is increased respiratory distress. The trachea is shifting to one side. This condition is called
    a. hemothorax
    b. simple pneumothorax
    c. tension pneumothorax
    d. flail chest

26. A patient with a spinal injury who cannot feel sensation in the legs and feet but can move his fingers and arms most likely has an injury to the ___ region of the spinal cord.
    a. cervical
    b. thoracic
    c. lumbar
    d. sacral

27. Define the following
    a. Sign_____
    b. Symptom_____

28. Match the sign/symptom to the injury/illness
    a. ___ cardiac arrest   1. dry, red face
    b. ___ heat stroke   2. charred tissue
    c. ___ fracture   3. pink fluid from ear or nose
    d. ___ dislocation   4. bleeding
    e. ___ hypothermia   5. position may be fixed
    f. ___ brain injury   6. shivering
    g. ___ laceration   7. deformity and swelling
    h. ___ third-degree burn   8. paradoxical breathing
    i. ___ shock   9. pale, clammy skin
    j. ___ flail chest   10. no pulse

29. Solid organs are more prone to rupture due to force than are hollow organs.
    a. true
    b. false

30. The purpose of the primary survey is to
    a. take and record vital signs
    b. carefully assess every part of the body so that no injury is overlooked
    c. obtain the patient's medical history
    d. immediately identify and treat life-threatening emergencies

31. In the primary survey, ABCDE stands for
    A. _____
    B. _____
    C. _____
    D. _____
    E. _____

32. In the context of obtaining a patient's medical history, the acronym AMPLE stands for
    A. _____
    M. _____
    P. _____
    L. _____
    E. _____

33. The five vital signs are
    a. area of injury, temperature, pulse, bleeding, level of responsiveness
    b. temperature, pulse, respiration, blood pressure, level of responsiveness
    c. pulse, respiration, skin color, blood pressure, level of responsiveness
    d. skin color, pulse, blood pressure, respiration, temperature

34. In the AVPU scale, used to determine level of responsiveness, the P stands for
    a. pulse
    b. pain response
    c. pupil reaction
    d. pressure

35. Match the following conditions and terms.
    a. ___ air in the pleural space
    b. ___ blood in the pleural space
    c. ___ accumulation of fluid in the subcutaneous fibrous
         sac surrounding the heart
    d. ___ air that escapes into the tissues and spreads as small
         bubbles into the subcutaneous tissues (Rice Krispies sounds)
    e. ___ an inflammation of the lining of the abdominal cavity

    1. peritonitis
    2. pharynx
    3. emphysema
    4. pneumothorax
    5. pericardial tamponade
    6. hemothorax
    7. myocardial contusion

36. Blood clots that form in other parts of the body then break away and become trapped in the lungs cause
    a. heart attack
    b. pulmonary edema
    c. pulmonary embolism
    d. arterial bleeding

37. A 26-year-old male complains of intense thirst, headache, and vomiting. His skin is red and dry. Respirations are deep and rapid, and there is a sweet or fruity smell on his breath. He is restless and merges into unresponsiveness. He is probably suffering from
    a. hypothermia
    b. hypoglycemia
    c. diabetic coma
    d. heat stroke

38. Signs and symptoms of narcotic use are likely to include
    a. a high level of excitement, agitation, and insomnia
    b. seizures, anxiety, and hyperactivity
    c. reddening of the whites of the eyes and anxiety
    d. slowed pulse and respirations, and lethargy

39. Intermittent, severe abdominal pain due to obstruction of a hollow muscular organ may cause
    a. colic
    b. constipation
    c. diarrhea
    d. cramping

40. The symptom of dysphasia is difficulty in
    a. speaking
    b. swallowing
    c. urinating
    d. flatulating

41. Dysuria is
    a. blood in the urine
    b. inability to urinate
    c. pain on urination
    d. sugar in the urine

42. Signs and symptoms of early acute mountain sickness include
    a. cyanosis, hunger, red eyes, headache
    b. headache, hunger, nausea, cyanosis
    c. red eyes, fatigue, inability to sleep, cyanosis
    d. fatigue, headache, inability to sleep, nausea

43. The temperature at which a patient moves from mild to profound hypothermia is
    a. 95 degrees F
    b. 90 degrees F
    c. 85 degrees F
    d. 80 degrees F

44. Structures attaching muscles to bone are
    a. tendons
    b. antagonists
    c. ligaments
    d. fascia

45. What are the three major body cavities? Also, name one major organ in each.
    1. _____, _____
    2. _____, _____
    3. _____, _____

46. The xiphoid process is ___ to the umbilicus.
    a. superior
    b. inferior
    c. posterior
    d. anterior

47. The term used to describe a patient who is lying down in a face-up position is
    a. prone
    b. supine
    c. dorsal
    d. posterior

48. In which circumstance should an injured person at a ski area be moved before completion of full and appropriate emergency care?
    a. high winds, 25 degrees F, light snow, open slope, no grade
    b. heavy snowfall, open and steep slope known to slide in similar conditions
    c. heavy snowfall, light winds, in trees, mild grade
    d. patient in severe shock with a bleeding head injury

49. Which toboggan position generally is more comfortable for a responsive victim of a heart attack?
    a. head uphill in a semi-sitting position
    b. head downhill, with feet raised to reduce shock
    c. on the side, with support under the head
    d. prone or semi-prone

50. In which case should transportation by ambulance be recommended (local protocol not withstanding)?
    a. suspected fractured humerus
    b. first-degree burns
    c. puncture wound of the hand
    d. suspected ruptured spleen

Emergency Care Scenarios

Please read the following scenarios and, for each, answer the eight general questions listed on the next page. Use additional paper, as necessary.

1. A frantic person approaches you as you come in from sweep at dusk. Her friend, who was skiing an intermediate nordic trail, is missing. A search and rescue is organized; you have two sectors to cover with another patroller. You are given a pack containing two blankets, splints, matches, and a radio. Two hours into the search you find the person lying semi-prone, left side down. Her left arm is straight out about 20 centimeters from her body. You begin your assessment. The patient is responsive only to pain. You discover an obvious deformity in the middle of her left humerus. The patient has a weak, slow pulse and shallow respirations. Your assessment further reveals frostbite on the hands, toes, and nose. You radio for a snowmobile, which will take 30 minutes to arrive.

2. You are called to respond to a traffic accident in the parking lot. When you arrive on the scene, you discover a skier lying next to a car. You identify yourself as a patroller and begin your assessment by asking the skier what happened. The skier tells you that he was changing a flat tire, when he saw an oncoming car getting too close. He tried to jump aside to avoid injury but the car struck him on his left side. He appears frightened and complains of extreme pain in the upper left leg. He is lying on his back. His left leg is slightly shortened and externally rotated, while the right knee is flexed approximately 15 centimeters off the ground. As time passes, you notice the patient becoming restless, breathing faster, and complaining of thirst. The patient responds normally to conversation.

3. A 22-year-old man is skiing down a groomed run at high speed when he loses control, falls, and crashes into the trees at the side of the trail. When you arrive, you note that both skis are off, the skier is sitting with his back against a tree, and a branch is impaled in his right chest. The skier's initial vital signs indicate a pulse of 120 and respirations of 24. He is coughing weakly when you arrive. Upon exposing the right chest, you find that the branch goes into the chest wall and blood is bubbling around it. Your assessment also reveals an obvious deformity in the middle of the right radius. As time passes, the frequency and forcefulness of the patient's coughing increases. After approximately 20 minutes, the patient is coughing blood and having difficulty breathing. His pulse is 180 and respirations are 40.

4. An 18-year-old man (Skier A) is skiing with reckless disregard for the safety of others. While skiing too fast through a crowded trail junction, he collides with another skier (B) who is literally sent flying off the trail into the trees and rocks at the trail's perimeter. You arrive moments after the accident.

   You begin your assessment with Skier B. He is responsive to questioning and other verbal stimuli but is slow, dazed, and not alert. He has no memory of what happened and thinks he may have been unconscious for a while. He knows his name and where he is but is uncertain about the date and time. After 10 minutes, he exhibits a deteriorating level of consciousness and becomes less responsive to verbal stimuli. He complains of pain in the pelvic region and screams when the pelvic bone is palpated. He also complains of tenderness at the back of his head, a headache, dizziness, "seeing stars," and memory loss. His initial vitals are a pulse of 95 and respirations of 20. After 15 minutes, his vitals are a pulse of 115 and respirations of 24.

   Skier A is aggressive, irritable, and appears confused. Your assessment reveals a medical-alert tag stating that he suffers from Type 1 diabetes. You learn that he took his regular insulin injection that morning, followed by a light breakfast. He skipped lunch; it is now 2 p.m. You also find an obvious, angulated boot-top deformity on the left leg. As you work on this problem, Skier A's vitals remain at a pulse of 95 with normal respirations.

General Questions

1. What problems does your overall assessment indicate?

2. What factors cause you to reach this conclusion? Include all evidence you have gathered from the dispatch and approach, mechanism of injury, primary and secondary assessment, and all other sources.

3. Are universal precautions appropriate in this circumstance? If so, describe which precautions you would take and why.

4. Is oxygen administration appropriate? If so, describe how to administer oxygen, the equipment you would use, and what flow and concentration you would give.

5. Explain the emergency care steps you would take and the order in which you would take them for this situation.

6. What common problems and complications might develop?

7. Describe the transportation decisions you would make.

8. What documentation is needed for this situation and why?

APPENDIX

J

Forms

This appendix contains the following forms that members commonly use at the national level of the NSP.

Associate Registration
Alumni Registration
Application for Affiliate Education Contract
Certified Candidate/Recertification Application
Senior Candidate Application
Senior Program/Division Activity Record
Instructor Application
Instructor Activity Sheet
Course Completion Record
Course Registration

NSP ASSOCIATE
REGISTRATION FORM

133 South Van Gordon Street, Suite 100
Lakewood, Colorado 80228
Phone (303) 988-1111

SOCIAL SECURITY NUMBER

DATE SUBMITTED

| MONTH | DAY | YEAR |

PERSONAL DATA

FIRST NAME	LAST NAME	HOME PHONE ( )
MAILING ADDRESS		WORK PHONE ( )
CITY	STATE	ZIP CODE + 4

DATE	$30 FEE
	FORM OF PAYMENT ☐ CHECK ☐ MC ☐ VISA SIGNATURE _____
MONTH DAY YEAR	CARD NUMBER _____ Exp. Date _____

SURVEY INTERVIEW (To be completed by all associate applicants)

1. How did you hear about the National Ski Patrol?

   ☐ from a friend   ☐ from an NSP member   ☐ at a ski area   ☐ at a ski show

   ☐ through another organization   ☐ through the media   ☐ Other _____

2. What is your primary reason for wanting to become an associate?

   ☐ to take an NSP education course   ☐ to teach an NSP education course

   ☐ to order from the *NSP Winter Catalog*   ☐ to receive *Ski Patrol Magazine*

   ☐ I'm interested in becoming a patroller   ☐ for personal fulfillment   ☐ Other _____

3. If you are interested in *taking* an NSP education course, which one?

   ☐ Outdoor Emergency Care   ☐ Outdoor First Care   ☐ Avalanche

   ☐ Mountaineering   Other _____

   Why? _____

4. If you are interested in *teaching* an NSP education course, which one?

   ☐ Outdoor Emergency Care   ☐ Outdoor First Care   ☐ Avalanche

   ☐ Mountaineering   Other _____

   Why? _____

5. Are you affiliated with any other outdoor recreation or rescue organization? Which one(s)?

   ☐ an outing club   ☐ emergency care providers   ☐ search and rescue   ☐ PSIA

   ☐ scouting   ☐ wilderness group   ☐ mountain biking   ☐ Other _____

DISCLAIMER

I understand this registration does not accord me all the rights, privileges, or responsibilities of an NSP member.

SIGNATURE OF APPLICANT	DATE

SPONSOR DATA

SPONSOR'S NAME	SPONSOR'S SIGNATURE	DATE

NATIONAL SKI PATROL
ALUMNI ASSOCIATION

133 South Van Gordon Street, Suite 100
Lakewood, Colorado 80228
Phone (303) 988-1111

PERSONAL DATA		
NAME		
ADDRESS	PHONE # (WITH AREA CODE) ( )	
CITY	STATE	ZIP CODE + 4
If re-registering as a member of the Alumni Association, provide registration number		

NEW ALUMNI MEMBERS PLEASE PROVIDE THE FOLLOWING INFORMATION:		
LAST NSP AFFILIATION: SKI PATROL	REGISTRATION NUMBER	
REGION	DIVISION	LAST YEAR REGISTERED
☐ ALPINE ☐ NORDIC	NATIONAL APPOINTMENT NUMBER. (ALUMNI)	

NATIONAL SKI PATROL
APPLICATION FOR AN EDUCATION CONTRACT
For Affiliate Organization
Desiring to Obtain NSP Education Programs for Its Members

The purpose of this application is to delineate the roles and responsibilities of the National Ski Patrol and the affiliate organization for planning, instructor training, quality management, and continuing education activity. (Requested information may be duplicated and submitted on disk, in an IBM-compatible format and accompanied by a hard copy, rather than by way of this form.)

GENERAL ORGANIZATION INFORMATION		
Name of Organization:		
Address (place of business):		
Organization Description:		
Organization History:		
Logistics for organization's existing courses:		
a) Types of courses taught	b) Location of courses	c) Frequency of course
d) Cost to student	e) Credential process, e.g. certification, (# of years), course completion	f) Instructor fees
Existing quality management policies and procedures:		
Agency contact:	Title:	
Address:		
Phone:	Fax:	
Accounting Contact:	Title:	
Address:		
Phone:	Fax:	

DESIRED NSP COURSE TITLE	
Instructor Contact:	Title:
Address:	
Phone:	Fax:

NSP Mission Statement

The National Ski Patrol is a leading partner in the ski and outdoor recreation community as an adaptable resource of valuable individuals benefiting this community. We are a member-driven association. Our members support and participate in the ski and outdoor recreation community by providing emergency care, rescue, and education services. Our association supports us by surpassing member expectations through the strategic intents: an esprit de corps that inspires members to belong, exceptional education programs, dynamic communication, outstanding membership support services, energetic interagency relations, and a strong financial position.

How does this organization "fit" with NSP's mission? _____

_____

Purpose for organization teaching an NSP education program _____

_____

_____

Needs Assessment

What methods will be used to identify the need for this course? _____

_____

Identify target audience (include anticipated numbers) _____

_____

Identify proposed locations for NSP course _____

_____

Fees expected to be charged students in program _____

_____

Instructional Design

Instructional facilities _____

_____

Educational resources (text, medical, audio-visual equipment, etc.) _____

_____

Negotiated agreement will define use of NSP educational resources. Please list additional resources. _____

_____

Instructional staff

a. Number _____

b. Qualifications _____

c. Training experience _____

_____

d. Anticipated fees to be paid to instructors _____

Define ability to deliver quality education program _____

_____

_____

Define student evaluation process _____

_____

_____

Instructor Recruitment and Training—Current instructor-based qualifications

1. Need NSP instructional orientation? ☐ Yes ☐ No
2. Need to complete NSP instructor development training? ☐ Yes ☐ No

Instructor certification maintenance and recertification

1. Need NSP to do this? ☐ Yes ☐ No
2. Need NSP to participate in organization's recertification program? ☐ Yes ☐ No
3. Need for organization's instructors to become individual associates of NSP? ☐ Yes ☐ No

Quality Management Agreement to have NSP evaluation of unstructors, students, and program integrity will be negotiated.

Approval for Affiliate Organization	Date
Approval for National Ski Patrol	Date
NSP Education Director	Date

NATIONAL SKI PATROL
EDUCATION PROGRAM

CERTIFIED CANDIDATE/RECERTIFICATION APPLICATION

PERSONAL DATA		
Name		Date
Address		NSP ID #
City, State, Zip		SS #
Daytime Phone	Evening Phone	

Please check as appropriate

New Application ☐ Yes ☐ No   Reapplication ☐ Yes ☐ No

Recertification ☐ Yes ☐ No   Reactivation ☐ Yes ☐ No

If for Recertification or Reactivation, please provide your Certified Number _____

Patrol history (List most recent first)

Total Years of Experience _____ Average Number of Days per Year _____

Patrol Name	Location	
From:	To:	☐ Full Time Paid ☐ Volunteer
Patrol Name	Location	
From:	To:	☐ Full Time Paid ☐ Volunteer
Patrol Name	Location	
From:	To:	☐ Full Time Paid ☐ Volunteer

Please check as appropriate

☐ Senior   ☐ Senior Ski and Toboggan Evaluator
☐ Senior OEC   ☐ Senior OEC Evaluator
                                                   ☐ OEC Instructor
                                                   ☐ OEC Instructor Trainer
☐ Phase I   ☐ Phase I Instructor
☐ Global Module: Phase II
☐ Advanced Instructional Skills Module: Phase II (discipline _____)
☐ Alpine Toboggan Instructor   ☐ Alpine Toboggan Instructor Trainer
☐ Basic Avalanche   ☐ Avalanche Instructor
☐ Advanced Avalanche   ☐ Advanced Avalanche Instructor
                                                   ☐ Avalanche Instructor Trainer
☐ Basic Mountaineering   ☐ Mountaineering Instructor
☐ Advanced Mountaineering   ☐ Mountaineering Instructor Trainer
☐ EMT   ☐ EMT Instructor
☐ Other _____

NSP CERTIFIED PROGRAM

List OEC, ski and toboggan, and other patrol-related activities during the last three years:

_____

_____

_____

_____

_____

_____

_____

To the best of my knowledge, the information on this application is accurate.

Applicant Signature _____ Date _____

To the best of my knowledge, this patroller is currently an NSP member in good standing. I have been directly or indirectly his/her supervisor for _____ years. During that time he/she has exhibited an attitude, work ethic, skill level, and dedication to patrolling at the highest level. I recommend this individual as a certified candidate.

Supervisor Signature _____ Title _____ Date _____

THE FOLLOWING IS FOR CERTIFIED COMMITTEE USE

Date Application Received _____

MODULE	DATE COMPLETED
Area Operations and Risk Management	
Avalanche Management	
Emergency Care	
Rope Rescue and Lift Evacuation	
Skiing	
Toboggan Handling	

Date Program Completed _____

Division Certified Coordinator _____

Certified Number Issued _____ Date _____

NATIONAL SKI PATROL
EDUCATION PROGRAM

SENIOR CANDIDATE APPLICATION

Date of Senior Candidate Application _____

PATROLLER INFORMATION

Name	NSP ID #
Address	Patrol
City, State, Zip	Years of Patrolling Experience
Daytime Phone	Evening/Weekend Phone

Senior Candidate Signature _____ Date _____

☐ Senior Alpine   ☐ Senior Nordic   ☐ Senior Auxiliary

DIVISION APPLICATION INFORMATION

This certifies that the above named candidate has demonstrated all the basic ski patroller or auxiliary skills and has sufficient knowledge, skills, and experience to participate in the national senior training program.

Patrol Director Signature _____ Date _____

NATIONAL SKI PATROL
EDUCATION PROGRAM

ACTIVITY RECORD
SENIOR CORE AND ELECTIVE COMPONENTS

A senior qualification log card will be developed after the transition senior program has been reviewed and the final program approved by the NSP Board of Directors. Use this form to keep the following pretraining and elective information with the appropriate instructor's signatures during the transition period.

PATROLLER INFORMATION

Senior Candidate

NSP ID #	Senior Program Application Date
Patrol	Division

☐ Senior Alpine ☐ Senior Nordic ☐ Senior Auxiliary

VERIFICATION OF COMPLETION

Senior Component	Instructor	Completion Date
Verify Basic OEC Skills		
Senior OEC		
Senior Alpine Skiing		
Senior Alpine Toboggan Handling		
Senior Nordic Skiing and Toboggan Handling		
Patroller Enrichment Seminar		
Elective 1		
Elective 2		
Elective 3		

Final Certification
I certify that the above candidate has completed all senior program requirements.

Patrol Director Signature _____

NATIONAL SKI PATROL
EDUCATION PROGRAM

INSTRUCTOR APPLICATION

PERSONAL DATA	
Name	NSP ID #
Address (street, city, state, zip)	Phone (Home)
	Phone (Work)
Patrol	Section
Division	Region

Instructor Speciality

☐ Instructor Development: Phase I

Phase II Program

☐ Global Module   ☐ Mountaineering

☐ Outdoor Emergency Care   ☐ Avalanche (Basic)

☐ Alpine Toboggan   ☐ Advanced Avalanche

    ☐ Ski   ☐ Snowboard   ☐ Patroller Enrichment Seminar

☐ Nordic Toboggan   ☐ Other

TECHNICAL DATA		
Initial Instructor Training and Prerequisites	**Instructor Trainer**	**Completion Date**
Instructor Development: Phase I		
Phase II		
Mentored Teaching		
Instructor Experience—Discipline		Year(s)

For additional information (e.g., other teaching experience or pertinent training) use signature page or additional paper.

Recommended by (Instructor Trainer, Region, Section, or Division Program Supervisor):

Name _____ Title _____ Date _____

THIS APPLICATION HAS BEEN REVIEWED AND APPROVED by Program Supervisor
(Region, Section, Division, National as appropriate)

Print Name _____ Signature _____ Date _____

Print Name _____ Signature _____ Date _____

Print Name _____ Signature _____ Date _____

Print Name _____ Signature _____ Date _____

Mentor Assigned Name	Date
Instructor Status Granted IT Signature	Date
Instructor Trainer Appointment IT/Supervisor Signature	Year(s)

Division program supervisor keeps instructor application following division procedures. Division program supervisor or designated instructor trainer submits Course Completion Record to national office for instructor data entry and generation of instructor cards.

Education Department
National Ski Patrol
133 South Van Gordon Street, Suite 100
Lakewood, CO 80228
FAX 1-800-222-4754 or 303-988-1111

NATIONAL SKI PATROL

INSTRUCTOR ACTIVITY REPORT

Name _____ NSP ID # _____

Date of Teaching Activity (Patrol and Location)	Course ☐	Challenge ☐	Refresher ☐	Subjects Taught Skills Demonstrated	Verification by Instructor of Record

A record to be maintained and kept on file by the instructor for recertification purposes.

Rev. 12/96

Fax on Demand Doc #0272

INSTRUCTOR ACTIVITY REPORT

(To be maintained by Instructor of Record)

Instructor of Record _____ NSP ID# _____

Course Name _____ Challenge ☐ NSP Course # _____ Refresher _____

Date Started _____ Date Completed _____ Patrol(s) _____

I certify that the following instructors (I) and instructor assistants (IA) participated in this program as listed below.

_____

Date   Signature of Instructor of Record

Instructor or Instructor Assistant	I	IA	Subject(s) Taught or Skills Demonstrated
	Check One		

Rev. 12/96   Fax on Demand Doc #0272

NATIONAL SKI PATROL EDUCATION PROGRAMS

COURSE COMPLETION RECORD

Check one box per record form

- ☐ Instructor Develop: Phase I

Phase II:
- ☐ Global Module
- ☐ Alpine Toboggan Module
- ☐ Avalanche Module
- ☐ Mountaineering Module
- ☐ Nordic Module
- ☐ OEC Module

- ☐ OEC Course or
  Challenge No. _____

- ☐ OEC Refresher
  Year _____ Cycle _____

- ☐ Outdoor First Care

Instructor Appointment
Type _____

- ☐ Basic Mountaineering
- ☐ Advanced Mountaineering

- ☐ Basic Avalanche
- ☐ Advanced Avalanche

- ☐ Patroller Enrichment
  Seminar

- ☐ Senior Module
  _____

- ☐ Certified Module
  _____

- ☐ Other Course Title
  _____
  _____

Instructor Of Record (please type or print)		NSP ID #	
Address (street, city, state, zip)		Daytime Phone	
		Evening Phone	

National Course #	Start Date	End Date	Total Passed	Total Enrolled

Course Location
Special Instructions or Comments
for National Office Processing

Member Type (See Key)	NSP ID NUMBER (and/or Social Security #)	Pass	Inc	Fail	Inst Appt Y/N	STUDENTS (Type or print, last name first)	ADDRESS (Street, City, State, Zip)

Member type key: M=NSP Member; A=Associate; AF=Affiliate Organization; N=Non-Member

I certify that this NSP education program was conducted in accordance with National Ski Patrol training standards and that the students have satisfied all knowledge and skills objectives and assessments.

Certifying Instructor (please print)		NSP ID #	
Instructor Signature	Division		Patrol

Mail original course completion record to: National Ski Patrol, 133 South Van Gordon Street, Suite 100, Lakewood, CO 80228. (Instructors: Please keep a copy of course records, and follow division guidelines and instructor manual for division distribution of course records.)

Rev. 12/96   Page ____ of ____   h:\all\tl\masters\course completion record.doc

COURSE COMPLETION RECORD
PAGE 2

Member Type (See Key)	NSP ID NUMBER (and/or Social Security #)	Pass	Inc	Fail	Inst Appt Y/N	STUDENTS (Type or print, last name first)	ADDRESS (Street, City, State, Zip)

NATIONAL SKI PATROL EDUCATION PROGRAMS
(ONLY for DIVISION use)

Course:	Location:	Instructor of Record:
Date:		Phone:

Course Instructors	NSP ID #	Topic(s)/Unit(s) Taught	Instr. Exp. Date or *Instr. Intern

Please attach this sheet to the course records before forwarding to the appropriate DIVISION advisor

Starting Date	Completion Date	Total Enrollment	Total Passed	Number of Hours

Division	Region	Patrol

Follow division distribution of course records per division policy and instructor manual.

Rev. 12/96   Page ____ of ____   h:\all\tl\masters\course completion record.doc

NATIONAL SKI PATROL
EDUCATION PROGRAMS

COURSE REGISTRATION
(For Instructor Use Only)

Fax: 800-222-I SKI or 303-988-3005   **Phone:** MIST 303-988-1646

Mail to: National Ski Patrol
133 South Van Gordon Street, Suite 100, Lakewood, CO 80228

Course Name	
Course Date(s)	
Course Location	
Instructor of Record: Name / NSP ID # Address City, State, Zip Phone (Daytime/Evening)	
Projected Enrollment	
Division	
Region	
Section	
Patrol	

For National Office Use Only

_____ Course information entered in computer

_____ Certificates of Achievement sent

_____ Course records received

_____ Postcard sent to instructor

OUTDOOR EMERGENCY CARE
ORDER FORM AND COURSE REGISTRATION
(For Instructor Use Only)

Fax: 800-222-I SKI (4754) or 303-988-3005 **Phone:** 303-988-1646
Mail: National Ski Patrol, 133 South Van Gordon Street, Suite 100, Lakewood, CO 80228

☐ Course ☐ Challenge

Course # (assigned by MIST) _____

Date (assigned by MIST) _____

Start Date _____

Instructor of Record _____

End Date _____

Member ID # _____

Projected Enrollment _____

Phone (Daytime) _____

Participating Patrol(s) _____

Billing Information

Invoice Name _____ Member ID # _____

Invoice Address _____

_____

Form of Payment: ☐ On Consignment (A backup credit card or purchase order number must be provided)

Charge to my ☐ VISA ☐ Mastercard Signature _____

Acct. # _____ Exp. Date _____

☐ Purchase Order # _____

☐ Full Payment Enclosed (Check or money order payable to: National Ski Patrol)

NO CASH or C.O.D. please!

Ship to: (if different from billing information)

Name _____ Member ID # _____

UPS Mailing Address _____

OEC Trainee Packet Order

Description	Unit Price	Quantity	Amount
#551 Outdoor Emergency Care	Check Current Price	_____	$ _____
#552 OEC Study Book	Check Current Price	_____	$ _____
#558 Enrollment Fee—NSP Member	$15	_____	$ _____
#560 Enrollment Fee—Affiliate/Associate	$30	_____	$ _____
Available at additional cost:			
#501 Ski Patroller's Manual	Check Current Price	_____	$ _____
#550 OEC Instructor's Manual	Check Current Price	_____	$ _____
		UPS 2nd Day Air	$ _____
		Overnight Air	$ _____
		TOTAL DUE	$ _____

Shipping costs are determined by weight for orders other than OEC Trainee Packets, and special shipping requests.

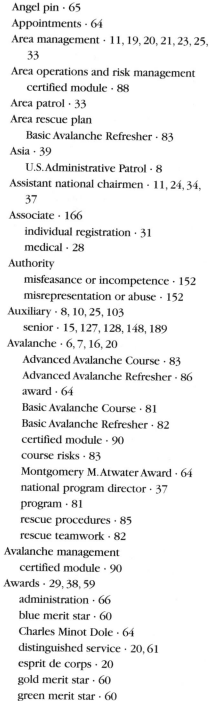

Index